7/03

Rethinking Home

The publisher gratefully acknowledges the generous contribution to this book provided by the General Endowment of the University of California Press Associates.

Rethinking Home

A Case for Writing Local History

Joseph A. Amato

UNIVERSITY OF CALIFORNIA PRESS
Berkeley · Los Angeles · London

University of California Press
Berkeley and Los Angeles, California

University of California Press, Ltd.
London, England

Library of Congress Cataloging-in-Publication Data

Amato, Joseph Anthony–.

Rethinking home : a case for writing local history / Joseph A. Amato.
p. cm.
Includes bibliographical references and index.
ISBN 0–520–22772–7 (cloth : alk. paper).
ISBN 0-520-23293-3 (paperback : alk. paper).
1. Minnesota—Civilization—Historiography. 2. Land settlement—Minnesota—Historiography. 3. Minnesota—History, Local—Philosophy. 4. Marshall (Minn.)—Historiography. 5. Local History—Philosophy. I. Title.

F605.2 .A43 2002
977.6′0072—dc21 2001027320

10 09 08 07 06 05 04 03 02
10 9 8 7 6 5 4 3 2

The paper used in this publication is both acid-free and totally chlorine-free (TCF). It meets the minimum requirements of ANSI/NISO Z39.48–1992 (R 1997) (*Permanence of Paper*).

To my mother and Vern, Bill, May, Jake,
and the other Lindsdeau and O'Brien family storytellers.
It is said that in those clans the tongue is the last "organ" to go.

The variety of historical evidence is nearly infinite. Everything that man says or writes, everything that he makes, everything he touches can and ought to teach us about him. It is curious to note how many people, unacquainted with our work, underestimate the true extent of its possibilities.

Marc Bloch, The Historian's Craft

Contents

Maps

Foreword

A newcomer's initial reaction to southwest Minnesota is that it is a bland and sedate place, dominated by endless fields devoted to the production of corn and soybeans. But this seemingly timeless region has for the past 150 years been in a state of pervasive transformation.

The region is no longer home exclusively to the traditional family farms of a few hundred acres. Vast drainage systems now crisscross the region, man-made adjuncts to the five rivers that flow through the area. Punctuating the rural vistas of enormous planted fields, each covering many square miles, are huge storage bins and silos, sprawling feedlots for beef cattle, and immense low-slung structures in which thousands of turkeys and hogs are raised with all the efficiency that contemporary agricultural science can muster.

About 150 miles southwest of the Twin Cities, beyond Marshall, the roads begin a steady 30-mile ascent of nearly seven hundred feet to the crest of the Coteau des Prairies—or Buffalo Ridge, as the locals call it. Coming over this rise, the visitor is met with a startling, even bizarre, sight. Stretching into the distance, as far as the eye can see, are enormous propellers perched atop hundred-foot towers, spinning relentlessly in the wind. There is justice in this unexpected and improbable transplantation of modern technology onto the prairie. For generations, farmers and villagers alike have cursed the incessant winds that whip across the region, bringing in winter harsh, subzero temperatures and heavy snowstorms and in summer the detested dust that accompanies the oppressive heat and humidity, which themselves can threaten crops and animals. Now independent farmers and corporations have leased parcels of land to utility companies, which are harnessing the wind to supply electricity to distant cities. At last, the wind has become a positive force.

The giant flapping wings of these aero-generators are but the latest innovation introduced in this region since the first white settlers arrived in the mid-nineteenth century. In the pages that follow, Joseph Amato traces the transformation of the material landscape of the nineteen-county area he identifies as southwestern Minnesota, blending his description of the physical landscape seamlessly into his equally acute analysis of social and cultural landscapes. He not only introduces us to the histories of small towns and important regional centers, notably Pipestone and Marshall, but also outlines the transformation of the senses, emotions, passions, and ideologies that have shaped the southwestern Minnesota mind since European settlement. Chapters on the senses, anger, insanity, the clandestine, and community inform Amato's bold vision.

Rethinking Home is the creation of a perceptive veteran scholar who refuses to work within the box. An academic maverick of the first order, Amato has produced a book that is unconventional and innovative scholarship at its best, the sort of work that comes along once in a great while. Although Amato's doctoral studies focused on contemporary French intellectual history, for the past quarter century he has dedicated himself to the history of southwestern Minnesota, where in the late 1960s he assumed a faculty position at the newly established Southwest State College, in Marshall. His efforts led to the creation of the Center for Rural and Regional Studies, which he now helps direct. He spearheaded the development of a dynamic interdisciplinary program that has produced an impressive collection of monographs and scholarly articles on the immediate region and beyond. Each year, visiting faculty and doctoral students pursue their research at the center and participate in seminars and symposia. Often collaborating with other scholars, Amato has published several books, whose subjects cover a broad spectrum of topics. They include a reflective social history of a particularly gruesome double murder; a serious, if not humorous, tale of a locally spawned multimillion-dollar horticultural hoax developed around the Jerusalem artichoke, which had worldwide implications; a pioneering analysis of rural and regional decline in the rural upper Midwest; and explorations of changes wrought by immigrants from Iceland, Norway, Germany, Denmark, Poland, and Belgium in the nineteenth century, and from Latin America, Southeast Asia, and Northeastern Africa in recent times.

In this wide-ranging and contemplative book, Amato draws heavily on these and other themes. The result is a compelling synthesis that sounds a call for dramatic new approaches to the way historians think about and write local and regional history. Readers should be prepared to have their imagination stretched. It is clear that Amato's recently published history of the miniature and unseen (*Dust: A History of the Small and Invisible,* 2000) opened up to him new ways of understanding often overlooked forces that have produced significant changes in twentieth-century America. Although he draws on the scholarship of natural scientists and social scientists, he is equally appreciative of the special insights provided by novelists and poets. The result is that in *Rethinking Home,* Amato presents a stirring call for a revival and renovation of that long-denigrated stepchild of the historical profession, local history.

Amato presents an engrossing view of a region that becomes ever more complex, ever more intriguing, and ever more elusive as its story unfolds. He demonstrates how local history can transcend tendencies toward provincialism and boosterism. *Rethinking Home* is thus much more than a history of southwest Minnesota, although residents of that region will find this book of infinite value. It is a pioneering work that will help transform the way local history is viewed and written everywhere.

Students of the Midwest and urban history will find *Rethinking Home* to be a companion piece to William Cronon's *Nature's Metropolis* (1991), a monumental study of Chicago and its influence on its hinterlands. From the earliest visits of white explorers to the present, southwest Minnesota has been shaped by elusive and distant forces from the Twin Cities, Chicago, and far beyond. Today, Marshall, with a population of twelve thousand, is one of the dominant communities in the region. Initially a county seat, railroad hub, and farming community, in recent decades it has undergone sweeping change. Since 1967 it has been home to a small and struggling state university that has been a decidedly mixed blessing for the town. In the past two decades, Marshall's ties to the nation and world have been intensified with the emergence of the family-owned corporation Schwan's as a producer and shipper of frozen foods—pizzas, sandwiches, ice cream, and an array of other goodies—to worldwide markets. Where local farmers once watched the Chicago commodities exchange with intense interest, now local corporate executives are tuned to sensitive agriculture and consumer markets around the globe.

Amato tells the story of these monumental changes and also homes in on smaller subjects, making such mundane things as sound, dirt, water, rocks, human anger, wild grasses, the macabre, gossip, hog manure, and muskrat populations come alive with meaning. As but one example: the warm summer evenings in contemporary Marshall are filled with man-made sounds—train whistles, the distant roar of trucks on the town by-pass, the whine of cutting chain saws, and the occasional siren of an ambulance on the way to the regional medical center. Each of these common sounds contributes to the warp and weft of contemporary daily life. But, as Amato points out, 150 years ago, before there were trucks and stereo systems, tract houses and motorcycles, the air was filled with other sounds. It was the roar of nature that set the evening ambience: a hubbub generated by millions of waterfowl, amphibians, beetles, bugs, birds, grasshoppers, and myriad other creatures that thrived in the small lakes and ponds and wetlands. These forces of nature are silent now because, from the very first, white settlers systematically set about to "conquer" the natural environment by draining the land of excess water so that crops could be planted and harvested.

Drawing on the work of environmental scientists and civil engineers, extension agents and agricultural historians, social scientists and poets, Amato demonstrates how, since white settlement, the physical environment of this area has been profoundly altered and restructured, driven by impulses emanating from distant economic and political capitals. And the meaning of that is revealed by recalling the natural sounds that once filled the air, replaced now by those of a society that has embraced the machine.

Rethinking Home is pioneering scholarship at its best. Amato makes his case for a new local history combining academic sophistication with a deft human touch, that can provide a new perspective on the way in which humans have interacted with their natural and created environments over the past 150 years. *Rethinking Home* is a tour de force that will require local and regional historians to expand their imaginations, and for national historians to reassess the role of localities in shaping American history. Amato's eloquent plea for scholars to rethink the intricate relationships between home, place, nation, and world is one that cannot be ignored.

Richard O. Davies

INTRODUCTION

The Concept and the Practitioners of Local History

This book is neither a manual nor a guide to writing local history; nor is it a theoretical treatise on the nature of local history.[1] Instead, it is intended as a book that evokes fresh themes for and alternative ways of writing about home. In an era when national and international forces hold sway everywhere, I try to foster a passion for the local, for reviving those particular people, places, and events past that don't demand but nevertheless need our careful attention.

I have drawn this material from two decades of teaching at Southwest State University in Marshall, Minnesota, and from my writing and other works on southwestern Minnesota published by the Society for the Study of Local and Regional History and my own Crossings Press. While at times I write of the rural world at large, I more often focus specifically on the northern prairie, which lies between the Midwest and the Great Plains.

A theme for this book is the transformation of the countryside. Through industrial, commercial, and democratic forces, contemporary civilization has metamorphosed the landscapes and peoples it has touched. Its settlement of the prairie occurred at the end of the Civil War with the coming of the railroad. Settlement meant the digging of wells, the draining of wetlands, the building of bridges and dams, and later the construction of water and sewage systems. Additionally, settlement brought churches, schools, newspapers, police, and multitudes of peoples with aspirations to have what "every civilized person and place should have."

Each chapter of this book forms a reflection on civilization's mounting control of waters and minds. My initial chapters explore civilization's shaping of natural and human environments. Then I explore in succession the promise of new histories of the senses, emotions, the clandestine, and the irrational. I conclude with an examination of literature and ideologies as conscious creations of the countryside. I draw my examples primarily from the region of southwestern Minnesota, which spares the reader a constant change of referent while allowing me the advantage of drawing on my own writing and knowledge of a particular place.

At points I do refer to other regions in order to suggest the applicability of this book to other places, especially rural places, which, I argue, have in the past half-century lost what political and cultural autonomy they may have achieved to national or commercial agencies and ideologies. Because I have taken rural environments and life to be distinctive, I have ignored local history in the cities, despite similarities between urban ethnic neighborhoods and rural ethnic communities, and despite local history's origin in the civic and political histories of the late medieval and Renaissance Italian city-states, with the writing of such Florentine humanists as Lorenzo Valla and Niccolò Machiavelli.

I wrote this book assuming that local history requires a corresponding mutation to match the mounting metamorphosis of the contemporary landscape. Everywhere, place is being superseded and reshaped. Home, locale, community, and region—and the landscape they collectively form—have entered a stage of transformation. People everywhere live in an increasingly disembodied world, their landscapes and minds increasingly falling under the persuasion and control of abstract agencies and virtual images. Like the ecologies they modified and supplanted, human places—homes, farms, villages, and towns—have increasingly lost autonomy. Space and time, which once isolated places and assured continuity to experience and intensity to face-to-face interaction, have been penetrated, segmented, and diminished by surrounding forces and words. The coordinates of community, place, and time no longer define identities and experience or contour desires and expectations. Even walking, the most literal measure of grounded experience, has vanished from everyday life in town and on the farm.

As more and more people embrace multiple localities, the big and innovative explodes the small and the traditional. Technologies, markets, laws, and expectations disrupt, alter, and transform rural life. They have done so at accelerating rates since the middle of the twentieth century.[2]

Against this background of change, turbulence, transformation, and metamorphosis, I propose rethinking home and the rewriting of local and regional history.

THE CONCEPT

People of every place and time deserve a history. Only local and regional history satisfies the need to remember the most intimate matters, the things of childhood. Local history carries with it the potential to reconstruct our ancestors' everyday lives: the goods, machines, and tools with which they worked, and the groups in which they were raised, in which they matured, celebrated, had ambitions, retired, and resigned themselves to their fates. It recaptures how they experienced the world through their senses: what they thought; how they felt; what they got angry, fought, and cursed about; what they prayed for; what drove them insane; and finally, how they died and were buried.

Every community has stories worthy of telling but few devoted historians worthy of telling them. On every front, local historians encounter dramatic change in environments, materials, technologies, institutions, and bureaucracies. In such a light, local historians cannot resist asking whether their subjects constitute a brand new order of society and culture in contrast to the one that existed until about a half century ago—one characterized, as French thinker Paul Valéry has noted, by "*interchangeability, interdependence,* and *uniformity* in customs, manners, and even in dreams."[3] In the course of its last 150 years, civilization has been measured by multiplying desires, by consumption and production, by new laws and government agencies. The past has been displaced at dizzying rates. Traditions and mentalities have been superseded, manners and crafts extinguished. Places and locales have been overrun as suburbs, subdivisions, and malls have expanded to satisfy and satiate an ever more powerful and demanding commercial civilization. Peasants and villages—the dominant class and the crucible of human life since the agricultural revolution of ten thousand years ago—have been commercialized and nationalized, diminished and destroyed. Ways of life that were unimagined in the countryside mere decades ago are now taken as the norm.

Local history focuses on the laboratory of change. It provides facts, comparisons, and contexts—the very pilings and piers of certain human knowledge—for the abstract reaches of contemporary social sciences and history. In the United States, historian Constance McLaughlin Green points out that "for any true understanding of American cultural development, the writing and study of American local history is of primary importance. There lie the grassroots of American civilization. . . . [There one finds] our varied population stocks and their sharply differentiated cultural inheritances, the widely differing environments and the rapidity of changes in our economic life."[4]

Local history satisfies an innate human desire to be connected to a place. It feeds our hunger to experience life directly and on intimate terms. It serves nostalgia, which (especially when one concedes nostalgia's political and literary cultivation and exploitation) is arguably as compelling a cultural force as the quest for progress.[5] Fostering loyalty to a unique climate of feelings and thoughts, it honors a kind of primal attraction one has to one's own youth—which is unique in the irreversible succession of life. In the words of early-twentieth-century French Catholic poet and essayist Charles Péguy: "One never makes friends except of the same age and time." Our only friends are contemporaries "of the same fellowship, of the same formation, of the same society, of the same world. . . . Friends of an only time are only friends." This singular friendship, mortal and fleeting, is a good without equivalent. It is "a cradle, a family, a people, a time, a date, an entire temporal order, of unique and irreplaceable importance."[6]

Local history serves more than personal desire and individual nostalgia, however. It meets groups' collective yearning to bring back to life departed people, places, and times, tempting nostalgia and commerce equally to exploit themes of inheritance and heritage with pageants, theme parks, and even real estate ventures. As Lewis Mumford pointed out, "Every old part of the country is filled with memorials of our past; tombstones and cottages and churches, names and legends, old roads and trails and abandoned mines, as well as the things we built and used yesterday. All these memorials bring us closer to the past, and, so doing, bring us closer to the present; for we are living history as well as recording it; and our memories are as necessary as our anticipations."[7] Local history—as I, along with my original colleagues in the history department, have discovered in a decade of teaching mandatory rural and regional courses at Southwest State University—provides the natural link between immediate experience and general history. It confirms the idea that one's own home is worthy of study and, again in the words of Mumford, promotes "a decent self-respect," and it is that "form of self-knowledge which is the beginning of sound knowledge about anyone else."[8]

THE PRACTITIONERS

Local history's topics are innumerable in their combinations. They arise from the desire to know, to explain, to preserve, to understand, and to commemorate. They flow out of interest in and curiosity about one's own place of worship, business, and civic and social organizations. Like the impulses that underpin journalism, local history takes form around the wish to document single episodes, which often teem with worlds of meaning, and is imbued with a sense of proprietorship in those episodes. A violent strike, a political massacre, a wildfire, or a sunken ship—all potentially win local historians' fidelity.

Local historians are driven to piece together a cherished and intimate past. They cannot quit themselves of their curiosity. This quest supersedes any desire to write critical history and often separates that desire from the professional historian's commitment either to a structured narrative of events or to a theory of development. In fact, local historians' concern for the unique person, singular place, or particular episode challenges them to satisfy the demands of both narrative and explanation.

Local historians' interests in traditions, legends, and rituals—the physical and mental landscapes of a place—resemble those of folklore or anthropology. Yet local historians commonly eschew theory. Their fidelity is not to ideology or methodology, to complex hypotheses, subtle generalizations, or protracted debates about sources, but to details, anecdotes, and particularities. Their concern for the particular can make them parochial. They risk mistaking what is common to an entire epoch and a whole nation as singular to their own place and time. Often, local historians' love of the past leads them to discount the present. Change, if they acknowledge it at all, is judged as decline from a pristine past, from a time when the world was whole. They discard the present, which is the spur to rethink the past, and, thus, escape a reconsideration of the present. And what is history without revision?

Enamored with the static past, local museums and historical societies can become mere attics for peoples and things of bygone times. Members, though not necessarily averse to today's inventions and progress, pledge themselves to collecting, storing, and reminiscing, to duplicating and reinforcing a frozen image of the past. Endless sheets of music, hats sufficient for a dozen Easter parades, uniforms and guns from all services, band instruments, and old Coke signs can cumulatively reiterate a single redundant point: mass-produced goods, along with national signs and slogans, had a profound effect everywhere.

In all likelihood, the present condition of local history will persist as long as local historians remain oblivious to the mutation, metamorphosis, and even obliteration of the contemporary countryside. Aside from sharing with most historians a disinterest in the changing present, they lack a stimulus, a minimal theoretical apparatus, and a guiding model. The field of local history by its nature is profoundly fragmented. Think of Thomas Jefferson's hold over the Charlottesville region of Virginia. Here, local history is dominated by the biography of a single individual. Think of Petersburg, Virginia. There, place is commanded by a single battle in the Civil War. In yet other places (I think of alternating stretches along the mid-Atlantic coast), local history is subsumed by concern for a changing ecology, the rise and fall of the fishing industry, or the dominance of an emerging beach-resort industry. Conversely, in Cape May, New Jersey, all efforts, historians' included, are dedicated to preserving the town's golden age of leisure for the sake of present tourism and community.

Many places in the Midwest likewise know and express themselves in relationship to stereotypic, often idealized and sentimentalized portraits of the past. One place focuses on its early settlement days; another commemorates the coming or rule of the railroad, or thriving times prior to the First World War. Such preoccupations can distort the entire history of a place. The commemorated past can spell disregard for the present, leaving great contemporary changes unperceived and undocumented. Traces of the changing world in the village vanish daily—and local historians do not take measure of them. And, like generations before us, we fail to grasp in detail what the world makes of us.

If local history is to be renovated, it will depend on the commitment of talented amateurs seeking to understand what has and truly is happening to home. These individuals will most likely be solitary and eclectic. They may be community college teachers, people from the ranks of the burgeoning retired, or stray and odd individuals intent on grasping the place where destiny has delivered them. Certainly they will arise unpredictably. Their passion will be to fathom the singular place that has imprinted their mind with indispensable memories and a willingness to rethink home.

Proving the old saw that historiographers rarely write good history and theorists seldom conduct good practice, a new and vibrant local history will not spring from those in popular or academic quarters who appropriate locales for their sweeping views of humanity. It will not come from those who harness their stories to myths of the early settlers' triumphant ordeal. Nor will it come from revisionists who turn the settlement narrative upside down by making it a hideous tale of destruction and exploitation. As practitioners of local history know, the history of one place is never quite that of another place. What they cherish is not theory and generalization, but difference and differentiation.

Yet there is a rub to repudiating theory. If local history is to be renewed, historians must first question the premises of their history. They cannot be isolated from the present and its changes. If the changing times prove worthy of their consideration at all, they must doubt the reasoning that locks place and nation in a single and progressive history. They must draw fresh inspiration from professional history, especially from the emerging field of environmental history.[9] Also, as I hope this work will testify, fresh work in cultural history, particularly in modern and contemporary European histories, can offer novel themes and angles for local historical composition.[10] Ever in need of invigorated concepts and broadened perspectives—not moral rage and metaphysical stammering—in order to provoke and excite, local historians must make sparks without appearing to grind an ax.

Local historians now find their communities caught up in a great transmutation. In the last two decades, in particular, they have found themselves bearing witness to the making of an entirely new rural order—characterized by decline, turnover, turbulence, and transformation. Local historians must recount the story of the growing penetration and dominance of outside powers over local minds and landscapes. They must describe agencies and effects of change unequaled since settlement itself; at least, that is the argument John Radzilowski and I make for Marshall and southwest Minnesota in our recent book *Community of Strangers*.[11]

Stories of local initiative and accomplishment have evaporated in the face of state-mandated programs, population decline, and the loss of the traditional business community. The nation and its rural communities no longer seem to walk hand-in-hand into the future. Their last shared triumph, to paraphrase historian Richard Davies, was over the Great Depression, with victory over the Axis and material achievement that placed a car in every garage and a flickering television in every living room.[12]

Local historians are seldom directly preoccupied with earth-shaking events or political maneuvering, although worldwide forces continually shape their homes and communities. Their subjects are usually far more modest: a family, a house of worship, a company, a bay of sailors, a valley of farms, the coming of a new technology, the passing of a venerated institution. It is precisely the limited focus of local history that makes it such a powerful anodyne in a mass era characterized by gigantic proportions and crushing statistics.[13]

Local historians do not court high, mighty, or even large audiences. Generally they keep their distance from the methodological fashions that pervade universities. In contrast to the exalted terrain over which academics vie, local historians hug the less sublime ground of anecdote. They often deserve their reputation for being commonplace, ho-hum, and tedious, because they concentrate on ordinary things. Not unlike social historians of everyday life, local historians pursue invisible men and women living their common lives, going about their pedestrian labors, and pursuing their daily bread and popular pleasures.

Offering a humble solace in this imperial age, local historians shape their work around items we can touch, personalities and institutions we have directly experienced. Resembling genealogies on this count, their best studies rest on precise connections. For these historians, theory always gives way to facts. At a time when encompassing ideologies and global sensibilities abound, the practitioners of local history strive to tell single stories in a straightforward manner.

For local historians, their rewards are as tangible as their subjects. They know in detail what contributions they have made by collecting, studying, and writing. They know what territories they have opened and what gaps they have filled. They know the communities their work serves. They know that their work in almost all cases is a singular, irreplaceable contribution. They are consoled to know that their publications, which rarely ever gain national or even regional notice, may outlast standard academic tomes dependent on the vagaries of academic fashions. More grandiosely, local historians can argue that their publications are indispensable contributions to the science of the singular in this age of abstraction. There is pride and pleasure in giving birth to a book about a place, community, person, or small region when society at large is agog over great ideas, startling developments, or all-embracing trends. Local historians can take satisfaction in helping to sustain a specific locale. They do what Guy Thuillier, master of French local and regional history, considers so important: they define the tissue and the memory of endangered local communities.[14]

Such high praise as this seldom, if ever, is heard from professional academic historians, who commonly disregard local and micro-regional history. They venture into regional history mainly to contend against a prevailing theory. The microcosm serves merely as a reflector of their macrocosm. If they bother even to notice local and regional historians, professional historians judge them to be narrowly focused fact gatherers and eccentric storytellers, or they are irritated by the disdain that amateur local historians show for the academy's No Trespassing signs. Lacking an effective and popular national association dedicated exclusively to local history, local historians go about their business as oblivious to professional historians and their canons as professional historians are indifferent to them. (State historians and their societies commonly find local histories too narrow and eccentric to merit their support. Additionally, local history might, by approach and subject, transcend state borders and prove indifferent to prevailing orthodoxies.)

Like any passion, writing local history can bring pain and disappointment. Aside from the lack of time, money, skills, and collaborators, local historians often find themselves writing for small, poor, and diminishing audiences. And even when supported by a rare university appointment, they may not find allies among administrators, students, or faculty members, who frequently have little historical understanding of or affection for the locale. The awareness of what is *not* being done to save the history they cherish keeps local historians constant companion. As in other fields of knowledge, accomplishment is often rewarded by an escalating sense of insufficiency.

Local historians must collect and preserve the primary and secondary documents of their locale. Over time, this can turn into a pressing obligation and even a matter of despair, as time sweeps things clean. Conscientious local historians sense that they must not only provide documents for their own works but also provision subsequent generations with abundant possible evidence. They grasp that those who come after may find the past inaccessible precisely on matters that we take for granted. Who, for instance, thinks of saving the records and catalogues of the local contractor, hardware store, or chamber of commerce? Who is undertaking the study of changing patterns of travel, use of psychological services, or turnover rates in diverse local industries? Duty simultaneously binds local historians to past, present, and future.

An irrevocable fidelity to a given place, time, landscape, and community—which as an ensemble might equal a childhood or adult home—makes capturing even the most everyday images and objects a matter of conscience. Local historians worry, often compulsively, that if they do not preserve a given past, it won't survive at all. At some point, they recognize themselves and their subjects as mutually precious, fragile, and temporal. Tedious, demanding, and exhausting, local history, like a consuming hobby, demands more work than any human can muster. Effort cannot keep pace with the desire, imagination, and conscience born of passion. Passion forces local historians to confront their finitude and mortality.[15]

Even as local historians shoulder the weight of their responsibility to their successors, they feel mortality strike at them from other dark quarters. The information they painstakingly research, collect, and write down won't endure forever. The living lose interest in the dead. Local historians' documents end up in dusty archives—and in the end, both the historians and their subjects vanish. How could it be otherwise, when whole civilizations—Elam, Nineveh, Babylon—fell into oblivion and remain for us but dry stones and "beautiful vague names"?[16]

Neither life nor work, neither memory nor the subject can last. All turns to dust in the mills of the contemporary market, state, technology, and bureaucracy. In the highest mountains of Sicily, the deepest recesses of Brazilian jungles, on this prairie, under its immense sky, change prevails. No heart secures permanence, no action assures continuity; even hope wavers with different wishes. All peripheries register the rhythms of Chicago, Los Angeles, New York, Washington, London, Paris, Rome, Tokyo, and other world-shaping cities. The river of change always spills over its banks, inundates the land, and eventually erodes even the most enduring promontories.

However, temporality does not weaken local historians' fidelity, at least as I have idealized it. On the contrary, it intensifies it. Mortality does not divest their hearts from earthly matters but rather stimulates their wish to preserve particular objects and temporal connections. They know that they have a singular duty to a singular place. They know that their work is uniquely valuable. They know themselves to be blessed in a protean age and amorphous world to offer a testimony that must be given—and that they alone, or with the help of a few friends, can do it. On this count, local history is a mission that belongs to committed and passionate amateurs.

DEFINING REGION

Local historians must stand ready to connect their locales to both immediate and distant worlds. Above all else, they must come to terms with the accordionlike notion of *region*—and its subsets, zones, belts, sectors—in order to understand the natural endowments and human actions that distinguish a place. Without this capacity, local historians will indeed be guilty of the parochialism for which they are often cited and will fail to extend the context of their work and thus give it the significance its deserves.

Local historians should not come to this task empty-handed. In all likelihood they are acquainted with how cotton determined the fate of the American South; how the milk cow made rural New England; how corn and pigs formed the Midwest and windmills and barbed wire allowed mastery of the Great Plains. With just a smattering of European history, local historians can grasp that the concept of region has been, for more than a thousand years, adjustable and omnipresent, for it was medieval Europe that witnessed the birth of regions. Regions took form in distinct environments: mountains, woods, plains, and lowlands. They were shaped by climate, vegetation, and oceans and rivers; they were defined by agriculture, forestry, and mining. Nature largely measured out subsistence and fertility, but culture, religion, economics, and politics also drew odd and capricious borders and created lasting affinities and aversions. Fiefdoms, duchies, principalities, islands, centralizing city-republics, and even empires defined regions in the maelstrom of European events. Nowhere as much as in the Balkans did cultural diversity, historical memory, and ideologies collide, as recent events have again brutally shown.

In early-modern European history, regions existed by virtue of participation in the Mediterranean or Atlantic economies and Catholic or Protestant faiths. The Atlantic community settled the New World. The people of northern France—especially Normandy and Brittany—settled the St. Lawrence Valley, traveled the rivers of the Midwest and northern prairie and explored my own local Minnesota River system. Names such as the Coteau des Prairies and Lac Qui Parle testify to the early presence of French explorers and traders in southwestern Minnesota.

Local historians must extend their reach to grasp the multiple and evolving definitions of the concept of *region*. They must grasp its relativity. They must make themselves at home with anthropologists' varied use of the term: both the traditionally employed definition that identifies the space of tribes and customs and, more recently, the constructed Marxist-inspired reference to staking out shared spatial and material realms of "peoples without history."[17] Linguists, in turn, define regions by similarities and differences in language, while demographers characterize them by numbers and types of people. Geographers place spatial boundaries around natural physiography or a region's economic resources and development, whereas historians cast temporal grids over political borders and cultural boundaries. Local historians must also grasp how politicians and chambers of commerce are master creators of regions. On occasion, both appear to conjure something out of nothing, or next to nothing; the former can excite armies to march, and the latter can fashion lake regions, cheese lands, and wine valleys out of landscape.

A term as variable as *region* requires dexterous use. Although commonly judged to be the most myopic of all historians, local historians must draw on the works of geologists, agronomists, hydrologists, and other students of the natural and constructed world. Using contemporary geography and demography, local historians can estimate and represent the shifting forces, changing institutions, and developing cultures of their locale. Finally, with the aid of other historians, local historians can establish contexts and narratives that link their subjects to other regions and the world at large.

Of course, local historians also need all sorts of maps, charts, and graphs to accustom themselves to the variety of perspectives defining a region. Natural features such as rainfall, vegetation, geologic structures, and water sources constitute elemental determinants of place. Maps and graphs of human activity—from those recording borders of tribal lands and nation-states to those charting early settlements, waterways, railways, and drainage systems—give different views of the human constructions of the landscape. Of course, no set of spatial coordinates and quantitative indicators can represent all aspects of a given place. They simply do not capture the dynamics of change that are so pertinent to all historical inquiry, especially for historians dedicated to understanding home and place at a time when accelerating change characterizes the entire world.

LOCAL HISTORY AND REGIONAL HISTORY

Local history calls for a clarification of the relationship between the local and the regional. I treat the region of southwest Minnesota (which has no singular definition) as if it were a locale itself. I see it as a micro-region composed of nineteen counties that share a common history by virtue of being in an agricultural zone within the state of Minnesota. I conceive it (as shown on the three maps in chapter 1) as belonging to and being encompassed by yet other and larger regions, such as the tall grass, or northern, prairie, or the Prairie Lake Region. I place it at the northwestern corner of the Midwest. A borderland between prairie and plain, wet and dry lands, I suggest it is a gateway to the Great Plains.

Yet, as a region comprising roughly ten thousand square miles, it is too large to count as a locale, insofar as a locale implies a place that one experiences and knows directly. Furthermore, southwest Minnesota's geography, ecology, towns, and ethnic settlements are diverse. Its economic, political, and cultural development provide it with a varied and changing historical definition, which I admittedly transform—or even create—by the very act of writing about it.

Sometimes I treat *local* and *regional* as synonyms, whereas at other times I underline their opposition. Operating under the truism that locales belong to regions and regions are composed of locales, readers are likely to assume that locales and regions, thus local and regional history, not only have much in common but are in many cases identical. This assumption, however, falls apart on close examination.

While definitions of a locale *can* prove problematic, definitions of regions invariably do. At the extreme, in fact, regional definitions are self-contradictory. On the one hand, a region can be conceived of as an entity sharing a common geographic, economic, political, or cultural center. On the other, a region can be understood as a macro-unit, embracing whole states, nations, and even vast and diverse geographic territories in which individual locales are unlikely to share a common geography, climate, culture, government, or historical experience. The very range of its diversity becomes a part of the region's definition.

Historians can disagree on definitions of locales. A given locale can be mapped differently when classified as a location, a site, or a place, for at issue is the definitional centrality of geography, economics, cultures, or community. The history of European names suggests that in the Middle Ages, particular and modest features of a landscape—a stream, a church on a stream, a marsh, or a single tree—were significant enough to provide villages and individuals with their names. In contrast, testifying to the tremendous transformative powers of contemporary civilization, whole regions have been temporarily identified by the nation that colonized them, like French West Africa, or the industry that has exploited them, like the coal region of northeastern Pennsylvania, which has been named the Anthracite Region. At the same time, national borders divide ecological zones, as shown by the division of the grassy plains by the United States and Canada and the arid plains of the Southwest by the United States and Mexico.

The physical geography and the history of a place are not identical. A place belongs similarly but never equally to the course of nature and human events. Topography, soils, and climate define conditions and set limits to human settlements. For instance, according to essayist and naturalist Joseph Wood Krutch, the American West begins where vegetation competes for water rather than sunlight.[18] Yet the West as a region cannot be understood independently from profound and ongoing economic and political efforts to shape and transform the land and its waters to suit its human wants and needs. The degree and manner to which nature and human work seem in harmony with each other, or stand defiantly at odds, form the histories of macro-regions.

From another perspective, the definition of a place—its borders, meaning, and use—is conferred by those who discover, conquer, and map it. Old World conceptions and ambitions defined New World realities and attractions. The fate of places depends on changing motives, developing interests, and even the skills of mapmakers.[19]

Historians do not escape these testing problems. To delineate a region is tantamount to determining which factors, natural or human, define it. In constructing regions—whether the Mediterranean or the Great Plains—historians fabricate unities and draw divisions between places. Situating a place in a region attributes to it an environment, a way of life, a fate, and can even predicate a distinct relationship between society and nature.

Regions also rise out of contested events. French Canada belongs to the history of French colonization, the British victory in North America, and above all else, the plight of a single Canadian province, Quebec. In Ukraine, recently born as an independent nation out of the ashes of the Soviet empire, local history thrives as fresh potentials are perceived and novel identities are required. All regions are subject to reinterpretation as events and politics mutate and elite groups foster fresh ideologies. All historians to a degree both record and invent pasts and presents for peoples, places, regions, and nations. They are makers of place and home.

In the hands of its definers, a region can be a micro- or a macrocosm. Environmentalists may equate a region with a distinct ecology or with one of its physical attributes, such as a chain of mountains, a body of water, or the specific mixture of them.[20] While some traditional practitioners identify regions with a combination of ecology and historical interaction, as in the cases of New England, the Southwest, the Midwest, and the Pacific Coast, other historians drape regions in timely ecological and environmental garb. They equip regions ethically and ethnically to fit their yearnings for yesteryear and their politics for tomorrow.

Historians of macro-regions like the West (such as Donald Worster, Richard White, and Patricia Limerick) create narratives to match vast historical processes.[21] They invent moral narratives and agents to express nation building, the expansion of democracy, and the establishment of new economic and industrial orders. The aim of their regional histories is to reflect critically the transformations of society and nature. Localities and micro-regions become forgotten stars in the movement of such immense heavens.

Local historians make a different use of the concept of region. They use it principally as a backdrop for their stories of places. Imprecise about where the surrounding region ends or begins, let alone how it fits into the nation, they articulate smaller, even minuscule, regions. They speak of micro-regions, such as a zone where two rivers join or one divides, where one or two crops controlled the economy for a century, or where a particular industry, such as iron mining, commanded life and settlement. The micro-region provides a kind of mediating identity between a collection of places and localities that have contact and share a common experience and yet are shaped (as all contemporary locales are) by an expanding metropolis, the history of the state, or the fate of a nation.

The need for a sense of place (as real and constructed) intensifies as impinging nations, economies, technologies, and ideologies get larger, more complex, and increasingly abstract.[22] In the last three to four decades in Europe, regionalism, despite moves toward overall unification, has exploded. Micro-regionalism does more than criticize centralization and excess taxes. It ignites passions, warms souls, and peddles politics. It also sells wine, cheese, and a lot more. The tourism industry often adds a picturesque distant past to eclipse a failed present. It sells stories of yesteryear's bandits in the mountains of Sardinia and train trips across the North American plains. Frequently, local and regional historians, with the goading of the chamber of commerce, conspire to provide local color and culture to freshly created places. Historians have yet to deliberate on the possibilities of creating electronic regions out of interactive Web pages—nor have they begun a fully critical discussion of how much "tradition" and "place" are recent creations.[23]

Wise local historians—I hope—will grasp all this. They will not sacrifice locale to region or region to locale. In fact, this conceptual complexity will lead them to a timely reformulation of home and place. It will enhance their sense as makers of places—as creators who must toggle between the immediate givens of place and experience and the profound influence of state, nation, and world. They will learn to use the notion of region—so important to contemporary environmental and economic history—to write their histories of individual places. Although complex issues lie outside their doors, they will not allow methodical argument and moral disputation to devour home and its stories. Even when perplexing theory, contradictions, and ambiguity nip at their heels, they must pursue their own path among details and particularities. They persist in their duty of getting right the names, places, deeds, motives, associations, circumstances, and events of a chosen place. This is the labor and reward of rethinking home.

CHAPTER I

A Place Called Home

Local historians are often historians of home. The meaning of home shapes their works. It is the source of first feelings and impressions, of primary encounters; it is the subject of first memories, deep senses, and enduring passions.[1] Simultaneously the object of the most profound feelings, the subject of the greatest nostalgia, and a topic for a lifetime of rethinking, home is local historians' measure of every other place.

Home is first and foremost the house into which one is born. A secure home allows a person to inhabit the universe safely. Composed of a singular set of objects, each home occupies space and anchors lifetimes in the same way a tuft of grass catches and holds particles of soil. Imprinted on a child's mind, home establishes vocabularies of senses, emotions, images, and metaphors that later express a lifetime's meaning.

Home also extends beyond the walls of a house and its garden. It gathers around itself orbits of sounds, smells, and sights. It embraces the environment, the historical era, and the temporal goods that fill it. Home is the site of natural epiphanies: the sky and the earth touch in a certain way, horizons are vast or impeded, light has a certain quality of radiance, rain comes in steady drizzles or drenching downpours.

In southwestern Minnesota, home is a place of winter blizzards, summer tornadoes, spring floods, and frequent droughts. My wife's shade garden testifies to the erratic turn of seasons here. As the snow melts in spring, she kneels on saturated ground to ready the soil, only to find herself in a matter of days lamenting the cracking ground and quarreling with the desiccating winds. She soon takes up her summer duty of hauling water to keep the garden alive.

Home is the place from which and to which all journeys lead. Home—in the form of mother and father—takes a child by the hand, marches him or her out into the surrounding world, and later offers a welcome back. It provides a touchstone, a template, so that when people travel away from home—their neighborhood, village, or farm—they can find elements in common with the place they came from. Home prepares people for their encounter with the world. It creates a code for deciphering new experiences. Migrants—which to some degree all of us in the contemporary world have become—carry a mental compass that spins toward familiarity and home as often as it pivots in the direction of difference. Only by understanding that does one grasp how immigrants succeed in taking root in a new place while striving to create home or at least its simulacrum.

The farmers and villagers of southwest Minnesota find common ground with all those who work the land, raise the same crops and animals, earn their profits from distant markets, and live in small settlements. And they understand the plight of other rural people who are experiencing a shrinking number of farms and agricultural communities. This familiarity explains why they find it an especially keen pleasure when traveling to encounter people from home, or from other rural towns. It's no coincidence that the Twin Cities of Minneapolis and St. Paul host dozens of annual reunions for rural Minnesotans who have been transplanted to the city.

EMBRACING A SECOND HOME

Homes can also be adopted. They can be more about sustenance than childhood experience. They can be more about vital relationships of work and family than birth and deepest memories of a given place and landscape.[2] A growing family attaches itself to a place as the tentacles of a husband and wife's work and activities and their children's play and schooling take hold of the world around them—at least that was my experience. The story of how the Minnesota prairie came to be home for me and my family highlights some of the elements of how an individual and family make a place home.

I came to southwestern Minnesota thirty years ago with my wife and two infant children. After having taught at the State University of New York in Binghamton and the University of California in Riverside, I had come to teach European intellectual and cultural history at a brand-new college on the prairie. My wife and I had no intention of staying at this small college for three years, much less thirty. Even less could I imagine dedicating a significant portion of my work to studying and defining a place whose cultural and material landscape seemed so distant from ours. I came from the working classes of Detroit, my wife from northeast Pennsylvania, the coal region.

Nevertheless, we stayed. A poor job market and two more children securely anchored us in this sea of corn and soybeans. I never expected to write a range of books on a murder, a crop scandal, an ethnic farming community, demographic decline, new immigrants, and economic and social turbulence in this region. Nor did I imagine that one day I would direct the university's program on rural and regional studies and help form a society for the study of local and regional history.

This place on the prairie—at the northwestern edge of the Midwest and the Corn Belt and at the doorway to the Great Plains—first meant for me open lands, endless fields, empty roads, and God's commanding sky. Here, openness and emptiness seemed to feed each other.

The region's constant wind pushes and presses everywhere, sharpening the edges of the climatic extremes of cold and hot. Tornadoes cut fickle and destructive swaths across the countryside in spring and summer. In winter, temperatures are commonly below freezing for months and may stay below zero for a week. Though winter can occasionally swaddle the countryside in soft and tempering flakes, more often it strangles the region with ice and snow. Blizzards turn fields into seas of frozen waves and freeze people to death within sight of their homes. Blizzards drive cattle into the fields, where with iced nostrils the animals are suffocated by the thousands, to remain buried in snow until the spring thaws exhume them.

Snowstorms also close roads, schools, and businesses for days at a time. They shut me and my family in our seventy-year-old home—in which our heating system, pushed to the limit, gurgles and bubbles like a swamp—as drafty cold enters through every crevice. With the outside world annulled by snow, our home expands to be the whole world. Winter tethers all to home and village.

Our first eight winters in southwestern Minnesota were spent in Cottonwood, an agricultural village of eight hundred inhabitants. We lived on East Main, a wide street bordered by homes built at the beginning of the twentieth century. Our house was a hundred yards from a major ditch dug around 1900 to drain twenty-five square miles of farmland into nearby Lake Cottonwood. Up and down our street, especially during harvest season, farmers drove their large machinery to the town grain elevator, which, along with the water tower, distinguished Cottonwood's skyline from other nearby villages.

Across the street to the north, behind the facing row of houses, was a mink farm whose odor on humid days engulfed our lives. At the west edge of the mink farm, in a small house facing the small furniture factory, which emitted strong paint fumes, lived the town policeman, Lowell Fenger, and his wife and three children.

Lowell grew a small garden and lived for hunting and fishing. He occasionally stopped at Andy's Pool Hall, where Andy, between serving up beer and pop and playing pinochle, held court. Andy believed that things were going to hell in a handbasket and the nation needed a purifying depression. His audience, shifting in and out across the day and evening, included at any one time a pipe-smoking bachelor who graded roads, a farmer who rented his land, several retired farmers, the town drunk, and a young man who was forever trading off the bike he had just bought for another one.

Across the road and down a ways, at the new municipal lounge, another part of the village humanity assembled. Perched on two stools were two heavy bachelor twins who dressed like cowboys and stank like polecats. Often next to them sat the local pollution control officer, who frequently polluted himself and got belligerent. Found on a few other stools, depending on the day and hour, were a butcher who was a former boxer (he once fought Golden Gloves), a successful farmer who had pitched in the St. Louis Cardinal farm system for a few years, and a hard-drinking Norwegian farmer who was familiar with the work of expansive prairie dreamer, moralist, and politician Ignatius Donelley. Once at the lounge I had a conversation with a Vietnam veteran who had sent his mother a bottle of ears. Frequently there were one, two, or even three promising students—"the best in the history of Cottonwood's high school"—who went away to college, only to return home for instructions on what they should do next in life.

Trying to chart the inner map of these people, I developed a technique for drawing out their stories. I would attribute some behavior—acceptable or unacceptable—to my relatives and then add that I was sure my listeners didn't have relatives like that. For example, after telling stories about how frugal my relatives were, I heard in response case after case of the niggardly behavior of others' relatives. On another occasion, I told the old, Belgian, part-time bartender at Andy's that, of all the strange things, my grandmother carried two chestnuts to ward off rheumatism.

As he reached into his pocket and pulled out two chestnuts, he responded, "These things don't work at all. But what does work," he added, "is this stony-hard spud of a potato," which he retrieved from his other pocket and held in front of my nose.

The village also provided other experiences worthy of reflection. Along with a handful of other faculty and a few students who lived in the village, I clashed with the local veterans' association over its intention to install a cannon in a small park adjacent to the principal highway crossing. A major subject in the town newspaper and the village gossip, "the battle of the cannon" played out locally the national ideological battle over Vietnam. The veterans passionately invoked the debt owed to those who had died for the nation, and we, outsiders all, called for guilt over the youth being sacrificed to an unjust and a futile war.[3]

Subsequently, I witnessed the election of a Catholic priest, Dennis Becker, as mayor of this Norwegian Lutheran town, whose government he transformed with new energy, direction, and popular support. I became friends with the town's most prominent Norwegian Lutheran, Bror Anderson, who was head of the local Norwegian Mutual Insurance Company and the dominant member of the all-important local Lions Club. Later Bror supported me—outsider, protesting professor, and Catholic—as head of a Cottonwood Lake study. The study of the lake introduced me to the complexity of conflicts over environmental issues, which in this case pitted village resident against village resident, city against state agency, one state agency against another, and county against county. It also showed me how controlled our waters have become, and yet how divided our opinion is about their use.

So in this village, where we found an affordable home for a family of six, I discovered, person by person, story by story, issue by issue, year in and year out, a rich texture of characters and cultures. Cottonwood indeed was a small world teeming with individuals and experiences, diverse attitudes and opinions, and they formed only the visible face of a village whose almost century-long history includes tales of changes in institutions, groups, politics, and attitudes, not to mention in the countryside around it. A study of Cottonwood could absorb decades of a historian's life.

DEFINING OUR REGION

On the one hand, my sense of locale grew out of the home I came to embrace in Cottonwood. On the other, I consciously constructed it out of discussions at the nearby college, in the regionally dominant city of Marshall, whose 1970 population of ten thousand made it the second-largest town and the approximate center of southwestern Minnesota. There, my history colleagues and I tried to give a more substantive meaning to "southwest Minnesota" than merely the nineteen counties defining the southwest corner of the state and the towns and communities our college was pledged, by its founding mission, to serve.[4] Did the borders of Iowa and South Dakota form the southern and western edges of this region? Did the higher, sandier, and less-productive grounds to our north constitute a northern border, or was it the trees and deeper lakes farther on? What would serve as our region's eastern border? Was there one? Where did we cross it along the three-hour drive to the Twin Cities, through a region characterized by a nearly static topography, the same crops, and villages that all appeared so similar? Perhaps it lay at that point in the journey when we momentarily dipped into the wooded Minnesota River Valley, which transects this corner of the state from northwest to southeast (see Map 1).

The more I sought to characterize this region, the more it eluded me. A single state like Minnesota can contain many regions, zones, sectors, and belts that can be differentiated by water, woods, prairie, soil, crops, mineral resources, size, and density of human settlement. The main ecological regions of prairie, deciduous forest, and northern coniferous forest are not contiguous with state or national boundaries.[5] And how was I to situate southwestern Minnesota, which belonged to the prairie and was door to the plains, in the Midwest or heartland?

James Malin, Kansas historian of the prairie and grasslands, got to the heart of the matter when he said, "No two criteria determine boundaries that coincide exactly."[6] In different combinations, terrain, climate, vegetation, soils, agriculture, and metropolitan influence all give rise to different regions. Adding a pinch of complexity to a pound of arbitrariness, Malin contended that a region is an interrelated whole in which all the parts form a singular situation and act simultaneously. Yet Malin acknowledged that a region can be a historical creation, and he implied that today's region might be yesterday's political or economic accident.[7]

Fortunately, we had a more tangible axis for our definitional work. It was the survival of our university, whose continued existence was called into question by declining student enrollments. We were compelled to identify our region as the surrounding nineteen counties. For political reasons, it had to encompass roughly ten thousand square miles and two hundred thousand people.

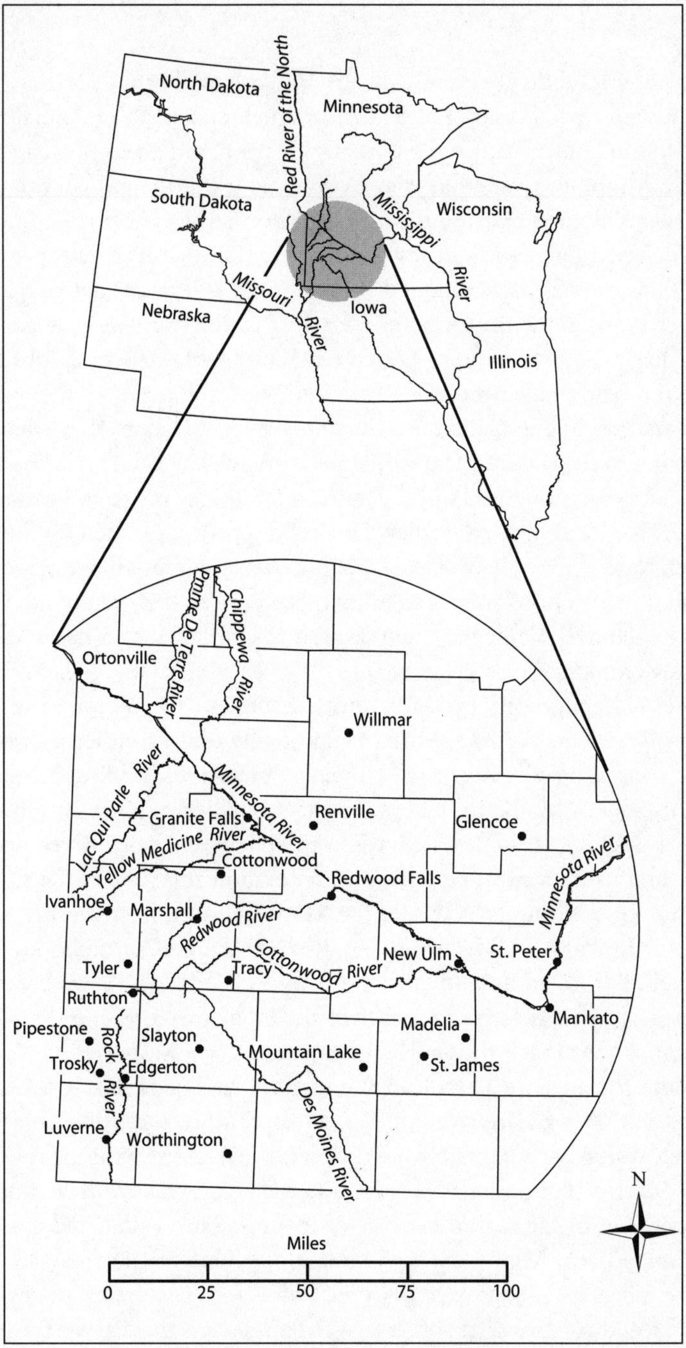

Map 1. Places and rivers of southwest Minnesota. *Sources:* ESRI base maps, USGS and SAST rivers, and MN Dot cities. Prepared by the GIS Center, Southwest State University.

But politics didn't prevent us from thinking of alternatives. For example, my fellow historian Ted Radzilowski (father of John Radzilowski, with whom I have coauthored two books) proposed an ethnic map of the region. Although aware that ethnicity is a malleable material out of which Americans fashion cultural identities, he argued that German communities encircled our region of diverse northern and eastern European ethnicities. Catholic, Lutheran, and Presbyterian—Germans define our borders, starting in the northeast and circling to the southwest, where they were displaced by a band of Dutch reaching from our region into Iowa. With the Scandinavians to the north and west, the region—like the little lakes that dimple its landscape—features a smorgasbord of settlements: Belgian, Czech, Dakota, Danish, Dutch, French Canadian, German, Icelandic, Norwegian, and Polish. These communities invite endless opportunities for local history studies. During the period of intense white settlement after the Civil War, cities, county seats, larger villages, and even certain farm sections were settled by the American children of ambitious New Englanders, while the countryside and smaller villages became home for new ethnic groups.

Physical geography presents another view of the region. The Minnesota River cuts across the area from northwest to southeast. It begins at the southern tip of Big Stone Lake, at Ortonville, and flows southeast until it reaches Mankato, where, taking a northerly course, it moves up to Fort Snelling to join the Mississippi. The Minnesota River was the route first used to explore, control, and exploit this part of the state. In addition, four tributary rivers of the Minnesota run from west to east—the Lac Qui Parle, Yellow Medicine, Redwood, and Cottonwood. These rivers flow from an upland glacial moraine called Coteau des Prairies—the largest geologic structure east of the Rockies—and end their rapid descent as they reach the gently rolling plains (see Map 2).

These features are a result of the region's geological history. Glaciers carved out the oversize river valleys. Most notably, the Minnesota River was excavated approximately ten thousand years ago by the great Glacial River Warren that drained the vast, ancient Lake Agassiz.[8] The most distinctive river of the region because of its impressive valley and extensive bottomlands, the Minnesota is 353 miles long, with a watershed of 26,000 square miles. Its valley is up to 5 miles wide and has vertical drops of up to 253 feet through a series of terraces.[9] The glaciers that carved the region also contoured it. They created the Coteau des Prairies along the western edge and pocketed the land with lakes and wetlands, prompting one author to define the region as the Prairie Lake Region.[10]

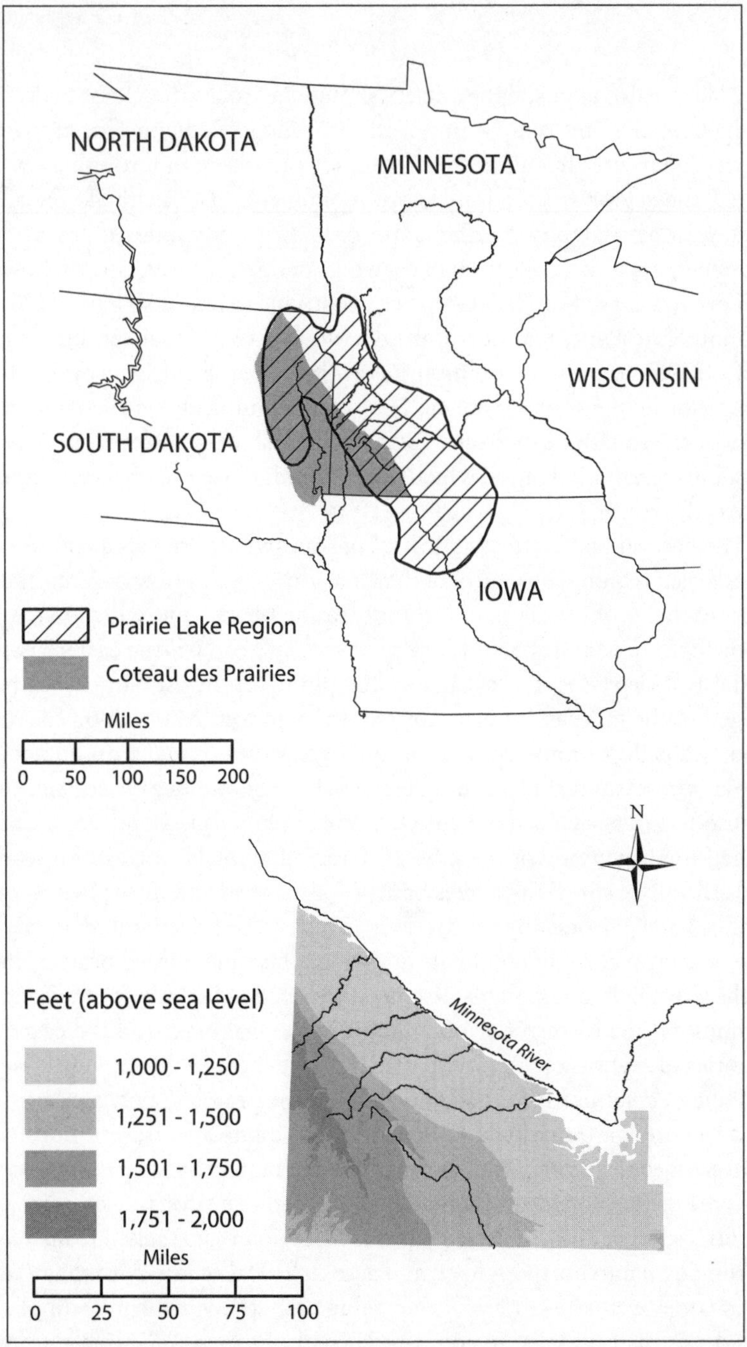

Map 2. Coteau des Prairies and Prairie Lake Region. *Sources:* USGS DEMs (30 meter resolution); Scott Anfinson, "The Prehistory of the Prairie Lake Region in the Northeastern Plains," Ph.D. diss., University of Minnesota, 1987; and the Northern Prairie Wildlife Research Center.

Glaciers also exposed the ancient granite bedrock (the oldest bedrock in the United States is at Granite Falls, in Yellow Medicine County) and the red quartzite, from another geologic era, whose outcroppings produced the region's most impressive monuments. For instance, Native American petroglyphs at Jeffers (approximately sixty miles southeast of Marshall) are a rich collection of drawings of thunderbirds, turtles, bows, and arrows carved on flat red rocks a thousand years or so ago. At Blue Mound State Park, just north of Luverne, red rock forms an imposing cliff off which, popular opinion has it, buffalo were driven by Native American hunters. At Pipestone National Monument, on the northern edge of the town of Pipestone, Indians still fashion a softer form of red rock into ceremonial pipes, which for hundreds of years have been traded across the continent.

The natural and cultivated grasses of southwest Minnesota connect it to a larger region, the prairie—that flat, open, and grass-covered land that reaches from Indiana and Illinois to the plains, and which extends from Texas to Manitoba and Saskatchewan and reaches the eastern edge of the Rockies (see Map 3). Before the plow, southwest Minnesota belonged to the tallgrass prairie. Grasses three to four feet high on the upland and eight to nine feet high in the river valleys created an immense sea in whose subterranean tangle existed a true biome. Of course, the prairie has not been a fixed entity. Climate altered it. Conditions challenged the hegemony of the grasses. Grazing animals, waves of insects, and advancing shrubs and trees battled for the land and their place in the sun. Indians periodically set fire to it, which also shaped and defined it. The new crop corn, in conjunction with pig farming, joined prairie land to the Corn Belt, a region historically developed to include southwestern Minnesota, the eastern tier of counties in the Dakotas, and the eastern counties of Nebraska.

Human creations have also laid claim to the prairie. Laws, bureaucracies, technologies, markets, rails, roads, real estate agents, and boosters have claimed the prairie as their own. Starting in the 1870s, a new rail system created the Northwest Empire. Bound together by iron tracks and market forces, town and countryside formed a region that reached from Wisconsin down into northern Iowa and across the Dakotas to Montana. The Twin Cities were the empire's principal focus—its engine, bank, supplier, and depot. Its railroads, in competition with those from Chicago, transformed prairie space. They linked and created prairie towns. They brought immigrants and gave full and immediate access to the goods of civilization, defining the primary commercial relationship between metropolis and

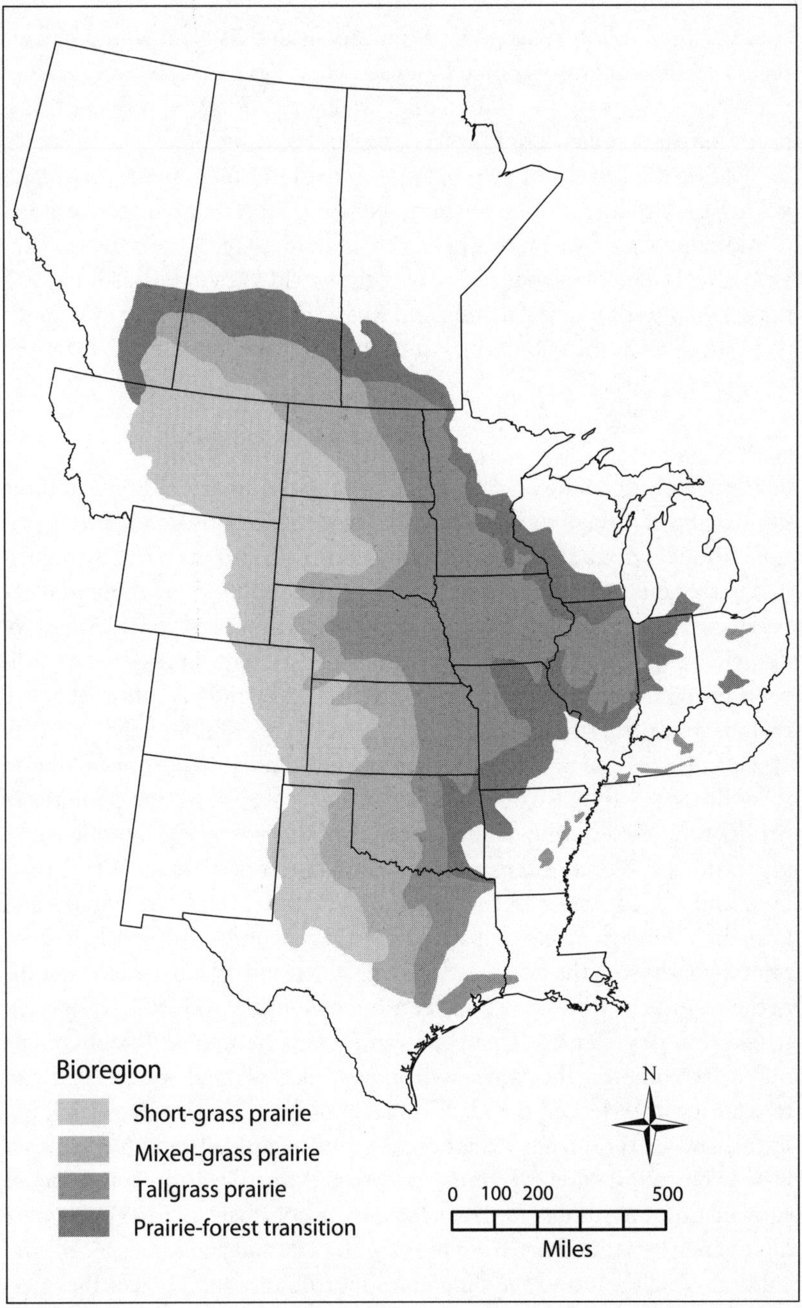

Map 3. The prairie bioregion. Prepared by the GIS Center, Southwest State University, based on the original work of the late professor David Costello and adapted by permission of his estate.

colony. In the following century, Minneapolis and St. Paul would make a region whose integration could be measured, for example, by frequency of telephone calls, patterns of banking, watershed districts, hubs of transportation, and audiences of professional sports teams.[11]

Writing the history of any region is a matter of telling the story of developing markets and new technologies, burgeoning democracies, and centralizing states. From this perspective, the fate of the southwest Minnesota region belongs to the history of the world's grasslands. Along with the grasslands of South America and Russia, North American grasslands were subdued at the end of the last century by an expanding civilization.

So the search to define place extends from the intimacy of home and the immediacy of village to far-reaching conceptualizations and generalizations about regions and a world in transition. It begins its reach by reflecting on the unmediated sensual experience of childhood, its elemental experiences, and fresh and dawning emotions. It moves to consideration of first encounters and initial formulations of different landscapes and diverse groups. It ends in speculation on the reality and invention of entire regions and rural orders caught up in a world of engulfing change.

This progression parallels the passage of the individual from childhood to adulthood. Molly Rozum makes this one of the informing premises of her doctoral dissertation.[12] She conceives of this passage as uniting entire generations in the same sensual foundation and process of identity formation, and she conceives of this process as crossing the United States and Canadian border and encompassing several generations of grassland-bred prairie youth from the last decades of the nineteenth century to the middle of the twentieth, when new and yet more revolutionary forces of differentiating change prevailed. These generations experienced, as Rozum points out, approximately the same environment of grass and water, road and town; they experienced the identical technological, economic, social, political, and cultural transformation. As centralizing altering forces penetrated the countryside ever more deeply and dissolved the autonomy of rural institutions, more recent generations, in contrast to earlier ones, were increasingly separated one from the other by mutating material, social, and cultural conditions and the different opportunities and choices they presented.

Technology, industry, commerce, government, and law continually transformed the prairie landscape. They entered home and hearth, altering ideas of power and right, shaping emotions and identities, aspirations and ambitions. Creating new communities and celebrations, they challenged older identities, affiliations, and loyalties. The changing prairie world established and then altered sensual worlds of sight, touch, taste, smell, and sound. These accounted for the modification and expression of such basic emotions as happiness, anger, and disgust. The evolving prairie society and conditions, as I will show in subsequent chapters, redefined experiences and expressions of fear, accounted for altered senses of the clandestine, and identified insanity and prescribed its treatment. At the same time, the larger meaning of the prairie and its places was consciously defined by articulate, imaginative, mythic, and stereotypic representations of it. On this count, the prairie and its meaning belong to literature, politics, and history.

To write local history (especially of prairie places) is to take the two opposite poles of rethinking home and place while defining this modern era and these contemporary times. It is to learn a place in detail while understanding it as part of an unprecedented mutation, transformation, and metamorphosis. Writing local history puts us in touch with the embodied child and the conjuring writer. It brings us to the common rural edge where village, region, and world meet.

CHAPTER 2

Grasses, Waters, and Muskrats

A Region's Compasses

In the decades immediately after the Civil War, American civilization exploded onto the Midwestern prairie and plains. Whole new orders of society were erected, and nature was irrevocably altered.[1] Native peoples of the prairie were driven to the margins. Soils and waters were transformed. Plants and animals from the Old World were introduced intentionally and unintentionally, while native tall grasses of the prairie were pushed out and native animals such as the wolf, the grizzly bear, the buffalo, and the elk became nearly extinct. Armies, railroads, markets, the government, and the plow made the prairie a docile servant of agriculture and expanding industrial society. In a matter of years, European settlement gave rise to capitalist agriculture, an immense, varied, and mutating system that overran an ecological system tens of thousands of years in the making.

In recent years, the national equation of European settlement with progress and God's will has been thrown into doubt. Local historians are now compelled to assess the impact of white settlement on nature according to new criteria. They must ask whether the settlement of the prairie and the arid plains, not to mention the discovery of the New World itself, was an unmitigated disaster for life on this planet.[2]

Reflection on the human consequences of settlement for native peoples may well lead local and regional historians to the position adopted by explorer and artist George Catlin, who visited southwestern Minnesota in the 1830s and was reputed to be the first white man to see the

Pipestone quarries, the primary northern American source of rock for pipes. Catlin wrote in *Letters and Notes on the Manners, Customs, and Conditions of North American Indians:*

> For the American citizens, who live every where proud of their growing wealth and their luxuries, over the bones of these poor fellows, who have surrendered their hunting-grounds and their lives, to the enjoyment of their cruel dispossessors, there is a lingering terror yet, I fear, for the reflecting minds, whose mortal bodies must soon take their places with their red but injured brethren, under the same glebe [soil]; to appear and stand, at last, with guilt's shivering conviction, amidst the myriad ranks of accusing spirits that are to rise in their own fields, at the final day of resurrection.[3]

The consequences of settlement force local historians to consider the costs of European civilization's spread to the Americas.[4] They may even induce historians to embrace the story of prairie and plains, as told by Patricia Limerick and Daniel Worster, as one of the victimization of natural and human landscapes.[5] As they do so, these consequences introduce historians to the complex and emerging field of environmental history. Students of this discipline, whose writings can be short on evidence and long on conjecture, now face a range of perplexing questions: How did native peoples alter landscapes prior to settlement? Especially, what use of fire did they make? To what degree were alterations of the prairie and plains environments caused by pressures from expanding French, British, and colonial civilizations and the new tools and animals they introduced?[6]

As prairie historians become aware of the scale of transformation brought about by contemporary life, they may reinterpret their subject. Abandoning the standard narrative of settlement's triumph, and shaken by the steady decline of the family farm, the rural town, and agricultural society, local historians may make an ecological judgment of the cost of civilization. In any case, the story of the settlers' unequivocal victory over nature, on which local and regional historians once relied, no longer holds. Historians of the prairie are called to consider their subjects anew.

ENVIRONMENTAL HISTORY

Rethinking settlement in terms of environmental history can provide a fresh perspective. It can stimulate historians to be more precise about the landscape, to approach agriculture in innovative ways, and to regain empirical and quantitative skills lost to the repetition of old myths or new fashions of historical rhetoric. Environmental history, with its preoccupation with biodiversity on the one hand, and agricultural history on the other, invites local historians to enhance the interdisciplinary character of their work.[7] It puts them in contact with geographers, demographers, anthropologists, rural sociologists, historians of agriculture, botanists, biologists, ecologists, and other scientists, encouraging them to look at complex systems of climates, soils, flora, and fauna and the effect of human action on all of them.

A historical approach to a region's ecology renders every ditch and wasteland a piece of evidence and a teaching prop. Every plant—from prairie grasses and forbs to wheat, corn, soybeans, sunflowers, flax, and Jerusalem artichokes—becomes a living text. In the same way, every animal—wild or domestic, large or small—provides a history lesson.[8] Animals form a picture of a region's biological history. A single species can function as the spine of that history, and the extinction of an animal or a set of animals can indicate the scale and speed of settlement. For example, in southwestern Minnesota, brown and black bears—more abundant in the woods and river valleys than on the open prairie—had already been killed off by the 1850s and 1860s.[9] The buffalo disappeared in the 1860s, and the last wolf bounties were paid in Lyon County in 1894.[10] These facts reveal the importance of historical records as seemingly insignificant as bounty documentation, trappers' ledgers, and taxidermists' logs.

A history of prairie animals would not be complete, of course, without information on small mammals such as the muskrat, weasel, gopher, shrew, mole, and vole. It also must cover the teeming multitudes of birds (now greatly diminished in number) that once made the grasslands and waters of southwest Minnesota part of one of the world's great flyways. And it must include the rich variety of fish in the region, and a few species of snakes, turtles, frogs, and clams, whose fates since settlement deserve their own histories.[11]

The history of animals reveals changes in habitats, and thus changes in environments. For example, deer, fox, rabbits, raccoons, skunks, rats, and other small mammals, which have become abundant in this region, thrive along the margins of agricultural lands.[12] Humans, for their part, are dependent on certain animals. The use of domestic animals such as the horse, ox, cow, sheep, pig, duck, and chicken would constitute additional chapters in the history of a region's fauna. Further chapters could cover the transformation these domestic animals have undergone as farms have grown in size, become systemized, and embraced technology to the point that they now resemble factories. Dairy cows have been turned into prodigious milk producers. Cattle and pigs, confined to yards and buildings, have become virtually new species. Hogs especially, once a free and rooting animal, have been altered in size, shape, and even behavior.

A history of a region's animals could be imaginatively expanded to include smaller, and even microscopic, creatures. One ecological history, for example, could focus on insects. A hearty test for the historian's imagination would be tracing the succession of species of insects to determine alterations in climate and changes in crops, as well as the changing uses of pesticides and herbicides. Such a history in southwestern Minnesota would recount, among other things, how the severe reduction in mosquitoes and dragonflies mirrors the increase in chemical applications and the decrease in wetlands. It would cover the puzzling phenomenon of grasshoppers swarming over this region in the 1870s.[13] It might also examine the introduction of the European honeybee with the coming of white agricultural settlement as another pollinator along with the indigenous wasp, butterfly, and bumblebee. A closer look at the spider, both a cousin to and predator of these insects, could punctuate the region's history of minute animals.

Environmental history also sheds light on human actions and attitudes that over decades have caused conflicts among farmers, sports enthusiasts, environmentalists, real estate developers, and government agents. Here in what remains a wet region of the prairie, an environmental history might examine battles over water, records of which abound in every courthouse. Neighbors, groups, agencies, and associations quarrel over dams, ditches, drainage, and anything else that alters the volume, surface, use, and flow of a body of water. In intensity and numbers, water battles exceed those over weeds, roaming animals, roads, bridges, and electrical cables.

Other types of conflict embroil regions as well. In Stearns County, farmers are still fighting battles over the erection in the 1970s of high-voltage power lines across their land by Northern States Power. In Yellow Medicine County, local citizens struggle against federal proposals to bury nuclear waste in the area's granite bedrock.

Currently, conflicts over large hog-confinement operations are igniting entire counties, pitting city against farm, neighbor against neighbor, friend against friend. The mayor of Pipestone reported that the establishment of four feedlots on the edge of town set the whole community astir. Supported on the one hand as the key to farm survival, the feedlots were attacked on the other for threatening the town's aquifer, polluting a nearby regional park, and destroying the environment of a grade school, golf course, and upscale subdivision. Detractors noted that the smell adversely affected the town's annual gathering of Civil War re-enactors; passions for and against the feedlots even set Pipestone's schoolchildren to fighting.[14]

Elsewhere in southern Minnesota, feedlots have been promoted as a way to save the family farm at the same time that they have been held responsible for killing fish and degrading a local cemetery—indeed, for destroying the overall quality of life. The issue has provoked heated conflicts in the Minnesota State Legislature. Surely there is enough stink here to win the attention of a dedicated regional historian. Someone should chart this tale of "new profits versus refined noses" as country and town encroach on one another.

Environmental conflicts such as these spawn citizens' groups, keep the lawyers busy, and nourish regulatory agencies, whose contested activities merit study. Minnesota still lacks succinct histories of the Department of Natural Resources (DNR), the Pollution Control Agency (PCA), and the state Department of Trade and Economic Development (DTED), not to mention solid accounts of environmental struggles that have embroiled county commissioners, watershed boards, advocacy groups, and nonprofit foundations. Environmental history abounds in conflict and thus in potential subjects—far more than there are historians to document them or archives to hold them. Yet no matter how outnumbered local historians are, they are not released from the obligation to provide a history of our changing landscape and the battles it arouses.

OF GRASSES I SING

As John James Ingalls wrote in "In Praise of Blue Grass," "Next in importance to the divine profusion of water, light, and air, those three great physical facts which render existence possible, may be reckoned the universal beneficence of grass."[15] With stories of grasses, historians can weave the intricate mat that joins native prairie and plains to evolving and diverse agriculture, and the boldest of them can seek to assess the costs of substituting the grasses of the market for those of nature.[16]

In the second half of the nineteenth century, modern civilization took control of all the earth's major grasslands, which occupy about a fifth of the earth's land surface.[17] (The world's tallgrass prairies are principally in central North America, European Russia, the South African veldt, and in the Argentine Pampas and neighboring Uruguay and Brazil.) In different ways and to varying degrees, settlement profoundly altered the North American prairie—the northern tallgrass prairie that reaches from western Indiana to the eastern portion of the Dakotas, and the short- and mixed-grass prairie of the more arid plains that extends from Texas north to Manitoba, Saskatchewan, and Alberta, and from the Rocky Mountains (from New Mexico to Montana) to the eastern Dakotas, central Nebraska, Kansas, and Oklahoma (see Map 3).

Prairie and plains historians must affirm that grasslands cannot be separated from the human life they support. The history of corn, wheat, oats, rye, barley, rice, sugarcane, and bamboo—all grasses—shapes and is shaped by human history. The Bible reminds us that all flesh is grass. Grasses make soils, which are the living skin of the earth. With three-quarters of their biomass below the ground, grasses determine soils' richness and integrity.[18] According to David Costello, in a square yard of prairie soil four inches deep, the roots "would stretch for twenty miles if all were placed end to end."[19] Grasses also nourish soils with residues and minerals and the worms, fungi, and bacteria that feed on them. Soils without grasses or other plants cease to be fertile; they erode and disappear, leaving only rock or sand. The entire biotic community of the prairie relies on its grasses.

The story of settlement on the prairie and plain cannot be reduced simply to the uprooting of wild grasses and planting of domestic grasses, wheat, and corn, in their stead. There is, to some minds, more to this history than the heroic tale of settlers' triumph over these grasses, which in the prairie and parts of the Great Plains were too vast to survey, too thick to penetrate, and too high to see over, with such dense and deep roots that it took plow teams of ten oxen to open up the rich black soil below. Historians must discuss more than the close relationship between grasses and pioneers—how grasses stoked their fires, stuffed their mattresses, furnished their brooms, and, as squares of sod, formed the walls of their temporary homes.[20] Historians must understand how human relations to grasses and animals, lands and waters, machines and markets, agricultural practices and personal desires, shaped and reshaped an environment, a way of life, and a state of mind.

The biosphere of the prairie, formed over millennia, was transformed in decades. Settlement divided the plant world into crops that make money, plants that don't make money, and weeds that cost money. Before this unprecedented division, multitudes of different plant species thrived on the prairie, and hundreds of them were considered useful.[21]

According to historian Allan Bogue, the distinguished student of the prairies Shimek Bohumil named 271 species in a list of "the typical prairie plants of Iowa."[22]

Perhaps the notes of the eccentric botanist, the dedicated gardener, or the odd weed inspector could serve someone who wished to write the history of a prairie region's flora. The botanist L. R. Moyer of Montevideo, Minnesota, hinted at the complexity of such an inventory in 1910 when he concluded, "No ecological survey of this region conducted according to modern ecological methods has ever been made, and it does not seem possible to make such a survey now."[23] If it were possible, such a history would inventory changing agricultural patterns, showing how soils, once opened by the plow, became receptive to the world's seeds. It would illustrate what George Perkins Marsh, a nineteenth-century father of ecological thinking, once noted: "Man is everywhere a disturbing agent. Wherever he plants his foot, the harmonies of nature are turned to discord."[24] This history—which would have to be extrapolated from the few remaining patches of native prairie—would examine indigenous terrestrial and aquatic plants as well as nonindigenous plants, both those introduced on purpose and surreptitious invaders like Russian thistle and crabgrass.

Grasses provide clues to a region's soils, climate, and fauna. Samuel Johnson may have said that "a blade of grass is a blade of grass," but prairie historians can use grasses to home in on their region.[25] In the Prairie Lake Region, tall grasses, particularly the native bluestem, characteristic of the eastern prairie, tended to cover lower ground; short grasses, identified with the high western plains, abounded on dry uplands. Indeed, the very mixture of grasses in southwest Minnesota marked out the region as a transition zone. In 1838, the explorer Joseph Nicollet noted the changing vegetation of the southwestern portion of the state as he moved "along the highest crests on this great plateau which separates the Mississippi and Missouri. . . . The grass of the prairie [here and farther west] is no more than 5 or 6 inches tall, a foot less than it was even yesterday."[26]

In combination with wetlands, tall grasses formed impenetrable barriers. This explains why buffalo and humans traversed the land along its ridges and crests, and why the original surveying of the land was such an arduous chore. Anthropologist Scott Anfinson speculates that the region's relative impenetrability accounted for the isolation of its early native inhabitants.[27]

Grasses also accounted for the prairie's consuming fires. Fire here, George Catlin wrote, "travels at an immense and frightful rate, and often destroys, on the fleetest horses, parties of Indians, who are so unlucky as to be overtaken by it; not that it travels as fast as a horse at full speed, but that the high grass is filled with wild ravines and other impediments which render it necessary for the rider to guide his horse in the zigzag paths of the deer and buffalo."[28] Fire encouraged native peoples to settle on islands or take refuge in the heavily wooded ravines.[29] Often, the only refuge from wildfire for settlers was a giant burnt circle of their own making.

Yet fire—so quick, so furious—did not destroy the vast subterranean root system of the prairie grasses. Nor were the fires intense enough to breach the insulating corky bark of the bur oaks, which, in the words of Aldo Leopold, were "the shock troops sent by invading forest to storm the prairie."[30] In fact, fire, as experimental burns in Minnesota, Kansas, and other states with prairie grasslands show, renewed the prairie. It burned away clogging brush and turned it into fertilizing charcoal, making room for the shoots of fresh grasses that attracted grazing animals, whose manure in turn fertilized the grasses.

For these and other ends, Indians burned the prairie. They used fire to shape their environment. Fire was their plow.[31] In fact, historian Stephen Pyne conceived of anthropogenic fire as extending the range of grasslands "north into Wisconsin, Michigan, and Minnesota, east through Illinois, Indiana, Ohio, and Kentucky, and south into central Alabama and Mississippi."[32] In some grasslands, white hunters and herders continued Indian fire practices, whereas on the prairie, farmers, who plowed and separated fields, both intentionally and unintentionally suppressed fire.

WATER, WATER, EVERYWHERE, BUT DROUGHT SOON TO COME

If grasses place southwest Minnesota on the prairie, water identifies its precise location. The Minnesota River and its tributaries, which at one time furnished the main routes into and out of this region, describe our location. The southernmost of the region's rivers, the Des Moines, flows not to the Minnesota and Mississippi Rivers but south and west to join the Missouri, and the Red River flows north to Canada. Thus, southwestern Minnesota is situated at the intersection of major national and international watersheds.

Tree-lined river valleys and creek bottoms zigzag across this region. Meager and unimposing in dry times, these rivers in wet spring seasons come roaring down from the uplands and produce floods that can quickly invade cities and linger for weeks on farm fields, as the region discovered in the floods of 1993 and again in 2001.[33]

The glaciers that scoured this landscape left a trail of small lakes, potholes, sloughs, marshlands, and seasonal ponds—wetlands whose size, number, and use warrant a local historian's interest. It is possible that, over the last 150 years, more than 25 percent of the wettest lands may have been covered with water during an exceptionally wet spring.[34]

In order to exploit such a wet landscape, settlers had to drain and tile. This process, which began around 1910, accounts for long and bitter struggles meriting study by a local historian.[35] Every significant ditch, which might have been decades in the making, has a story. Local residents can tell you who wanted the ditch, who paid for it, and who benefits from it. And since the extension, deepening, or cleaning of a ditch can bring to the surface deep currents of anger, such tales usually include accounts of upstream farmers fighting downstream farmers, farmers fighting conservationists, and conservationists arguing with real estate dealers. The stories can involve battles between cities and farmers, or between farmers of one watershed and those of another. Throw in county commissioners, ditch inspectors, the courts, agents from the Department of Natural Resources, the Pollution Control Agency, the Army Corps of Engineers, and state and national legislators, and even a short and shallow ditch can acquire a long and sinuous history.

Water is this region's passion. Changes in the course or elevation of water raise such ire because they affect farm profits. In comparison to the American West, where water is scarce, water here—at least in the spring—is too plentiful. Our ruling water philosophy is no mystery. Everyone upstream should be an ecologist—a lover of marshes and a breeder of ducks—and everyone downstream should be an engineer, removing floodwaters as quickly as possible.

Given the importance of water, this region should be labeled as much by its lakes and rivers as by its grasses. Indeed, Scott Anfinson identifies southwestern Minnesota as the "Prairie Lake Region" (see Map 2). It is considerably smaller than the Prairie Pothole Region, which includes three hundred thousand square miles from Iowa through Minnesota, the Dakotas, and Montana to three Canadian provinces. Anfinson describes the much more constructed Prairie Lake Region as wetlands characterized by a string of lakes extending from north central Iowa across southern and western Minnesota into eastern South Dakota.[36]

Water in this region tends to be either plentiful or scarce. In contrast to the eastern areas of the state, which receive approximately thirty inches of rainfall annually, the region along the Dakota border gets only twenty inches. Usually, after spring rains, this land is like a great sheet hung out to dry in constant winds—baked by a bleaching summer sun. As every farmer and gardener in these parts knows, we are caught up in the cycle of a wetland turning dry and a dry land becoming wet.

The wetlands, when they are wet, are rich in aquatic plants and animals, especially waterfowl and muskrats.[37] Plant and animal populations wax and wane with wet and dry times. Water dictates to insects, worms, and microorganisms, particularly fungi, their life cycles. It also accounts for the onset, spread, and severity of plant diseases, which affect agriculture. Further, just as plants reach a wilting point at differing percentages of atmospheric moisture, so the moisture content for optimal microbial growth varies among different materials.[38]

Water highlights this region's membership in Minnesota, "the land of sky-blue waters," "the land of ten thousand lakes," and "the headwaters of the Mississippi." With a history inseparable from that of Lake Superior and the Boundary Waters—indeed, so rich in shoreline, rivers, groundwater, and wetlands—Minnesota invites us to write its history not as a succession of governors and state legislatures but as a story of people and water. The chapters of such a history would cover rivers as the roads of exploration, trade, and empire; lakes used for transportation and recreation; agriculture and drainage; and controversy over the future of the state's waters. Flooding, pollution, and industrial water use would provide ample material for a conclusion.

THE UNSUNG MUSKRAT

Arguably, more than any other animal, the muskrat, grazer of the region's aquatic plants, defines the prairie, especially the Prairie Lake Region.[39] In wet times, muskrats multiply and seek out new ponds, and when their numbers become too great and aquatic grasses too scarce, their numbers contract.[40] Muskrats devour and cart away plants to build feeding huts, platforms, and winter lodges, which themselves are cycled into the detritus food web.[41] They graze wetlands into lakes, and they eat themselves out of den and pond.

The native peoples of the Prairie Lake Region depended far more on the muskrat than on the buffalo for their food. Skewered and skinned, with head and claws left on, muskrats were commonly roasted on Indian campfires. To the dismay of weary and hungry Europeans, muskrat meat was the first thing offered them by their Indian hosts. The Europeans were interested not in the flesh but in the hides—which traded at about sixteen muskrats to one mink. In the 1830s, Joseph Laframboise, the first French-Canadian trader in the area and an agent of the American Fur Company, sent muskrat skins by the thousands out of this region from his outpost at the Great Oasis, the site of what was once Murray County's second-largest lake, until it was drained in 1913.[42] The muskrat abounded in the region long after European settlement. In Jackson County, one resident wrote that "lawyers, ministers, and if we had [them,] doctors . . . [are] compelled to catch muskrats to make a living." A politician who lost an election to a trapper declared that a candidate "almost needed to smell of muskrat to get elected."[43]

The role the muskrat played in the region belies the conventional wisdom about the decline of the buffalo, that grazer of terrestrial grasses. Muskrats were not like the glorious but elusive buffalo, for which pursuers needed horses and sustenance for their long hunts.[44] Rather, muskrats, at least in wet times, were a standby. They were plentiful in lakes and marshes. Slow, waddling walkers, they made easy targets—although their taste and hide were least appealing at the height of summer. Even in harsh winters, breaking into their dens was not impossible. Muskrats were daily fare for those who lived off the land.

Although it is not easy to determine the muskrat's place in Indian prairie culture, it is certain that it lacked the spiritual prestige of the buffalo and the beaver.[45] In one Sioux story a muskrat spirit outdid the evil spirit Ictinike in the production of wild rice, but its powers did not rival that of the buffalo's. The Indians did not base an elaborate material culture on the muskrat's body as they did on the hide, bones, horns, and sinews of the buffalo. They did not make it an important part of their ceremonies, nor did they attribute to it any supernatural power. The muskrat was humble fare, accessible to a solitary boy with a club and able to fill a man's stomach.

The muskrat proliferated until the start of large-scale drainage at the beginning of the twentieth century. The buffalo, by comparison, began to vanish from this region well in advance of white settlement in the 1860s. Alan and Nancy Woolworth concluded that by the mid-1830s bison were gone from most of Minnesota. They had already vanished from the culture of the more eastern and southern Mdewakanton Dakota, though they still were important to the Sisseton and Wahpeton living on the upper reaches of the Minnesota River. There, on the eastern fringe of the Dakota buffalo range, the Dakota used horses to pursue buffalo out onto the Coteau des Prairies, also known as Buffalo Ridge.[46]

The arrival of white civilization meant local extinction for the buffalo, along with the elk, lynx, wolf, bear, and passenger pigeon. In 1858, a herd of buffalo was sighted in the western Lac Qui Parle area. In 1863, a herd of seven hundred to eight hundred buffalo were seen on the Coteau des Prairies.[47] In the winter of 1864–1865, the *Pioneer Press* was filled with accounts of buffalo hunts in western Minnesota. Then, as if to show how quickly man disposeth of what nature giveth, the Traverse County newspaper reported on the last buffalo hunt in 1866. In the same year a single buffalo was killed in Lyon County. In Lincoln County, transected by Buffalo Ridge, the last kill, of seven buffalo, was recorded in 1869.

Although the mounted buffalo hunter stands as the idealized image of the American Plains Indian, local historians must recognize that he was not the primary inhabitant of the prairie.[48] In this region straddling prairie and woods, the eastern Dakota and the nearby Ojibway lived off any flesh they could put their hands on—"not only deer, bear, and squirrels, grouse, ducks, and geese, but muskrats, otters, wolves, foxes and badgers, cranes, hawks, and owls."[49] At the onset of winter, they foraged for deer, muskrats, and whatever else they could find. In the spring, they took advantage of abundant fish, ducks, roots, and delicacies such as mud hen eggs. In the summer, they added fish, wild pigeons, and cranes to their diet; in autumn, they hunted wild ducks, geese, and again muskrats. The whole cycle was supported by the arduous autumn deer hunts. If deer, rabbits, raccoons, bears, or other mammals were unavailable, hunts ended in starvation. By mid-March, the hunting bands split and set off in opposite directions. One group went muskrat hunting, while the other made maple sugar or foraged for wild fruit, berries, and other foods.[50]

Though not principally agriculturalists, the Indians did grow some food along river bottoms: corn, beans, sunflowers, pumpkins, and squash. Other than these, they took what they found. Roaming widely over the landscape, they tapped trees, dug for turnips, and picked mushrooms, wild fruit, berries, and onions. In ponds they harvested wild rice and young cattails and waded for the roots of aquatic plants. Nothing was so hidden or so hard to come by that they did not try to get it.[51] In

Food Plants of the North American Indians (1936), Elias Yanovsky listed 1,112 species of plants that were used for food.[52] Many other plants were used for medicine and decoration. The Indians sought tradable items as well, hunting for pearls until some had, in the words of one historian, "quite a collection of pink and white beauties."[53]

Local historians must acknowledge that there were some exceptionally bad times before agriculture. Drought and freezing winters often reduced native peoples to starvation. They ate bark and the skins of animals. In September 1842, the Indian agent Amos Bruce from St. Peter's Agency in Iowa Territory described the bleak condition of the Sioux all the way from St. Peter, 250 miles up the Minnesota River, to those gathered at Lac Qui Parle: "The corn crops have almost entirely failed, and game being too scarce in the country to furnish food for so large a number, unless some means are placed at the disposal of this agency for the succor of those in distress, there is much reason to fear that many will perish from actual starvation."[54] Bruce distinguished between those who now lived primarily on corn and those who, owning horses, would undertake the mortal perils of the distant winter hunt for the vanished buffalo. (He noted: "I cannot tell the cause of the buffaloe leaving it, nor exactly the time, but it seems probable they were becoming comparatively scarce upward of thirty years ago, for it is more than that since the Sioux, who had long occupied the country moved into the plains of the west and the south."[55]) For the sedentary and isolated bands that remained at Big Stone Lake and Lac Traverse, he asked for clothing and plenty of fish spears, hooks, and line, remarking that many would perish unless efficiently aided by the government. Bruce attributes the famine partly to the low price of muskrat hides but also to a drought that had lasted several years: it had "diminished water, dried up beautiful lakes, entire rivers have evaporated, and watering holes for human and beast. The muskrat ponds have of course dried up, and the muskrats that were in them have perished, or gone, nobody knows where."[56]

Perhaps calling the peoples of this region the sons and daughters of the muskrat identifies the region itself as a transitional zone between prairie and woodland.[57] At least it challenges the audiences of local historians to reconsider the current interpretation of Midwestern history and concede that perhaps local historian James Gilronan of Lincoln County was correct when he wrote, "The disappearance of the rats was a greater loss to the Indians than the loss of buffalo. They got more money and food from the muskrats."[58]

CHAPTER 3

The Rule of Market and the Law of the Land

In rural areas, unless local historians choose irrelevance, they must suggest how the entire landscape has been molded by advancing civilization and how its cultivators—called yeomen, farmers, or agricultural operators—have been mutated into the servants of engulfing markets, intervening politics, and transforming sciences and technologies.

In the decades preceding World War I, Western civilization converted entire ecosystems into croplands. Daniel Worster wrote: "About 432 million hectares (or about 1,067 billion acres of land) were converted worldwide to regular cropping. Of that total, 164 hectares were converted in North America, 88 million in Russia, and 84 million in Asia, and the rest were scattered across the remaining continents."[1] These were the decades during which southern and western Minnesota was settled. The 160 acres offered to individuals by the 1862 Homestead Act, the end of the Civil War in 1865, and the subsequent coming of the railroads had the effect of bringing people west who had the wish to claim land, get rich, and start life afresh.

Settlement was an explosion, a big bang that brought permanent change. The suns in this man-made galaxy were the cities—Chicago, Minneapolis–St. Paul, and St. Louis. Each metropolis claimed the surrounding land, crops, and people as its own. The cities set the terms of successful farming while simultaneously transforming the desires and expectations of the rural environment. No rural locality was entirely isolated from this narrative.

As William Cronon has shown for Chicago and John Borchert for the Twin Cities, metropolises organized and colonized the countryside.[2] They reached out into their surrounding hinterlands and formed empires that competed against one another to monopolize the countryside. They were the hubs of the railroads that populated the countryside with standardized town plans and delivered to it prefabricated houses and churches. They supplied fresh impulses, recent ideas, and novel inventions. They defined laws and jurisdictions, issued calls for national patriotism, implemented the draft, and issued public health codes. In a matter of decades they provided automobiles, paved roads, buses (now largely vanished), and airports. Most recently, they have added pollution control officers, travel agents, branch banks, and computer technicians, along with weight-lifting studios, karate classes, coffee shops, and aromatherapists, all of which form intriguing topics for the enterprising local historian. The rapid rate of acceptance of city ways in the countryside reveals not just the cities' power to transform but also how the deepest wishes of rural folks included keeping up with their innovative and fun-loving urban cousins.[3]

RAILROADS AND ROADWAYS CRISSCROSS THE COUNTRYSIDE

With simplified cursive, the civilizing force of cities wrote efficiency across the countryside. Mothered by profit and fathered by machine, efficiency triumphed over distance in the rural world. Efficiency intensified interaction; interaction invited efficiency. At accelerating speeds—which a local historian might chart—civilization joined work, time, and profits in one equation.

The 1785 Northwest Ordinance and the 1862 Homestead Act imposed a uniform grid of control and ownership on the landscape. The land was first surveyed and then parceled out in terms of quarter sections of 160 acres, a whole section equaling 640 acres, or a square mile. Every six-mile square formed a township for the purpose of establishing a local government and maintaining public schools and roads. Homestead grants were first offered in quarter sections. Roads, usually no more than pathways for horse and wagon, were formed along these sections and so generally bisected the countryside at right angles. Straight furrows, with occasional curves to ward off erosion, still run to the horizon. Drainage ditches commonly form grids of intersecting straight lines, as do the underground tile drainage lines that regularly feed the ditches at right angles. Thus, an elemental geometry of straight lines appears to divide and rule the land. Only the sinuous and oversize river valleys and shallow lakes and wetlands dramatically interrupt the straight edges imposed with settlement.

No cursor cut across the countryside as deeply as the railroads. They partitioned the region to fit dreams of economic empires. Tracks were railroad companies' megalomaniacal conceptions of total and efficient exploitation.[4] Grandiose visions and fervor pushed the companies to build beyond the chance of making any possible profit. Prairie railroad towns, designed to be functional and efficient, were simply too numerous and close together.[5] In southwestern Minnesota, the railroad companies usually sited them seven miles apart, based on calculations of future field production. They were laid out according to familiar grid patterns. Street names came from a standard collection, which meant that every railroad town ended up with a set of "president streets" and "tree streets." These similarities supplied the prairie and plains residents with a sense of instant familiarity wherever they traveled and allowed outsiders to quip of Main Street: You've seen one, you've seen them all. It also forces many local historians today to concede that their town was superfluous and to a degree a failure from the day it was founded.

These towns were constructed according to the railroads' visions of what regional agricultural service centers should be. Every Main Street, no matter how small the hamlet, was wide enough to allow a wagon to turn around in it. Almost all the towns had a substantial brick commercial block. The lumberyard sat adjacent to the tracks; the bank was always at First and Main. The first churches (Episcopal, Presbyterian, and Methodist) were built in the vicinity of Third Street. Homes, stores, and churches were built to standard designs and in some cases were prefabricated in the metropolis and shipped in. Dedicated to supplying the city with goods and to gathering the countryside's products, these depot towns left nothing to chance. They were essentially standardized places where fortunes were to be made.

Yet as local historians know, there was more to these prairie towns than duplication. Their individual histories involved diverse intentions and actions. They were spawned by single-minded competition; driven by greed, deception, and illusion; built with mighty enthusiasm, high speculation, and constant boosting. Booms frequently busted, yet over the decades, speculators, town merchants, and citizens kept faith in their individual town's growth and success and persisted in denying that they were small fry in a big game. Here and there, the illusion produced lovely Main Streets, buildings with artful façades, and business communities that showed a novel capacity to innovate and sustain themselves against the odds. They also produced more than ephemeral attachments to one's hometown.

But many of the towns laid out by the railroads did not survive. Some achieved their maximum size in their first decade. In the Dakotas, as John C. Hudson points out in *Plains Country Towns,* the railroad towns rose and fell in a few years. Some even were aborted on company drafting boards.[6] Simply put, there wasn't enough "gold in them thar hills." Or, there no longer existed another town or place worth getting to farther along the line. That was the case when the railroad reached Marshall, in southwestern Minnesota. There was no reason to extend the tracks westward other than that the company had contracted with the federal government to do so. As every historian of the prairie grasps, there remains in the countryside a point beyond which no profit lies, where even the mightiest civilization must honor the theory of diminishing returns and the greatest boosters lack sufficient faith to keep boosting.

THE RISING INFLUENCE OF THE METROPOLIS

Civilization has drawn many defining lines across the rural countryside. In addition to roads and drainage ditches, it has run telephone, electric, water, and sewage lines. Radio, television, and now cell phone antennas dot the countryside, and aerial photographs and satellite images capture every detail of the tamed landscape.

Other agents systematize the countryside as well. Their targets include such ethereal qualities as behavior, culture, and community. The laws and bureaucracies imposed by civilization, for example, aspire to similarity and conformity. Our democracy builds national unity by fostering shared rights, sentiments, and expectations. Public schools consolidate identities, inheritances, and even ambitions. Commerce, with the help of science and technology, provides uniform products that flood the countryside.

New technologies usually arrive without significant opposition. In fact, machines are almost always welcomed, when money is available, because they mean less work and more leisure. Examining a rural town's adoption of and adaptation to machines or, more recently, computer software would be a topic worthy of study.

On the other hand, occasional acts of resistance against new technology merit the historian's interest as well, for they reveal the other side of the regional mind. For instance, it might be worthwhile to examine the fight against vaccination in the countryside before World War I, or a town's lingering battle against fluoridation after World War II. Often, acceptance and resistance characterize the same community.

Local historians lack a central axis for many chapters of their studies, unless they pay attention to local reactions to metropolitan influences. As quickly as it adopts the posthole digger, wire stretcher, stove, and gasoline tractor (all labor-saving devices), a rural town might resist certain civic amenities. A new proposal might be said to cost too much, or to require raising taxes, or to take away traditional freedoms and independence.

My deceased Cottonwood neighbor, Mr. Stellmacher, who served in World War I and got around town on his large tricycle well into the 1970s, loved tinkering with machines and was among the first in the region to pilot a plane. He was adamant, however, that city garbage collection was a communist operation, and he showed his nasty temper at the mere mention of labor unions or civic protest.

In some cases, as in the drafts for World War I and World War II, the metropolis coerces consent, turning authority for implementation over to the ways of local boards. In others, however, open defiance may characterize the countryside's reaction to the claims of the outside world. No case of opposition was as stunning as that of the 1930s Farm Holiday Movement, during which armed farmers, protesting the declining prices paid for their commodities and their resulting incapacity to make their mortgage payments, stopped sheriff auctions, closed stores, and temporarily took over towns.

In a study of the transformation of the rural north from 1870 to 1930, Hal Barron offers an accounting of the resistance to and accommodation of the new, which together underpin modern rural life. Starting in the last quarter of the nineteenth century with the emergence and consolidation of large-scale national businesses such as Sears, Roebuck and Company; Montgomery Ward; and the Standard Oil Company, this process continued into the twentieth century as new classes of managers and professionals attempted to refashion other aspects of American life along similar lines. At the same time, the growing centrality of cities and the rise of consumer culture threatened to erode traditional sources of authority and diminish the social and cultural primacy of local communities. These changes recast the United States into a centralized and national society at the expense of what Robert Wiebe has termed the "isolated community"; taken together, they represented a second great transformation of American society, equal to the initial spread of industrial capitalism earlier in the century.[7]

Barron elaborates on how localities and regions counterbalanced the centralizing powers of this "second great transformation":

> Farmers resisted attempts to improve local roads, which reflected the agendas of townspeople, professional engineers, and members of the urban "new middle class," and they resented greater state interference in what had been the province of local government. Yet, rural northerners willingly became integrated into a burgeoning consumer economy, largely through catalogue houses, even though this posed a threat to local merchants and eclipsed their importance as arbiters of taste and value. And, as farmers confronted an agricultural marketplace that was increasingly dominated by new monopolistic and oligopolistic corporations, they, too, organized in new ways and struggled with a fundamentally different understanding of their place in American society and of the role of their local communities.[8]

Although the dominance and eventual victory of the metropolis in most things cannot be questioned, local and micro-regional historians cannot reduce themselves to merely recording civilization's remorseless advance into the countryside. Instead, they must narrate, as I suggest in the following section, a tale composed of acts of resistance and compromise resulting in distinct local and regional hybrid structures.

AGRICULTURE MEETS THE MARKET

Agriculture has been civilization's greatest stamp on the land. It accounted for the digging up of soils, the draining of waters, and the transformation of woodlands and prairies. It introduced new plants and, over time, rewrote the genetic script not only of plant species but also of animals, insects, molds, and bacteria. Throughout the twentieth century—especially following World War II—it irreversibly altered southwest Minnesota's soils at accelerating rates and on increasingly large scales as the science and technology of agriculture delivered the countryside into the hands of the world's markets.

If agriculture is lord of the countryside, the market is king. At times fluctuating and fickle and at times rock-solid, the market repudiates and invites, expands and eliminates crops, animals, and types of farms. It dictates who survives and prospers and who doesn't. It imposes the implacable laws of profit and fevers and fears about the future of farmer and countryside. With money being the first and last measure of agriculture, the market determines the expansion and contraction of an agricultural region. Farmers need cash to expand their farms, to live well, and to keep up with the times. Those who endure over the long term learn to work with the market's vicissitudes. In light of this, rural historians often find themselves writing economic histories, whether they intended to or not.

Markets determine every aspect of farming. Although for the greater part of the century farmers sang the song of parity—a favorable ratio between the price of farm commodities and manufactured goods—they actually danced to a different tune. Farmers knew—or eventually were forced to learn—that their complaints about a lack of parity would not achieve what increasing production would. The market beat out the tune of grow-more-to-get-more. The song went something like this: First, you get bigger; then you plant fencerow to fencerow; and then you use all the chemicals you can. That is doing the farm shuffle. Dance as they would, farmers saw the shadow of overproduction lengthening over agriculture, but government storage and price support programs made it apparent that they couldn't produce their way out of overproduction and the eventual lowering of prices that went with it.

The market determines the types of crops that are planted. Just as Midwestern agricultural lands spelled the decline of agriculture in the East and Northeast, so mounting surpluses and declining prices for wheat pushed the eastern and northern sectors of the Midwest to join the Corn Belt. The Corn Belt, as depicted by John Hudson, was created out of hybrid short-maturation corn and pigs. It was successful for at least a decade because it allowed farmers to play the meat and grain markets against each other: early surpluses in the new, quickly growing corn allowed farmers to easily fatten their hogs, which were also in demand.[9] The dramatic decline of corn and hog prices—and other agricultural commodities—during the depression of the 1920s and 1930s, however, caused farmers to look elsewhere for cash.[10] In the 1950s and 1960s, they found their savior in the oil-producing soybean, whose complete regional and local history is yet to be told. Today, in the wake of long-depressed prices for corn and soybeans (held down by world surpluses), farmers at experimental stations and research laboratories again seek new magic seeds and the promise of profitable crops.

So the market dictates the fate of farms. It prescribes, although not consistently, the profitable farm size and commands that fields be drained, tiled, and fertilized. At the same time, the market turns farmland into real estate, equating it with its sale price, the cost of rent, and the rate of taxes. Over time the cost of capital exceeds the value of labor, shaping the very character of farm work and families. Supplemental income from gardening, egg sales, and secondary crops and animals, which once so occupied farm women and children, diminishes proportionately to an expanding need for larger sums of cash than such efforts can supply.[11] As local historians could trace for an individual farm or an entire region, the success of family farms increasingly depends on external sources of income and on banks and lending agencies. In the late 1990s, the first calculation banks made when considering a farm loan was not assets and debts but projected annual costs and profits.

The farm crisis of the 1980s provided graphic instruction in the influence of the market on agriculture. It was an engrossing emotional matter, as I discovered at a demonstration in St. Paul contesting farm conditions, on a picket line protesting the closing of a local and well-liked farm implement dealer, and in writing a book on the alleged murder on a farm of two bankers by a father and son. Yet the whole crisis boiled down to money: Too many farmers had borrowed too much cash at a time when prices were depressed and farm assets devalued. Debt split rural communities and divided farmers among themselves. Not all farmers were broke; not all bankers were deeply invested in failing farms; not all businesspeople had an equal understanding of or compassion for the situation. When city lenders called in the loans of rural lenders, rural banks called in the loans of farmers and indebted businesses—or simply declined to offer new loans. Credit determined survivability. Farmers who had the capacity to borrow more survived; those who were highly leveraged lost their land. Credit status became the arbiter of agricultural triage. Relatively debt-free farmers survived the crisis of the 1980s to prosper in the middle 1990s, when expansion again became the rule. With dramatic consequences for rural communities and associations of every sort, farm size roughly doubled in the 1980s and 1990s, whereas it had increased by only 20 percent in each of the three preceding decades. Both farm debt and its effect on farm size are topics greatly in need of a local historian's interest.

Local historians also have yet to elaborate on the countryside's accelerated decline in response to the farm crisis of the 1980s and subsequent changes in farming brought about in the middle and late 1990s by market forces. Rural populations shrank as farm family sizes grew smaller and the farm population aged. These changes affected rural communities, as rural banks, businesses, co-ops, schools, and churches closed or were consolidated.[12]

Today, the countryside is marching toward an agriculture without farmers, towns without people, and a landscape of cities populated by strangers. This metamorphosis is intensified by the presence of the thriving regional metropolises, flush with the influx of new industries, the spread of franchises, and the coming of peoples from around the globe to serve an expanding and decentralizing meatpacking industry. Since the late 1980s and early 1990s, the meat and poultry industries have been opening plants in the Midwestern countryside in order to escape unions, find a new labor force, and gain a competitive business advantage from near-to-site processing. However, unanticipated full employment and the relatively low wages they were offering for difficult and distasteful work have driven them to find and even develop labor sources among Hispanic, African, and Asian immigrants.[13]

MARKETS ARE MANY, REACTIONS ARE MULTIPLE

The market does not cut a uniform swath across the countryside, of course, and farmers are not simply balls on a billiard table. They insulate themselves against the immediate and long-term effects of the market by mixing crops and hedging one market against another. Differences in family, ethnicity, and locale support varying attitudes about risk, cooperation, and persistence. As a local historian could show, individual farmers are not mechanical in their reactions to the market.[14]

In fact, "the market" is not so much one entity as it is an array of markets, all of which affect agriculture, as local historians should explore.[15] And all these markets speak with different voices. They can counsel risk and caution simultaneously and advocate brutal resignation while causing whirlpools of anxiety and fear. Although railroads led to the undisputed dominance of the national market over local markets, the history of the countryside is not a mechanical story of unvarying compliance to the market. Every farm budget indicates that agriculture involves a subtle weighing of diverse incomes against varied expenses. In truth, no one knows exactly where to draw the bottom line. Farm budgeting at times amounts to so much shooting in the dark, since conclusions are predicated on guessing future markets and government policies.

The factors that affect markets are as varied as the farms. Markets are a mixture of projections of long-term trends and daily predictions. The value of crops fluctuates according to the size of the crop, weather predictions, surpluses, industrial needs, and national agricultural policies. All this makes commodity markets, eerily called futures markets, volatile. Although at any given moment markets can reflect value to a penny, they are no more constant than opinion and no more stable than speculation. When they are not rigged, markets are magisterially indifferent to who survives in the countryside.

Because markets are so indifferent, government often has to intervene, and the countryside abides in a paradox: the more the market penetrates and disrupts the countryside, the more the state, which is increasingly responsible for national coherence, irrationally intervenes to ameliorate the worst contradictions and most flagrant injustices of the market. Even without taking the extreme examples offered by such totalitarian regimes as the former Soviet Union and communist China, rural life in the twentieth century featured a central state trying to undo what the market had done. Local historians would do well to illustrate this concept with concrete histories of the economic, social, and cultural effects of national farm bills.

Some of the variation in farmers' reactions to the market is due to differing experiences of political protest in the countryside. "Despite technical assistance and educational programs," David Nass wrote, "the modernization of commercial agriculture over the past century spawned economic and political conflicts."[16] Over the years, farmers have lashed out at creditors, railroads, middlemen, and the grain trusts. Since the nineteenth century, Minnesota farmers have embraced various political opposition groups, seeking to vent their frustration over low crop prices, tight credit, and high freight charges. After the Civil War they supported the Greenbackers' protest of governmental monetary policies; in the 1880s they were attracted to the antitrust movement of the Farmers' Alliance; and in the 1890s the Populist Party drew their support with its attempts at radical agricultural-policy reform.[17] At the start of the twentieth century, farmers were turning to the American Society of Equity, founded in 1902, which had devoted itself to the idea of farm cooperatives. The society organized pooled marketing, urged holding actions, and fought against railroads, bankers, grain merchants, and the Minnesota State Grading and Inspection Board.

The farm protests of the 1890s, 1930s, 1960s, and 1980s offer a rich comparative field for local historians who wish to plumb the inner side of complaint (see chapter 5).[18] These protests are differentiated by numbers and percentages of protesting farmers, the farmers' average age and dominant ethnicity, and the type and size of farms. These differences allow historians to explore and distinguish the countryside's changing body and mind.

In the late 1980s, the state of Minnesota responded to the farmers' pleas with a unique program that "promoted mediation between creditors and lenders as well as an interest buy-down program to help restructure farm debt."[19] This program allowed a certain number of farmers on the edge to till and toil another day. As careful historical analysis would show, however, the majority of farmers have been economically weakened over recent decades. At the same time, variations in wealth, education, and types of farming operations have progressively differentiated farmer from farmer. In 1999 farmers constituted only about 1 percent of the entire national population. Their average age was around sixty. The only thing for sure now is that in the event of another farm crisis, today's farmers are more likely to die, and less likely to carry on a good fight, than were their predecessors. Detailed studies of what this means for rural communities and entire regions are required.[20]

SERVANTS OF THE LAND

Protest is not the sole indicator of the countryside's reaction to markets. The history of land ownership—who owns and keeps the land over the long haul—also accounts for significant local variations. In effect, local historians must acknowledge that an ethnic factor differentiates those who serve the land—those who want, get, and keep it over generations—from those who fail to secure the land. Certain ethnic groups, as local studies can confirm, have survived better on the land than others, and ethnicity forms an important determinant in long-term landholding.[21] Some groups persisted through good times and bad, despite the market.

For example, in southwest Minnesota, Yankee settlers (of American-English descent) were among the first to arrive, but most of them seemed more interested in profiting from real estate than forming communities (though we need careful studies); they came and departed quickly. A considerable number of Irish arrived as well; they were brought to select railroad sites throughout southwestern Minnesota by Archbishop John Ireland, who was intent on the Catholic colonization of the Minnesota countryside—but only a few remained for long.[22] Residents of the urban east, they lacked the agricultural skills and capital to farm the prairie. They were lucky after one winter to get out of Minnesota with their lives. The Norwegians came and stayed in the area, but not necessarily on the land as farmers. They viewed their farms as life rafts offering them the chance to reach career opportunities on other shores.

In contrast, a close examination of 130 years of plat books of land ownership in Lyon County, Minnesota, revealed that Belgians and Dutch

Catholics—also brought by Archbishop Ireland—were as a group the most faithful and enduring servants of the land.[23] In the course of a century they became Lyon County's dominant landowners. Like the successful Germans, Dutch Protestants, Poles, and other southwestern ethnic farm groups, the Belgians wanted to farm the land. They dedicated themselves to making southwestern Minnesota home.

Local historians would do well to explore the attributes of the ethnic groups who prospered on the land. Certain traits rendered the Belgians able both to survive and to exploit the market. To an unusual degree, they were depression- and inflation-proof. They saved money. They frowned on borrowing unless absolutely necessary, and when they did borrow they preferred to borrow from family rather than from banks. Their farms were rich with animals and gardens. They shared goods and machines. In bad times, such as the Great Depression, they hunkered down on the land. They ate gruel, planted larger gardens, did without, worked harder, and said the rosary. In good times, their aggressiveness came to the fore. They frequently mortgaged their farms and leveraged their assets to purchase more land. Simultaneously peasants and capitalists, they demonstrated how ethnicity can foil the determinations of market.

MAGIC CROPS

Local variations in agriculture are also brought about by a region's choice of plants and animals to raise. Just as humans have no history without plants (and animals), so every plant that comes into contact with humans gets a history.[24] Human society selects and rejects plants according to myriad factors. A plant considered a weed to one generation may be a profitable crop to the next.[25]

Every region has a story of plants of magic promise—and a Jack and the Beanstalk story for every inquiring local historian. In the end, most of these miracle crops are disappointments. The soil proves wrong. The weather fails to cooperate. The plant's primary promoter takes to drinking and runs off with the profits. Seeded in mania, the plant of promise is frequently harvested in depression. So it was with the tulip in Holland in the early seventeenth century and the Jerusalem artichoke in the Midwest in the 1980s.[26]

The fortunes of plants, whether in century-long efforts to introduce grapes in the American South or episodic attempts to reintroduce hemp in Minnesota, provide delicious tales worthy of keen regional narratives. Beginning in the early 1970s, the tumultuous twenty-five-year history of the sugar beet in southwestern Minnesota was focused around the town of Renville. Fluctuating sugar prices altered relationships between renter and tenant, changed institutions (especially co-ops and agricultural service agencies), and made and unmade regional economic leaders. North Dakota University historian Thomas Isern summed up the connection between crops and regions when he concluded that a new crop equals new agricultural frontiers, for a new crop means new minds and machines, different uses of the land, fresh markets, and new peoples.[27]

The frontier expands, contracts, and mutates with the fortunes of its crops. Unfavorable prices for a "savior" crop over a sustained period can squeeze the promise out of it and put its sponsors—farmers, horticulturists, engineers, processors—on the wrong side of the market. Survival then requires reversion to traditional crops. Processing plants and cooperatives are sold off at severe discounts. So Jack falls from his beanstalk back to the earth one cow poorer.

Southwestern Minnesota provides a wealth of crop narratives.[28] The story of corn, one major successful crop, contains chapters on hybridization, agronomic development, changing relationships to supportive rotating crops (such as legumes, clover, and genetically improved alfalfa), and corn's role as feed for hogs. Early surpluses led growers to conclude that the best way to get corn to market was in the form of fat cattle and hogs.[29] Eventually, though, the surpluses were too great; corn saved farmers from wheat surpluses only to deliver them corn surpluses.

Historian David Nass describes the shift away from wheat and toward corn and other crops:

> As wheat production exhausted older lands, many farmers had to choose between moving west or north and investing in new equipment or livestock. Reluctant to change their methods, many opted to move. Others began to diversify—to oats, corn, potatoes, barley, flax, and rye, or to dairying and livestock. In 1900 wheat was the dominant crop, accounting for about half of cultivated land [in Minnesota], but by 1910 acreage [in wheat] had declined to about 25 percent. The largest decrease occurred in southwestern Minnesota, where by 1910 about as much land was devoted to oats as wheat. The increased production of hay and forage crops reflected the practice of rotation and a growth in dairying and livestock farming.[30]

As corn and other crops diminished, however, disappointed farmers took to the soybean. The story of this engagement, which defines the

Midwestern market, is yet to be told locally. The soybean is an oil plant that served as a new cash crop to replace oats and to bolster faltering corn income. It delivered a triple benefit to the region: It offered a crucial alternative to national corn surpluses that started in the 1920s. It replenished the nitrogen corn depleted from the soil. And the whole plant was useful; its roughage furnished usable hay for livestock, while its seeds yielded oil with a high protein content.[31]

With a long genetic and agronomic development dating back to the start of the twentieth century, the soybean spread across the Corn Belt in the 1950s and 1960s. A micro-narrative of its introduction would require explaining when and where it replaced oats, and how and when it became the region's cash crop second only to corn. Local historians would identify which farmers grew it first, which elevators first accepted it, and how the crop spread to other farms and elevators. Local chapters of soybean associations would reveal this history.

A history of any crop requires research in a variety of academic fields. Historians must consider the genetic and agronomic domestication of a plant and how it is industrially processed.[32] It also demands that historians grasp the mechanization of farming, asking who acquired which machines when, and what the machines meant for the crops, production, labor, farm buildings, and the farm family.[33]

Tales of lesser crops than the soybean might prove equally fertile to the historian's imagination.[34] One such story in southwestern Minnesota might be about the region's off-and-on relationship with the sunflower, a promising oil crop in the 1970s that raised its bright head again in the 1990s. The local search to find economic value not just in plants but also in their wastes takes many forms. Another regional story yet to be written would focus on the commercial manufacturing plant at Dassel, thirty miles west of Willmar, that processed corn smut in the 1920s to produce a medicine for treating shell shock, a common condition among veterans returning from the trenches of northeastern France and Belgium.

A history of garden plants would provide a different perspective on the relationship between agriculture and the market.[35] In the fate of the garden, local historians could also find the changing character of farm women's economic contributions to the farm family, especially in light of their need to work off the farm for cash and to obtain ever more costly health insurance.[36] The decline of gardens reveals a countryside that increasingly lives by and for distant markets, reserving only small plots for leisure and aesthetic purposes. Likely candidates for select studies of garden crops are strawberries, apples, watermelons, cabbages, green beans, and peas. Potatoes would be of interest for a variety of reasons, as they straddle garden and field.[37]

A history of gardening would ask who—which groups—grew what kinds of gardens, what amount of money was spent on seed, where the seed was bought, what the specific gardening practices were, and whether gardens represented family seed inheritances. A history of gardening would also run parallel to that of the fields, asking about the adoption of machines, chemicals, and genetics. In the end, it might tell the story of regional farmers whose separation from animals and plants leaves them almost as ignorant of gardening as their city cousins.

There are also tales of lowly weeds to be written. Stealing precious soil, choking out crops, spoiling harvests, and even killing animals, weeds may be the enemies of farming but not of historians' curiosity. Their story, in part, is documented by the records and deeds of local weed inspectors. It concludes with the extensive use of chemical fertilizers and herbicides.[38] All these stories to be written in their varied details can be rendered only in conjunction with changing market prices and the increasing demand for cash in the countryside.

SEEDING HOPE

Residents of the countryside work according to the discipline of national and international markets. Yet at the same time, some part of the countryside—imaginatively, defiantly, foolishly—is always planting the biblical grains of mustard seed that will move mountains and markets. It does this when it tries its hand at organic farming, enters value-added activities, or starts large turkey and hog operations, as it has during the last two decades. It plants seeds of hope when it invests in llamas, emus, and Jerusalem artichokes. It planted hope in the 1980s when a few farmers sought to establish a mushroom industry in Lincoln County, when individuals prospected for gold in Murray County and for oil in Stearns County, or when town leaders of Boyd considered building a crematorium for human body parts as a path to economic development. At times, especially at bad times, the countryside becomes a hatchery of silly wishes and illusions. Local histories could be written about farmers being taken in by bizarre ideas, stupid schemes, and outright fraud.

Saving the countryside forms a common parlance. It is the rhetorical spine of many rural institutions. It gives rise to the vernacular of chambers of commerce and town boosters. It equips public and private agencies with the language of goodwill and justification. Many politicians earnestly talk the talk of economic redemption. All sorts of groups and agencies (usually based in metropolitan centers) commit money to reversing decline in the countryside. The promise of economic development is truly the shibboleth of the failing rural world.

Claiming to save nearly everything and effecting virtually nothing is a great sleight of hand by the magicians of economic development. Itinerant hawkers and peddlers of hope—who so deserve a good history—have always filled the countryside. New industries and markets are espied on every horizon, and every plant and animal is culled and reculled in the name of economic renaissance. The rural university must not allow its own mission to be hijacked by fantasies of rural development, and local historians must forever (with care for themselves and their associations) find a way of saying, "It ain't necessarily so!"

None of this should surprise the student of the countryside. The market draws erratic lines. The historian must learn to read the handwriting of those who try to survive and prosper on the land. Indeed, the local historian must learn to switch between two narratives of the countryside. The first is the story of the dominance of outside forces. The second is the story of unique local people and their singular experiences. As the first narrative destroys local history's integrity by rendering local places and events redundant microcosms of the world at large, overlooking the history of successful resistance, defiance, compromise, and even transformation of the countryside, so the second narrative produces eccentric histories that exclude the larger world.

This polarity is embodied in the dual meaning rural people attribute to the land itself. They work the land with machines and chemicals while equally cultivating it as an object of deep and lasting personal emotions. No matter how rural people shape their land to serve the abstract laws of the marketplace and the sciences of productivity, they rhetorically treat the land as an underlying moral substratum. While they can, and do, argue that the land is a repository of national virtue, and even a living organism, they nearly uniformly presume that it bears the personal and spiritual signature of the farm family's worth. (Only a few here who bring to the land a philosophy of organic farming and soil conservation would want to turn the clock back.)[39]

This means that local historians must learn to read between the lines of bold print of market and nation and the cursive script of individual, community, and region. Somehow, they must shape the text of their stories to the movements of a civilization and the contours of a place. This proves no easy task to do in thought, spirit, or word—and, in fact, because it is so difficult, good contemporary local history remains challenging and precious.

CHAPTER 4

Writing History through the Senses

Sounds

The countryside today is softer, quieter, and more colorful than it was a century ago, because of the immense economic and technological transformation of rural work and life. The control of water and fire, the introduction of electricity, the spread of public health reform, and the plethora of new materials and machines have altered the environments in which our senses operate. Today, rural residents hear, see, smell, taste, and touch a different world from that of their parents and grandparents. During the course of a mere century, rural people and their environments—every bit as much as urban people and cities—were transformed, prompting their senses to experience the world anew. With this chapter, I hope to inspire the local historian to conceive of the possibilities for writing innovative histories of places based on accounts of our changing sensory experiences.[1]

Take sight. Although the diversity of nature's wildflowers has been lost to monoculture, the contemporary countryside still strikes the observer as more transparent, translucent, and colorful than the countryside of settlement times. There is more light and there are more bright surfaces. Dirt has been beaten back from the thresholds of homes and the veneer of ever present dust removed from many of the indoor surfaces of rural life.[2] Houses are filled with light and color. Cars, children, and men and women are dressed more brightly than ever before. Rural residents see a world lit up by electricity, no longer dependent on the weak light of fires, candles, and lanterns.

As much as urban dwellers put themselves on display, country residents took to gazing at themselves in mirrors and learned from magazines and photographs to measure their own images against those of others. Their eyes became more demanding of perfection, quicker in their glances as they habituated to darting images and speeding machines. Optometry and ophthalmology improved and sharpened sight. Indoor lighting took the glare off things in general and accented things in particular.

The rural nose, too, smells differently than it once did. An olfactory history of the countryside would reveal not only new things to smell but also new ways of sniffing. As with the transformation of sight, this metamorphosis had its origin in a material revolution. Refrigeration and food packaging were important steps on the way to a less stinky environment. The outhouse vanished; underwear, frequently changed, became fashionable; and the fragrances of soaps, air fresheners, and perfumes now rise where nasal abominations once hovered. Foul-smelling clothes are no longer part and parcel of everyday experience. Even dogs and cats are given regular baths. The fragrant has supplanted the foul.

At the same time, of course, some of the most pleasant smells, such as burning leaves and freshly cut clover, have disappeared, while other foul ones remain and even increase, as animal confinement and sewage ponds increase. Indeed, conflicts multiplied across the countryside in the late 1990s as noses got finer and profit demanded greater concentrations of animals.

In Marshall, giant diesel trucks on their way to the local meatpacking plant roll up Main Street, leaving behind them a trail of fecal odor to assault the nostrils of customers at the new café as they savor their gourmet coffee and almond *biscotti.* Nearby, a turkey plant emits the stench of scorched feathers. On the other end of town, a corn processing plant saturates the atmosphere with the sweet, sickening aroma of corn syrup.

Changing taste offers another perspective for writing a history of the senses in the countryside. Such a history would have to be written with reference to ethnic groups and classes and the diverse crops and food they raised and cooked. The voyage of an individual's, a family's, or a region's trip from potato to tomato, and from there to pizza and tacos, would reveal a lot about changing tastes. (The arrival of the tomato in our region of dominantly northern European, especially Scandinavian, stock would fill a chapter on its own.) A study of the history of taste in the rural Midwest would establish the conjunction between national and local diets, between foods grown in local gardens and prepackaged and nationally advertised foods sold in the modern grocery store. The role of university home extension services, the place of county fairs, and the function of church socials in the dissemination of recipes and cooking instructions would all have a place in such a study. In any case, this story would have a lot more solid fare to it than state and local writers' constant jokes about the culinary hegemony of tasteless "hot dish."

NATURE SOUNDS

Of all the possible histories of the senses, I have chosen sound to illustrate how a changed environment and society transforms the auditory experience. On the prairie, wind dominates the auditory field. It blows in the dry grass and shakes the trees of the river valleys, especially the large cottonwoods. It drags and scrapes itself along plowed fields, whistles around the corners of villages built out of wood, pounds in and out of metal structures, and swirls up against one's ears. Natives say you hear the wind here even when it isn't blowing. It ranges from gentle breezes that barely disperse smoke to tornadoes that destroy everything in their path. Average wind speeds that approach maritime velocities turn the two-hundred-plus turbines of the giant windmills on Buffalo Ridge.[3]

Advancing civilization imposes acoustic and auditory changes on rural life. Human-made sounds eclipse natural sounds, which have diminished like the droves of birds that once passed overhead. The howls of gathering wolves were last heard in Marshall in 1874, according to the town newspaper. The disappearance of the last baying elk was not recorded. Even the drone of the once omnipresent mosquito no longer fills the summer air. Where wetlands have been drained, the cacophony of singing birds, chirping and croaking frogs, and buzzing and crackling insects has grown quiet. The ducks, the pelicans, the honking geese, all the migrating birds, have shifted the main paths of their flyways west.

The ponds that dotted our region once teemed with noisy life. They were nature's open orchestra pit. Vibrating, full of dissonance, marked by their own anarchic rhythms, they never assembled themselves into the symphony they promised, yet there was a sort of development to their daily songs and seasonal music. Now, the hum of electric machines and the pulsating beep of the backing construction truck often form the background sounds that water, wind, and bird once did.

Still, nature has not entirely lost its voice, although few are attentive to it (in fact, some are bothered by it). Birds still sing, especially in spring and early summer and again in the fall as they gather for migration. Early spring is still announced in wetlands by frogs and peepers. "Truly, spring belongs to the frogs and toads," observed Vincent Dethier recently. "Except for them, nature has not found her voice."[4] Summer belongs to the electric sound of the cricket. "One day," Dethier wrote, "the crickets are mute nymphs; then, as if by some agreed-upon signal curse by the season, they molt, become adults, and celebrate the occasion in song."[5] The Richardson ground squirrel still sends out a piercing whistle to signal danger. In response to the jay's taunting of the cat and the cawing of assembling crows, the tired mother of two children who lives in the house behind ours screams out, "Shut up, you birds!"

FARM SOUNDS

European settlement began the change in the countryside's sounds. Noisy raccoons were drawn to the marginal lands created by farms. The Chinese pheasant and Hungarian partridge cooed and gobbled in ditches. Domestic animals chimed in. The crowing rooster, snorting pig, lowing cow, baaing sheep, braying horse, chattering chicken, and barking dog formed a new aural tapestry. The flap of the immigrant pigeon from barn to barn became commonplace. Noisy squirrels living in the new windbreaks chattered down from trees. The constant chirping of the plain brown sparrow and the continual squawking of nagging starlings—both nineteenth-century imports from England—supplanted the sounds of native songsters.

White settlers brought new languages to echo across the prairie. They put new names to things; they cried, shouted, and made love with different words and tones. They braided together sounds, actions, and meanings. With sound, music, and noise, they shaped a new world to be heard.

Men, women, and children made their own sounds. In happiness and anger, they registered different tones and words. Their voices reached, echoed, and implored. Culture allocated to each a way of teasing, shouting, complaining, and crying. The clothes they wore, the objects they worked with, and the things they did set myriad auditory horizons. To be human is to make and hear sounds; each place, each time, and every set of circumstances leaves aural prints in the mind.

Farmyards were stages for concerts of sound. Doors squeaked and slammed. Boards were sawed and hammered. Boots made great sucking sounds when pulled out of the mud. Sweeping was a snare drum, raising clouds of dust. Rocks were broken and foundations were poured.

Restive horses whinnied and neighed, cows bellowed, and the pigs, sensing that they were soon to be slaughtered, wailed pitifully. All the while, the clinking and sucking pump filled buckets with splashing and swirling water.

Every new machine has changed the auditory composition of farm life. First the gasoline and now the diesel engine of the tractor and combine testify that farm fields are agricultural factories. Indeed, farmers must take care that their machines do not make too much noise, lest they themselves go deaf or their cows reduce their milk production or abort. Today, agricultural producers live in an environment with no resemblance to the preindustrial village, whose sounds are estimated to have been a mere forty decibels (dB)—except at sunrise, when roosters, lambs, and cows announced themselves to the world. A 1968 national hearing examination discovered that of all working groups, the farmers most frequently suffered hearing impairment. University of Nebraska researchers have reported that tractors, with decibel levels of 90 to 114, can cause permanent hearing loss for those who use them over extended periods.[6]

SMALL-TOWN SOUNDS

Noises from the farm carried over into rural towns. Carts creaked; adults and children shouted; dogs and harness horses in the streets created their own chorus. Hammers pounded and saws sawed. The thud of splitting logs filled the air. Brass bands, proof of the small town's claim to culture, played for special occasions. Women beat rugs, whisked brooms across wooden floors, and clinked metal buckets full of soapy water. Men played pool at the local saloon, knocking balls about; they shuffled cards, spitting and cursing, or fired rifles in the fields. At the end of the nineteenth century and the first part of the twentieth, local police officers made their living charging young men with being "drunken, loud, and disorderly."[7]

Families have their distinct sounds as well, and their characteristic ways of making, hearing, recording, and reacting to sounds. People's ears are trained to be acute to certain noises, based on where and how they live. Happy families are tuned to chatter and banter around the dinner table. Troubled families know the sounds of the faltering return of a drunken father or a mother's cold silence or screams of rage.

These individual differences do not deny a certain commonality to prairie sounds, however, one brought about by universal pursuits that change with the seasons. The crack of the baseball bat (even if the bat is now dinging metal) announces spring all over southwest Minnesota. Late summer brings the paced and taciturn announcements of the riding contests at every county fair, the roar of go-carts and the demolition derby, and the amplified voice of the best-known country-western singer the fair can attract. The report of the rifle (now more of a crack than a boom, because of faster, smokeless powder) signals autumn in the fields. And cracking ice beneath skate blades announces that winter has arrived in earnest.

Some of the sounds that once made up this auditory environment have disappeared. Parades and town celebrations are largely gone, fewer guns are discharged in the countryside, the ax no longer swings, and the boom of dynamite is rare. Public ceremonies are fewer. People no longer gather along Main Street, whose shops closed years ago. Few artisans remain to bang and clang. Many gas stations are closed. Village projects no longer sustain conversation, rancor, or celebration. With fewer young people in town and the local school closed, the staccato voices of children at play are no longer heard. Parents no longer retrieve their children from the streets with calls that lilt over the rooftops. A nocturnal quiet characterizes small villages today.

In times past, the quiet of small towns meant subservience and tedium. Silence was a way of paying respect. Landlords and parents, courts, banks, funeral homes, and cemeteries encouraged hushed whispers. But humans could tolerate only so much silence. Even solemn churches came to life with bells, organs, sermons, and choirs. Aside from sleeping, quiet and tranquility meant boredom and tedium, which were experienced as steps descending to death. As every kid knew, quiet simply meant that nothing was happening. Noise, conversely, meant life and action. Like smoke to fire, noise revealed the presence of change with which comes the promise of profit and progress. Town boosters habitually equated banging and chugging with the coming of civilization.

So each town on the prairie has its own tapestry of sound and deserves a history of it. Its bells ring as distinctly as its fire siren blares.[8] Its vegetation and trees form a singular whistle in the wind. The town's residents have lived among the unique reverberating echoes of their mill and the peculiar melodic quality of their ethnic chorus. Their memories are etched with singular events, such as the cicadas singing louder than ever the spring their grain mill exploded.

As the naturalist must grow accustomed to the chirps, snaps, zips, and buzzes that make up the calls of particular birds, so the local historian must learn the unique sounds of a town.[9] The ears of each generation have been implored and chastened by changing styles of sermons, excited and flattered by varied political rhetoric, and coaxed and seduced by the invitations of changing breeds of merchants. Each generation has been allured by its own music and fought its own war against new intrusions of noise.

TRAIN SOUNDS

The clarion sound of arrival in the countryside was the train, the bringer of a new symphony of steel, steam, and machine in motion. Train sounds were many: shrill signaling whistles, grinding engines, hissing and sighing steam valves. Setting those tons of steel in motion required a lot of creaking and groaning. Their shaking and churning set the whole countryside shuddering. At full speed, their rhythmic clickety-clack counted off the miles. Stopping required screeching, shuddering, and scraping. Rusty metal doors were pushed open. Ramps banged and clanked as luggage and goods were unloaded. Many a yardman went deaf from years of serving the iron horse.

In his essay "Sounds," Henry David Thoreau—the premier nineteenth-century Northeastern localist and regionalist—speculated that everywhere on the Massachusetts landscape the train's whistle had joined the acoustic landscape of hooting owls, baying dogs, trumping bullfrogs, and rumbling carts. "The whistle of the locomotive penetrates my woods summer and winter, sounding like the scream of a hawk sailing over some farmer's yard, informing me that many restless city merchants are arriving within the circle of the town or adventurous country traders from the other side," he wrote.[10] Residents learned to set their clocks by the train whistle, which came and went with the regularity of the rising sun, causing Thoreau to ask whether trains had taught men to think faster and move more quickly. He knew that trains were constructing a way of life from which there was no turning back.

Thoreau measured the effects of trains in terms of the mute goods and bleating animals they transported. Connecting distant places and minds, trains, for Thoreau, marked a transformed relationship between humans and earth. "When I hear the iron horse make the hills echo with his snort like thunder, shaking the earth with his feet, and breathing fire and smoke from his nostrils (what kind of winged horse or fiery dragon they put into the new Mythology I don't know), it seems," Thoreau noted, "as if the earth had got a race now worthy to inhabit it."[11]

The train spoke of the annihilation of local places and the commingling of distant spaces. It brought the city into the countryside; it *was* the city in the countryside. The train took away one sense of time and imported another. Its whistle punctuated the day. It instructed everyone along its path to internalize industrial time.

The train ended one kind of local history and began another. The steam engine, off its mooring, put on wheels, and turned loose in the countryside, trumpeted the triumph of the Industrial Revolution. It represented the roaring blast furnace, the shaking stamp press, and the grinding room. The train led the parade of vehicles that would come to speed through modern life. It refashioned lives, lands, and minds. It accounted for the dust and din of constructing hundreds of thousands of miles of beds, trestles, and bridges, the leveling of hills, the tunneling of mountains, and the filling of valleys. The train marked the beginning of the machine's acoustic tyranny over the landscape.

AUTOMOTIVE SOUNDS

The automobile furthered this tyranny and increased movement and choice in rural life. The coming of a car—perhaps the postman's—was heard from afar and was announced by the yapping yard dog. It could make one's day or undo one's life. The car took people places. It joined farm to village and village to city. The crunch of tires on gravel and later their hum on asphalt became common, and people riding in cars ceased to hear the sounds one hears when walking.

As the system of local, state, and national roads spread, the drone of rubber tires became a background sound of the countryside, as birds and insects had once been. The pitch of the drone measured the distance to the highway, and its magnitude measured the volume of traffic, which in turn differentiated the hours of the day, the days of the week, and the seasons of the year. Each generation of cars left its own auditory signature on the countryside. It changed with the models of automobiles and trucks, styles of driving, alterations made to cars (especially the addition of mufflers), and the music that poured out of car windows.

Other vehicles added their stamp to the auditory experience. Every villager knows the late-night rumble of the neighbor's idling diesel truck, the high-pitched roar of the snowmobile, the beeping of the backing construction vehicle, and the drone of the jet passing high above. The sounds of these metal locusts add to both the pleasure and the pain of many a rural resident.

"DON'T TOUCH THAT DIAL!"

The intellectual Max Picard was not alone in attacking the radio as the primary instrument of contemporary auditory anarchy. In *Le monde du silence* (written in 1953, before television had engulfed the French nation), Picard attacked the hold radio had secured on the human mind. Devoid of content, he claimed, its sole purpose was uninterrupted noise: "With radio there is no longer silence. . . . Radio has occupied all the space of silence." Contemporary man, Picard said, is born of its uninterrupted buzz. It mediates the human relationship with the world. It offers a senseless stream of sound and chatter in place of truth and reality. "The entire world," Picard concluded, "has become the sound of the radio. . . . Like a nest of machine guns, radio directs uninterrupted fire against silence, its dreaded nemesis."[12]

As much as Picard and others cursed the radio, the masses fell in love with it. An oddity in the countryside in the 1920s, by the early 1930s it had become a "necessity," even though listeners often had access to only one frequency and this meant listening, with or without choice, to news broadcasts and summaries of hog prices. "A survey of nine hundred farm families in Wisconsin found that they spent an average of 200 hours per year listening to the radio and 292 per person reading. Near Marathon, New York, 10.5 percent of the families had their radios on five or more hours per day."[13] Though radio listening cut into community time, rural folks undoubtedly saved money by staying at home to tune in.

The radio was advertised for its utility. What better way than the radio to alert farmers to bad weather and provide vital information about crops? Radio farm shows and sectional and regional programs provided entertainment as well. The radio put people in contact with distant and interesting places. It provided a giant step away from boredom.

The affordable radio assured membership in a greater community even during bad times. It created standard auditory fare to which the whole family, and the whole town, tuned in. The sound of the radio passed through uninsulated walls and open windows into the street. In the summer, with radios tuned to the league championship, a passerby could follow the game just by walking down the street. The army quickly discovered the link between radio and home. It formed its own stations and made the radio the frontline buddy of the World War II American soldier.

The radio over time came to support individual choice, and in that sense it went hand in hand with the privatization of contemporary life. Stations began to offer a range of selections. An individual with just the family radio could listen alone, late at night, with the volume turned down low, to whatever station he or she wished.

The transistor, invented in 1948, vastly extended radio's reach into the countryside. Cheaper and smaller than the earlier radios, the transistor radio went wherever people did. Individual listeners defined their environment (much as a dog marks out his territory) with their radios.

Starting in the 1940s and 1950s, successive generations of teens built their identities on their favorite radio programs. With boom boxes, ever louder car radios, and shuddering vibro-tactile beats, youth culture began using radio to declare war against village and town, despite the vigilance of the local police, especially on the first warm nights of May, when graduation was drawing near. They carried to an extreme what commercial, rock, and sports cultures do: they made an ear-splitting, body-shaking, dissonant bid for attention.

The radio was the twentieth century's first auditory imperialist. It permeated rural life. It accompanied chores, enhanced the pleasure of baseball and football games, and supplied barbershops and offices with cheap distraction. It still keeps town swimmers afloat and skaters in rhythm. It stimulates shoppers and comforts banking customers and supposedly helps soothe the impatience of those waiting on the phone.

Although there were arguments about whether the radio lured people away to cities or kept them at home listening, it certainly got rural people to listen to strangers.[14] It joined them to a world in which somebody was always talking—or singing—about something. The radio taught them and the nation at large that everybody has the right to express his or her opinion. Dull and repetitious local conversation now finds it hard to compete, as radio gathers local people into national networks of ideas and fashions. Radio programming forms auditory ensembles humming the same tunes and engrossed in the same news and fiction. In this way it really has, as Picard warned, taken hold of minds.

SUDDENLY, LESS CLANGING AND BANGING

The modern sounds of our technological society have begun to take over from the natural and human-made sounds of earlier times. In doing so, they have quieted the countryside. All sorts of familiar sounds from the rural world of old have been replaced by less noisy counterparts, thanks to new materials and new technologies.

To begin with, innovative materials have transformed water sounds. Although brooks and rivers still rush over rocks and through rapids with a roar sufficient to stifle the May chorus of birds, and rains still pound thunderously on roofs, water has been made, like everything else, into a quieter and more docile servant. It is heard less as its flows underground and is disciplined by tile and ditch, gutter and spout. Water that once freely coursed through the countryside is now sequestered by mains, pipes, valves, and nozzles. Encased, pressurized, and in every other sense regulated, water splashes, bubbles, drips, and drops less. It has lost its relationship to the shuddering windmill and the clanging handle of the pump. Water heaters, dishwashers, and showers have superseded the water sounds of old.

Heavy industrial sounds have also been muffled. Metals are used less frequently. The clang of hard iron and steel does not ring sharply across the countryside as it once did. The blacksmith, the iron timpanist of villages past, is as still on the prairie as Dakota drums. The immense metal machines of mashing gears, boring bits, crushing jaws, and straining cables lie in rust. Rails, once the synapses of the countryside, have been largely removed.

Asphalt roads are quieter than gravel and concrete roads. Traffic has been shifted to highways. Main Street is quieter, with the banishment of horses and carts and, with only a token presence of stores and shoppers remaining, fewer cars and trucks. Those that remain make less noise than their predecessors. The shooting and snapping piston-driven truck, which occasionally made it to Main Street, has been replaced by the humming and vibrating diesel. Engines in general have been muffled, even as the need for horsepower has grown. Indeed, motors in general have become less mechanical, less a matter of moving and turning parts than a system of circuits and components. More precise fittings, better lubrication, improved insulation, and better mufflers have contributed to the quiet.

Even auto repair shops have grown quiet. Better roads and rubber mean fewer frames to straighten and tires to change. Hammer, pry bar, drill, and torch have been replaced by ready-made parts and muted air drills. Where once the auto repair shop served the rural village as a place of conversation and gossip, customers today sit in well-padded chairs in music-filled rooms, reading magazines.

Outdoors, the lawn mower, chain saw, and snowmobile have grown quieter; indoors, dishwashers, refrigerators, furnaces, and stoves create only subdued household hums. Electric clocks have replaced the noisy ticking of old wind-up clocks, though they still can hum loudly.

Laser printers have quieted the ripping staccato of early dot-matrix printers.

Another significant quieting factor in the countryside is that construction takes place less and less on site. Materials arrive prefabricated from the factory, and precut materials are glued together, rather than noisily hammered and drilled. In contrast to the cacophony of building sites years ago, where cement was mixed, steel welded, and rafters, walls, and floors sawed and hammered, the contemporary construction site stands as a relatively tranquil place, except for the blare of radios. And even though the high-winding sound of the Skil saw and the popping thud of the new air hammer and nail gun form a loud trio, they don't match in pandemonium the construction sites of old.

Metallic sounds as well reverberate less frequently in the countryside and town. On bulldozers, rubber tracks have replaced clanging metal cleats. Salvage yards use hydraulic power and magnets, eliminating the straining and clanging steel cables of cranes. In newsrooms, the clicking and clacking of linotype has met the same fate as the earlier tip-tapping typewriter: it lost out to the computer. Quieter production of newspapers squares with that medium's softer opinions.

The world of medicine too has grown quieter. Gone from the hospital are the sharp metallic sounds of metal bed frames being raised and lowered and the clang of accidentally dropped metal bedpans on hardwood or stone floors. Even the patients, thanks to painkillers and psychotropic medicines, are less likely to moan and shout. Now plush carpets, thicker walls, and private rooms give hospitals a sense of hush, though the chatter of the television may be constant.

Much of this quiet has been made possible by plastics and other synthetics. They have replaced steel and iron as piping and tubing, screws, nuts, bolts, and fan and motor parts. They form scrub buckets, brooms, garbage cans, and containers of all sorts. Plastics even make fencing, ladders, wheelbarrows, and furniture. These materials create smaller, more intimate noises.

In the kitchen, whose sounds are worthy of an essay in themselves, the creaking pump no longer commands. Whistling teakettles are no longer the norm, and few coffee percolators gurgle anymore. Pots and pans bang and clank less, with the disappearance of steel utensils and cast-iron stoves. Cabinet doors open and shut more quietly. Prepared foods require less cutting, stirring, beating, or chopping. Canning sounds—the hissing kettle and metallic snapping of jar lids sealing—have all but vanished.

Objects that have been in use for decades, such as pumps and drills, are now made smaller and lighter, have fewer gears and moving parts, and, thus, are quieter. Light switches make little noise, springs on doors have disappeared, and even zippers, buckles, and snaps are fewer and quieter. Horns, signals, microphones, and speakers are all smoother and mellower than their predecessors. The ringing bells at railroad crossings have been replaced by flashing lights. And so, even the world of the machine collaborates in making a more peaceful environment.

SOUND AND CULTURE

Each society creates a distinct auditory order out of its technologies, materials, and goods. And every locale in that society forms its own particular aural tapestry. Looked at one way, sounds spontaneously take possession of space. They blend and collide independently of human intervention. Looked at another way, the mix of sounds in a particular place is a result of conscious human choices. Each machine, every zoning ordinance, every radio station adds to the local fabric of sound. Choice—individual and collective—governs the design of a home or office, the placement and regulation of a factory or shop, the creation and maintenance of a park, a highway, or, to take the most dramatic contemporary example, an airport, whose jets—120 decibels at takeoff—are the loudest sound of all.[15]

Architects and engineers study the auditory implications of their designs. They know that the selection of a site, the design of a landscape, the choice of materials used, and the number, location, and function of rooms in any building determine the noises its inhabitants will hear. Auditory engineers concern themselves with sound insofar as it affects occupational safety and office behavior. Codes aimed at controlling sound regulate insulation; the thickness of walls, floors, and doors; and the resonance of surfaces.

As society articulates its auditory environment, so individuals personalize their auditory locales, partitioning them and isolating themselves. Each pair of ears becomes a distinct portal of all sound. For example, individuals personalize their music experience. Students can play their own instruments in soundproofed studios. Commuters listen to music through headphones. Music played and listened to, although it still retains a communal function, develops a private side.

At the same time that society multiplies and individualizes the sounds it makes, its diverse cultures (with exceptions) strive to form pleasant and sonorous auditory experiences. Culture monitors the sounds humans emit and receive and establishes rules for sounds that are acceptable and those that are not. The same culture that allows babies to coo, gurgle, and pass gas instructs older children to watch their language and teaches adults not to yawn, spit, or holler except at baseball games. It tells members when and how to talk, sing, shout, curse, and moan, and defines the limits and boundaries of sound. Cultures generally require women to be more reserved in speech and sound than men, except in childbirth and mourning.

European upper-class settlers brought a restrictive culture of sound to the prairie, one that judged Native American dance and song to be chaotic and disorderly and similarly judged prairie ethnic cultures to be rude and loud. Advocating softer and more enunciated speech and less gesturing with hand and body, the proponents of upper-class culture idealized self-control. No sooner did schoolteachers, lawyers, and doctors—often the vehicles of upper-class cultural values—arrive in rural towns than they unpacked what could be called official and fashionable American culture. With schools, newspapers, and churches largely under their control, the cultured leaders of the countryside preached a quieter, more polite, and more sedate rural society.

Etiquette, whose composition and dissemination on the prairie would be a delight to study, taught a polite person to speak in a firm and modulated voice (except when at war or when ordering others about). This person would not holler, whine, whimper, whisper behind a cupped hand, or mumble. The civilized man would also refrain from making disorderly sounds or gestures such as washing his face in his hands (as my father and I did), blowing bubbles in his drink, slurping his soup, or loudly devouring his food. Also off limits, especially for women, were cracking knuckles, hacking up phlegm, and loud nose blowing.

Nevertheless, ethnic rural communities filled the Minnesota countryside with millions of words and trillions of sounds and echoes. European immigrant languages were multiple. (Indian languages were as well, but the sounds of their everyday lives and ceremonies are beyond ethnographic reconstitution.) Voting instructions for Minnesota state elections were issued at the end of the nineteenth century in eight languages. Minnesota's polyglot human communities were truly as rich in song and sound as its wetlands.

Settlements once formed distinct sonorous centers on the plains. Over time, however, they, like sound waves themselves, were deflected, transformed, and swallowed up. Folk and local culture were supplanted by national tapestries of sound and a common language and literature. Local sounds gave way to external control. Outside markets, creeds, and fashions prevailed.

The comings and goings of peoples and changing technologies, businesses, and crafts all invite acoustic and auditory histories. If done well, these histories would inspire the sensual resurrection of lost times and places. An entire childhood—like Proust's *petite madeleine*—can be evoked by the sounds of beeping and blaring cars trailing back home from the winning baseball game.[16] Writing of Sicily, an island of many regions, Gaetano Pennino remarks that sound deposits a symbolic bank of meanings.[17] Local historians could create such a bank, saving for future generations the aural symbolism of times gone by.

WILL YOU PLEASE SPEAK UP!

The leading causes of deafness were once occupational, whether in farming, dentistry, aviation, or industry. Railroad workers led the occupationally deaf. Now, those who suffer hearing loss are more likely to be victims of their play than of their work. Shooting (its side effects recently mitigated by sound-protection devices) and snowmobiling are harmful to the ears, but music is the biggest culprit. Three generations of deaf young people are "music's victims." Daily, a nation of youth assault their own eardrums in the confines of their cars or bedrooms, or in public at ear-splitting rock concerts or sporting events where amplifying devices magnify natural enthusiasms. Deafening and deafened are workers in the music industry—musicians, sound crews, disk jockeys, restaurant and dance club employees—a group that by now probably outnumbers the nation's farmers. Audiologists sell them sophisticated earplugs to protect against the music that may exalt the mind but surely deafens the ear.[18]

As the world grew louder and more variegated in manufactured sounds, so advancing civilization sought to help the deaf and hard of hearing. In the second half of the twentieth century the ability to aid hearing improved dramatically. Diagnosis and treatment of hearing problems, along with control of infections, reduction of sinus ailments, and the implantation of artificial organs, have meant a more distinct acoustic environment for many who would not have enjoyed it before.

Yet, rude sounds still assault the ear. Reflected, refracted, absorbed, concentrated and rarefied, magnified and amplified, sounds in contemporary society come from all quarters. Traversing air and gases, liquids and solids, sound literally moves from molecule to molecule. Industrial sounds are heard around the clock in the city and even in the countryside, especially during harvest.

Of course, quarter must be given to relativism. The barking dog makes music to its owner's ears, but not to its neighbor's. A factory's ceaseless, dominant, and brute noises sound like audible progress and money to the ears of industry or the chamber of commerce, even though they drive others to distraction. A neighbor of mine who lived near a service station claimed that the sound of wrenches being dropped on concrete in the early morning was more disturbing than the daylong hum of an air conditioner.

Noise in some form or other will always exist for those who have ears to hear it. The word *noise*—which derives from the Latin word for *nausea*—is not etymologically connected to *noisome*.[19] But it should be. Noise constitutes a contemporary pathogen. Measured as pollution in decibels, it can leave industrial workers and rock musicians, as already noted, stone deaf. (In 1970, the Acoustical Society of America found that the noise level of rock-and-roll bands in Minneapolis ranged from 105 to 120 dB, "only about 10 decibels less than the maximum noise level observed in a boiler shop.")[20] Though noise is intended to alert people to danger, in contemporary society the sheer volume of it endangers life. It invades sleep, steals attention, disorients, and even precipitates suicide. Noise control has become an important issue as scientists explore the effects of noise on our minds and bodies. Noise is believed to affect vasoconstriction, hormone levels, heart rates, and blood pressure. It may aggravate heart ailments and trigger ulcers and hives. It apparently has an effect on unborn children, and it has psychological effects causing irritability, nervousness, and anxiety.[21]

The auditory signature of the contemporary world is traffic, with automobile and truck noise resonating across the land wherever there are roads. Of all traffic sounds, the exploding noise of the motorcycle is perhaps the most searing to the nerves. However, those who find themselves living on a flight path near an airport might prefer the sound of constant traffic to the crushing and shaking noise of low-flying jets, which, according to an English survey, causes cows to abort their calves and hens to stop laying eggs.[22]

THE SOUND OF MUSIC

Members of the same civilization of course do not march to the same beat, even in the countryside. The real and imagined pandemonium of the trailer court on the edge of every rural town is considered a problem by the people of Main Street. In fact, more than one might imagine, the countryside fights over noises. Neighbors and neighborhoods, merchants, crafts, and industries have found themselves entirely at odds over what constitutes "too loud."[23]

In truth, the countryside is subject to a conceptual quarrel over the meaning of sound. Rural people (who may love shooting guns and driving snowmobiles) trumpet the quiet of the countryside as proof of its safety and serenity. City people equate rural quiet with boredom, a place where nothing is happening. Such a debate is predicated on the notion that somehow the countryside is the same everywhere, and it distracts one from observing how rural communities are embroiled in struggles over sound. Indeed, as I wrote this essay, I received the text of the city of Marshall's brand-new noise ordinance "providing for the elimination and prevention of noise, and imposing penalties for violation."[24] The ordinance cast its net as wide as possible, making it unlawful and a misdemeanor for "any person to make or cause to be made any loud, unnecessary or unusual noise which either annoys, disturbs, or affects the comfort, repose, health, or peace of others." In its illustrative enumeration, it mentions "horns and signaling devices" and "radios, tape and disk players" that make sounds audible from fifty feet away. Exempted from the ordinance are amplifying equipment authorized by the city, church bells and chimes, school bells, and warning devices. This ordinance supplements older city codes that prohibit loud gatherings and disorderly conduct, a category that includes brawling, using boisterous and obscene language, disturbing an assembly, racing a car motor, or spinning or skidding tires.[25]

As the nation is further populated, industrialized, urbanized, specialized, individualized, and privatized, one can expect that more municipalities will enact laws regulating sound. The countryside—thriving in its bigger towns and dramatically declining in its villages—will continue to differentiate itself into pockets of quiet and noise. As the rural world continues to be transformed, local historians will have a unique opportunity to record a changing history of sound and senses.

CHAPTER 5

Anger

Mapping the Emotional Landscape

As environmental control progressively transformed the landscape, so it correspondingly altered the range of human experience and expression. At least, I make that argument hoping it will stimulate local historians to consider writing of primary emotions and elemental human dispositions. Of course, by focusing here on anger, I do not wish to block historians from taking a more cheery route. I hope to set them also to writing about emotions such as love, happiness, and fear, and such dispositions as kindness, sympathy, and even sadness, jealousy, embarrassment, and guilt.

As I write here of the gradual constriction of anger on the rural landscape, local historians might attempt to document a corresponding expansion of friendly feelings among rural people. Indeed, they might venture an outline of the development of rural happiness in a place. The components of their story would include pleasure, comfort, sensual delight, intimacy, and optimism. Historians might first record who smiled and laughed, when, where, how, and at what. They might consider how happiness increased with a changed environment, which meant, at least for a sizable majority, less pain, more goods and opportunities, less tedious labor, and fewer familial obligations.

Emotions, it must be acknowledged, don't permit an easy study. They are not easily identified or classified. Any one emotion can be expanded, accordionlike, to encompass a whole range of what are essentially different states. Anger, for instance, expands from mild irritation to fury, from being hateful at the core to a generalized "outrage." Further confounding historians' study, emotions can be either spontaneous or calculated. Anger, which appears to strike out like a reflex, also can arise out of smoldering resentment and take the form of a long-incubated insult. Hate can flower into treachery, an art as refined as that of lovers who braid their passions into poetry. Even if emotions are spontaneous in their first expression, they become over time part of an individual's character and narrative.

A child's anger is not a man's anger, and a man's anger is not a woman's, and one woman's anger is not the same as another's. Situation, occasion, and gender determine their myriad origins, combinations, and expressions, as do intensity, frequency, and predictability. Emotions cluster around differing biological states and involve varying degrees of consciousness, fit together in diverse ways with other emotions, and command or are recessive in different temperaments. In turn, emotions are shaped by character, can be transformed by enlightenment and forgiveness, and are animated and modified by the stories individuals weave.

Groups, classes, and cultures also determine the expression of and reaction to differing emotions. Cultures validate emotions, distinguishing proper occasions, certifying legitimate motives, and establishing acceptable forms. Likewise, eras also birth and kill emotions. Period books, songs, and films propagate select feelings. Epochal movements—none as much in modern history as Romanticism, which can be understood to span the entire nineteenth century—can constitute a reordering of the constellations of emotions. Events such as wars, revolutions, and depressions can bring to the fore hidden emotions and give them fresh faces and gestures. Vietnam veterans, for example, brought new orders of emotion and expression to rural places.

As emotions are formed by distinct times, so they are embedded in unique social situations, institutions, and movements. A group's existence can be accounted for by a specific configuration of emotions. Some—such as farm groups, tax protest groups, or veterans—coalesce around complaints. They thrive on resentment. They not only gather hostility but focus it. In intense forms, complaint and its remedy can lead groups to declare war against remote markets and distant governments, adding desperate conspiratorial and paranoid views to their anger.

In this chapter, additional philosophical considerations are kept to a minimum. I try to stay closer to the ground by comparing past and present expressions of public anger. In the end I draw the modest though debatable conclusion that over the course of the twentieth century, country people, insofar as I can make them one, became less angry and more refined and sensitive.

"LAKE WOBEGON"

Americans, at least those who listen to Garrison Keillor, think Minnesota is "nice." In Keillor's invented folklore, tinged with occasional moments of dark passion, Minnesotans are depicted as the emotionlessly toothless descendents of their fierce Viking forebears. They don't loot, pillage, or rape; they avoid public disagreement at all costs. If we are to believe local humorist Howard Mohr's invented depiction *How to Talk Minnesotan,* they utter, ad nauseam, the noncommittal "Whatever" to avoid making a distinction that might solicit disagreement, ignite controversy, and so give rise to anything similar to anger. For a good time, Minnesotans gather in church basements, eat hot dishes of noodles and tuna fish as bland as their conversations, and, for a real thrill, sneak a second dessert. Adventure for them focuses on the weather that closes schools, leaving children stranded along the road, and sometimes shuts down towns. The strongest of passions comes wrapped in nostalgia for the simple life of Lake Wobegon.

Radio audiences from coast to coast have been wooed into believing that Minnesota has an undisturbed core of niceness.[1] Repressed, their baser emotions sublimated, Minnesotans are archetypically Midwestern and quintessentially antithetical to Easterners, with their sharp outbursts of anger, and Southerners, who brood with smoldering hatred. Niceness forms a moral mist covering Minnesota's population. It crosses class boundaries, envelops all industries, and observes not religious, nor ethnic, nor sexual, nor racial difference. Boosters market Minnesota in a Scandinavian wrapper despite its large population of Germans (the state's dominant ethnic group); Czechs, Italians, and Slavs in the Iron Range; African Americans from Chicago; and newly arrived Hmong and Somalis. They all are presumed according to the Minnesota stereotype of niceness to be equal in emotional blandness. The state's reputation abides in stereotypic nicety despite the rapes, murders, and armed robberies; independent of the long histories of farm, labor, and environmental conflict; and in contrast to long-standing virulent strains of anti–Native American, anti-Catholic, and anti-Semitic sentiments.

Increasingly, Minnesota functions as home in a world in which nation is too large and village too small. Minnesota is small enough to gather hearts and big enough to win minds. Though idealized in the media—

and in a sense invented by it—contemporary Minnesota serves as a moral compass in a changing, disorienting, and overwhelming era.

Historians, not immune to false generalizations, also construct a benign Minnesota emotional landscape. Particularly when they traverse the southern part of the state, they construe its flatness and openness as defining aspects of a candid terrain. The countryside "nearly always exudes an air of innocence."[2] Its plowed fields are vast, unbounded by deep woods or uncut by sharp ravines, which might shelter (if the mind is allowed to run wild) menacing fugitives and outlaws.

NOT SO NICE AFTER ALL

Having lived in the open land of southwest Minnesota for more than thirty years, I have learned the limits of Minnesota nice. Residents of this region make their living in a climate that is extreme and unforgiving, and though civilization's conveniences have made struggles for daily bread easier than they were in the past, anger still has numerous opportunities to take root and grow. Bosses are still unfair, wages are suppressed, neighbors quarrel over lot lines, and divorces—ever common—are rancorous, perhaps even especially bitter when children are battled over. Jealousies over land acquisition, conflicts of culture, and ancient family feuds abound.

To the passerby's superficial glance, southwest Minnesota appears devoid of class warfare, but inequality can't be missed. It shows on the faces and in the clothing of those who gather at the doors of the food processing plant. It is expressed by the rusted car that turns off into a trailer park, in the large and luxurious farm homes that stand down the road from run-down farmhouses surrounded by dilapidated animal pens and old machinery. Fences and walls between such farms testify to conflicts over ownership and the all-important rural separation of animals and crops.[3] Even without the tangible evidence of fences, hostility can be extrapolated, for land always provokes conflicts of interest. Land owned and land desired will forever nurture rivalries. Though today this region produces far fewer animals than in the past, and weeds are better controlled, property lines still mark claims and counterclaims and feed the resentments that naturally accompany differences between mine and thine.

Every countryside has its spite lanes. Even if these bands of anger are not to be read literally in the plowed stretches of land separating the fields of rival neighbors, as they are in the West, they do exist. By knowing the hostilities and aggressions, the conflicts and grudges of their friends and neighbors, local people make of the landscape an emotional territory. Families use stories to extend their anger over generations—and in the countryside, land (falsely inherited, bought with bad money, abused) underlies the dark and enduring conflicts from which literature frequently borrows.

Money also leaves trails of anger. Fluctuating grain markets, the influence of international capital, and disputes with railroads over prices are part of the narrative of communities trying to survive on the land. Membership in and the policies of local cooperatives and elevators can stir up memories of fights and abiding ill will. The question of who did and did not join farm movements in times of crisis can emotionally partition the countryside for decades.

Although ethnic and religious differences and rivalries between farm and town have significantly diminished since the 1950s and 1960s, such group rivalries remain. Intermarriages between Catholics and Protestants are more frequent, but still far from prevalent. The success of Belgian and Dutch Catholics in farming is less resented now, no doubt in part because their rivals—Scandinavian and French-Canadian farmers—have vanished from the countryside. Still, everyone in a county observes individual progress—material goods on display at an auction, or the erection of a new barn—and it awakens envy. My ninety-seven-year-old Cottonwood friend Torgny Anderson related a classic story of rural envy from his youth. In bare feet a neighbor woman walked a quarter mile from the road across his family's stubble field to deliver a single sentence: "I see you bought this new binder to make us feel bad." Then she turned on her heel and walked back across the stubble to the road.

TROUBLED WATERS

Perhaps no part of the landscape engenders as much hostility in rural regions as water. Struggles over weeds, roads, and schools—surely fertile subjects for the local historians of anger—don't even come close to water battles. It is no great exaggeration to say that every dam, "damn" ditch, and tile—its diameter and grade—has been contested. In contrast to the arid West, where farmers have killed to acquire water, farmers in rural Minnesota have all but killed to get rid of it. Draining water has been a necessary path to financial success, and for many a farmer, removing water from the land became a personal obsession. One local figure won himself the nickname "Jimmy Ditch, the Diggin' Son of a Bitch."

As in eastern agricultural states, the first farmers in Minnesota to ditch their land were the richest. They started their drainage systems in the early decades of the twentieth century. Poor commodity prices and bad times in the 1920s, and the drought of the 1930s, forced them to set their shovels and dredges down until the 1950s, when good times and a need for greater production led them to resume ditching and tiling with a passion. More land in production meant more profits and more capital for ditching. In rich and exceptionally flat Redwood County, there still are more ditches than roads.

As surely as water flows downhill, county ditches and judicial ditches (ditches that cross county lines and require court establishment) pitted farmer against farmer. Losers in the ditch battles, those who were flooded by water or sucked dry by taxes (or both), invariably petitioned and went to court to reroute a ditch or alter the cost of its maintenance. Ditch cases filled court dockets, leaving behind more evidence than any historian could digest and producing sufficient money to furnish every county with at least one lawyer who made a living off drainage cases.

Every county in the region has a ditch or two that remains a stream of angry memories. The mere mention of it—to say nothing of a proposal to expand, clean, or flood it—can reawaken decades-long fights between folks upstream and downstream, between townships and counties, and, in the past few decades, between watershed districts. Vocal meetings, bitter litigation, and detailed newspaper articles etch in the mind acrimony over water.

Controversy over drainage might lead a farmer to brandish a gun or start a fistfight. Neighbors once friendly might never talk to each other again. One notoriously angry farmer was consumed with bitterness for fifteen years because of the five acres of land he lost to flooding. He blamed his neighbors and the government agencies that had allowed this injustice. He boasted that he had hounded people out of their jobs, claimed that he once had thrown a dead cow in the water, and flew an Afghani flag on his lawn (to symbolize his fight against government tyranny). He even threatened that murders would occur unless his grievance was remedied.

Water fights still boil in the blood of wronged farmers, but more and more the source and the resolution of their fights lies with government agencies. Water battles increasingly pit the state's watershed districts, created in the 1970s, against one another and place them on the opposite side of a freshly articulated environmentalism supported by yet another set of government agencies, including the Army Corps of Engineers and Minnesota's Pollution Control Agency and Department of Natural Resources. The DNR's charge to protect native plants and wildlife and its overall defense of wetlands puts it in frequent conflict with farmers' drainage and tiling plans. Although none of its officers have been beaten or killed, the DNR has been locked in a low-grade war with farmers, who defied its authority in one local instance by dynamiting a dam the DNR had built.

Lakes also occasion fights over water, and no fight has been as significant as the draining of the "Great Oasis," a large lake in Murray County, in the early part of the twentieth century. This struggle of several years presaged later battles, pitting early environmentalists and recreationists against land-hungry farmers and real estate speculators.[4] Throughout the century, and throughout the southwestern Minnesota region, battles over drainage, the creation of new lakes (especially the Lac Qui Parle, in the county of the same name), the dredging of canals, and the straightening of rivers have upheld the truth of Mark Twain's quip, "Whiskey's for drinkin'; water's for fightin'."[5]

Floods, which inundate fields, towns, and homes, also provoke conflict and exacerbate divisions, as the 1997 flood along the Red River demonstrated. Long after the flood subsided, it lingered in raging legal and political quarrels over past and potential damages. This ability of floods to set watershed district against watershed district, farmer against farmer, farmer against town, and neighbor against neighbor is illustrated in my book *At the Headwaters,* an account of the 1993 floods in southwestern Minnesota.

Such conflicts do not belong to southwestern Minnesota alone. In myriad forms they are fought throughout the Minnesota and Mississippi River watersheds. Seeking resolution, advocates on both sides turn to politics and the law, which embroil their struggles in abstract state and national debates over the administration of water. In this way, water battles are fought and resolved, if at all, in distant forums.

FROM DEFIANCE TO THERAPY

As our society broadens its control over the countryside—its waters, lands, and peoples—so it correspondingly expands its influence over human feelings and their expression. Indeed, it appears that the more society has access to and takes control of human and natural environments, the more it moves from the external regulation of things to the internal influence over minds and feelings. In other words, modern society has shifted broadly from legal and administrative regulation to pacification through psychological gratification, making the majority of its people, if not happy, at least compliant. A history of southwest Minnesota farm protest from the depression to the present offers partial proof of this societal shift from the strength of collective action and confrontation to the relative impotence of individual resolution and therapy.

The Farm Holiday Movement of the 1930s, dedicated to stopping lenders from repossessing farms and to suspending farmers' payments of mortgages, was popular and confrontational in its tactics.[6] It brought together farmers who feared the loss of their land, which constituted everything they had, especially in that epoch of national unemployment and depressed agricultural prices. The boldness of the Holiday activists' tactics underscored their desperate condition. They pushed and shoved their adversaries and blocked the passage of trucks and commodities. They openly defied auctions against indebted farms, ordered by the courts on behalf of banks and suppliers, by threatening the lives of auctioneers and others. They assembled armed and intimidating crowds, which made the last and final bid for a farm a nickel or dime, and concluded the auctions by returning the farm to its owner. They also threatened and manhandled sheriffs who sought to carry out auctions. In one instance, in the vicinity of Granite Falls, thirty miles north of Marshall, the Holiday activists locked up the sheriff who had been directed by the court to supervise an auction.

And the protestors did not stop there. They dumped rivers of their own milk on the ground to show how unprofitable dairy farming had become. In further protest of the low prices paid for farm commodities, they formed a caravan that traveled around Lyon County, shutting down elevators, food-processing plants, and other purchasers of farm goods. In 1933, they overran the town of Marshall in order to close the local Swift meat-processing plant, making national news. More than ten thousand farmers from Minnesota, Iowa, and the Dakotas converged on Marshall, disarmed the sheriff and his men, and drove away the supporting firefighters and cut their hoses. Having successfully closed the Swift plant, they paraded down Main Street, snaking in and out of town stores, and, as one oral account has it, appropriating occasional goods.

The farm protest of the 1960s was far less spontaneous, popular, violent, and even confrontational than the Farm Holiday Movement. Rising up in a far less severe and engulfing agricultural depression, the protestors and their sympathizers were fewer in number and less dramatic in action. The nature of the protest varied considerably from county to county, although its goals and direction were orchestrated by the National Farmers Organization (NFO). Born of depressed prices and the overall dismal conditions facing small-scale grain and dairy farmers in an era of expanding farm production, the NFO tried to imitate what organized labor had accomplished in the 1930s by promoting collective bargaining between farmers and buyers. Here too, however, its tactics were less confrontational.

The NFO had an aggressive and large chapter in Lyon County.[7] Its membership comprised as many as 30 percent of Lyon County's farmers, including a considerable number of the county's large and young Belgian farm families. Nevertheless, their pushing, shoving, road blocking, and three holding actions in the early and middle 1960s, which aimed to block the shipment of cattle and milk off the farms, did not approach the Holiday Movement's level of aggression. Their principal tools, identical to those of the NFO at large, were nonviolent and democratic. They withheld crops and livestock from the market and tried to persuade others not to ship their goods. For dramatic effect, and to display their frustration, they too dumped their own milk by the truckload. In the end, however, their tactics failed to alter the market or convince fellow farmers that collective bargaining pointed the way to improved prices.

In the 1980s, against the backdrop of high interest rates, low prices, and the devaluing of farm assets by half, a great number of the farmers in southwest Minnesota went bankrupt or quit farming. Even though farms were being lost, there were far fewer farmers in the region and nation to protest against ever more imposing and complex markets. As a result, although there was protest, it was feeble and unorganized compared with that of earlier decades. It lacked a clear principle and never gathered a large or cohesive following.

That is not to say farmers were not angry. What differed was the expression of their anger. Farmers quietly rode buses to St. Paul, the state capital, to hear speeches and look for public help where they could get it. The sole organization that emerged out of the protest, Groundswell, was poorly organized and had few members.[8] They conducted their protests on moral and symbolic grounds. In their complaints, they depicted themselves as a group of victims rather than as the backbone of the nation, as earlier protesting farmers had done. Their major play was for media attention. Aside from the trip to St. Paul and a ceremony on the capitol steps, there were staged events featuring protest celebrities such as the Reverend Jesse Jackson and United States senator Paul Wellstone. Willie Nelson sang his heart out for the farmers at a special concert in Iowa.

In their attempt to capture media attention, launched in the autumn of 1983, the emerging leaders of Groundswell transformed the murder of two bankers by a mentally ill father and son in Lincoln County into an expression of the farm crisis. Taking only the selective facts that the father had been a farmer, and that the dual murder had occurred on his former farmstead, the Groundswell leaders cautioned the world at large and regional bankers in particular that you can push farmers only so far. They ignored other, less convenient facts, as I point out in *When Father and Son Conspire:*[9] the father had been a deadbeat farmer even in the best of times, during the preceding decade and a half. He'd worked an impossibly small farm of thirty acres and had fewer than forty cows. He had willingly returned the farm to the bank two years before, in the wake of a divorce and before the onset of the latest crisis. Groundswell also overlooked the son, who was the actual killer. He was a loner who had spent most of his time learning to shoot and playing soldier. He had trained himself to shoot an M-1, in fact, in emulation of soldiers of fortune. In sum, Groundswell took an exceptionally odd father and son, who were pathetically alone and lost in anger, and made them part of the farmers' cause. In a similar vein, they later repeatedly attributed contemporary farm suicides to the crisis, although the evidence of any change in the rate of farmer suicide was scanty or nonexistent.

Publicly, the farmers sought sympathy and support. They decried the death of the family farm. They looked in all possible directions for favorable legislation. Consciously imitating the Farm Holiday Movement, protesting Minnesota farmers hit at least a small jackpot when they called for a moratorium on farm debt and their cry was heard by the Minnesota legislature, which passed a farm negotiation act requiring arbitration between farmers and creditors before foreclosure. At the same time, on an individual level, debt-laden farmers (caught in an immense credit crunch produced by low prices on the one hand and depreciated assets on the other) used what individual means the law and society afforded to keep themselves afloat. They resorted to their own or a pro bono lawyer to salvage what cash they could from their indebted farms, while turning to their ministers, priests, and psychologists to aid them with the emotional aspects of their loss. At the same time, farmers returned to school in appreciable numbers for job training and became even more dependent on their working wives to provide the family with money and benefits.

In effect, farmers protested less in the 1980s than their predecessors had, although with good reason. They simply weren't as numerous, their absolute and proportionate numbers having been in decline since the middle of the century. They constituted less than 2.5 percent of the national population. What's more, several factors prevented their ever coalescing. As a group they were profoundly divided and differentiated by size and type of farm. They had varying goals and allegiances to farm organizations and political parties. And they were differentiated by the extent of their debt. At the same time, they confronted a more remote and powerful world. They faced vast markets enhanced by international competition, including European grain and Latin American soybeans. They had to deal with an ever more complex government and society. And at the most immediate level, armed and efficient local and state police, as well as the army, were ready to meet radical protest.

Lacking muscle and unity, these farmers were too weak to successfully protest or even sustain their resentments. They weren't nearly equal to the forces they faced. They had become bystanders to their own fate. A new profession, consoling words, and therapy were essentially all that remained for those facing the loss of their farm.

The 1980s saw the death of collective and angry farm protest and the undeniable decline of rural life in southwestern Minnesota. Farmers, for the greatest part, learned that farming was a business—and when the books didn't add up, it was time to move on. Speaking volumes about the plight of effective protest, Groundswell activists in the Redwood Falls area met the renewed farm crisis of the 1990s by operating a "Used-a-Little-Bit" shop and offering one-on-one counseling to troubled farmers, thanks to a grant from the Minnesota Department of Agriculture.[10]

DEFINING THE LIMITS OF ANGER

Today, expressions of anger in southwest Minnesota, or in any region for that matter, have their genesis in the interaction between cultures and institutions. Right from settlement times, an elite of bankers, schoolteachers, newspaper editors, doctors, state lawmakers, sheriffs, judges, and merchants of Yankee stock created the Main Street of larger towns such as Marshall, Granite Falls, Pipestone, and Redwood Falls. For the prairie, and especially for the newly arrived immigrants who filled the countryside and helped form the outlying farm villages, they defined the norms and ideals of the new republic. Through laws, patriotic celebrations such as for the Fourth of July, and preachments from the pulpit and local newspaper, they taught the newcomers what it meant to be a respectable citizen.

Immigrants, in turn, looked to the representative institutions of their new land—especially its schools, laws, courts, media, and business community—to instruct them on how to be good Americans. The immigrants, especially the wealthier ones, came from rural locales in Poland, Germany, the Netherlands, and Scandinavia, which not only had their own communal and family norms, but also had been shaped by spreading urban culture and newly emerging democratic ideals. Nevertheless, while some did form their own churches and schools, overall their goal was to assimilate. For those who did not conform—most often single men who were farmhands or from the laboring classes—police and authority were always present in the towns. The high number of arrests for assault, drunkenness, and disorderly conduct among the immigrants recorded in Lyon County's Prison Calendar from the 1890s through World War I suggests that American law and order did indeed discipline these newcomers.[11]

As the nineteenth and twentieth centuries progressed, society, starting in the cities and spreading to the remote countryside in Europe and the United States, transformed people's behavior and shaped their emotions. Almost everyone was made more polite, more genteel, and, in effect, more "civilized."[12] Or, to express this pervasive yet diffuse transformation in other terms, local peoples and cultures increasingly adopted the ways of—and began to resemble—the urban middle-class cultures.

Beginning at settlement and extending through the second half of the nineteenth century, society cleaned up both emotion and behavior. People were taught to wash more often; shout, spit, fight, and gesticulate less; and, finally, to repress and disguise their more coarse and aggressive feelings. Anger especially became more controlled. Any display of out-of-control behavior—fighting, assault, public urination, and drunkenness—was not tolerated.

Laws and etiquette spread from city to town to village. Rural people mimicked the self-controlled upper class and, over time, saw no reason why they should not be as clean, restrained, and, thus, sophisticated as their city cousins. The metamorphosis of the emotions and behavior of rural folk reflects the civilizing process of rural life. Historians of feelings must reach back to the Middle Ages to explore the formation and transmission of manners, sensibilities, and social control.[13] The modern conquest of feelings and impulses developed in conjunction with the expanding powers of court, state, commerce, democracy, and education. In the nineteenth century, civilizing processes reached and started to transform coarse peasants into law-abiding citizens and respectable and even sensitive individuals.[14]

In order to follow this theme in rural Minnesota and the Midwest, local and regional historians must follow this society's evolution from one that accepted many forms of violence—brutal fistfights, deadly beatings, cruelty to animals, baseball brawls, great wedding fights, and rumbles between the young people of rival towns—to one that tolerates violence directed against wartime enemies of the state. In the twentieth century, most rural Minnesota towns had only a murder or two over the entire hundred years, although that's counting only those that were reported. Aside from recording violence's retreat from the public eye, historians, with an eye to parallel developments in other regions and times, must focus on the diminution of open physical aggression between individuals, neighbors, extended families, villages, and parishes. Gender provokes its own, separate line of inquiry. When did women—which women—quit fighting? How did women continue to express their anger and vent their rage at home, in public, and toward their husbands, children, neighbors, and public officials? Deciphering such expressions of anger as stony silence, scorn, and even fury and physical assault would also be part of the local historian's study of the nature and transformation of anger.

One European historian on the subtle trail of the mollification of anger framed his inquiry around telling questions: When was brawling criminalized? Where and between whom did public fights begin to lead to imprisonment and lawsuits? When did assault begin to be treated consistently as a crime?[15] A similar sort of framework could apply in studies of rural Minnesota towns. When did fighting stop in churches, cemeteries, and other public places? When did individuals begin to think they should fight fair—not kicking, not surprising their opponents or ambushing them when they were in the most compromised biological positions? This line of inquiry follows nineteenth-century society's mounting success in imposing order.[16]

As the nineteenth century progressed, society redefined itself. Individuals became increasingly preoccupied with their own pleasures, though politics, laws, and codes of punishment made everyone part of the same collectivity. The triumph of the public order accompanied the spread of social manners, the articulation of individual rights, increased concern for the suffering of fellow humans, and in certain quarters, a nascent concern for animal suffering. Death itself was dressed up with the use of the ornaments and paraphernalia of a good Victorian funeral.[17]

By the 1880s, Western civilization—from Eastern Europe to the "wild" American West—had advanced considerably and rapidly. Control of the environment and of human conduct went hand in hand. At the time rural Minnesota was being settled, American society was leaving behind biting, eye-gouging, bare-knuckle fighting, and bear baiting. (In truth, Minnesota never was much of a wild frontier. Pianos and French lessons arrived on the prairie with the first riverboats and trains. Indeed, the first major trapper in the area, Joseph Laframboise, educated himself and made sure his daughters were formally educated back East.)

By the end of the century the state had grown strong enough to forgo public execution. In 1862, the federal government had publicly hanged thirty-eight Sioux Indians in Mankato for their part in the Minnesota Uprising, in which hundreds of white settlers were slaughtered up and down the Minnesota River Valley by young braves infuriated by mistreatment and the threat of a degrading life. State hangings continued throughout the 1870s and 1880s, but by the 1890s they were on the way out of fashion. The last public hanging in southwestern Minnesota took place in 1898 in Granite Falls. The victim had bludgeoned his wife to death.

The civilizing process and the settlement of the Trans-Mississippi West coincided, and so did the decisive transformation of the European countryside. This was not accidental. Thanks to the industrial revolution, both continents experienced interior colonization by nation and law, goods and markets, values and taste. As historians have yet to explore, this link was reinforced in the Midwest by European immigration. In this sense, it fell to Minnesota and other Midwestern states—their laws and statutes, agencies and bureaucracies—to continue the civilizing processes begun back East or in Europe. The young American civilization might have been heard to invoke Europe in these terms: "Send to us your teeming masses. Even if they have not been refined in your rural locales, they will be uplifted, mannered, and tamed here in the new land."

THE STRUGGLE FOR EMOTIONAL CONTROL

The refinement of emotions parallels the overall evolution of civilization toward control. It conforms to Carol and Peter Stearns's fourth stage of anger in the United States.[18] According to the Stearnses, the first stage of the history of American anger control occurred in colonial America among the dominant upper-class Protestant and northern European cultures. During this stage, Americans (and their contemporaries in Western Europe) showed little concern about anger. It was natural and expected. The second stage, which covered the second half of the nineteenth century, preached the virtues of the anger-free home. During the third stage, which lasted until the First World War, Americans continued to focus on familial control of anger, especially in socializing children, while remaining ambivalent about public anger. For example, public lynching and fistfighting were tolerated, if they expressed a righteous wrath. In the fourth stage, which began in the 1920s and arrived in the Midwestern countryside in the 1960s, American culture defined anger, one of the most difficult emotions to master, as a problem and sought to treat it therapeutically.

Local histories of gestures could prove insightful in demonstrating that displays of anger have become less acceptable. No longer can one spit on others, abruptly turn one's head away from an enemy, kick dirt, throw down one's hat, or even shout or gesticulate without being judged to be out of control. Displaying anger is thought to manifest character weakness. Anger can be aroused by taxes, pollution, land use, and ditches, and passions can be publicly vented about proposals—as was the case in Marshall—for a new incineration plant, sidewalks, or a housing project for the poor, but it is never acted out. The disputants may fire off, if they dare, a few argumentative letters to the newspaper. If they are really angry, they may retain lawyers, who have become the main contemporary conduit of grievances.

Even when there are matters that justify anger—the lack of support for family farms, for example—rural people find it difficult to articulate their anger. They do not constitute a distinct class. They have no natural leaders. They are not unionized, and no radical party has gathered them up. The institutions that for generations have been setting the limits on anger are well organized, numerous, and connected with law enforcement. Society knows how to put a damper on protest merely by supporting the belief that happiness is possible and that anger is out of place in an age of good feelings.

This artificially pacific atmosphere leaves rural people with few outlets for their irritations, disappointments, and humiliations. They pour their resentments into the streams of gossip that turn the mills of the local coffee klatches, whose diversity, membership, and functions deserve careful local study. Gossip may well create more troubled waters than does politics.[19]

THE NEW FACE OF VIOLENCE

The most emphatic displays of anger—acts of violence—are as much out of favor as are more subtle expressions of anger. Society demands that violence be curbed by laws and public pressure. In the country, barn burnings are not unusual and fistfights, once common, are now rare. Flashing weapons to get attention is quickly judged as evidence of mental imbalance. Of course, there are still small groups of young men who have drunken brawls, but they are far outnumbered by the good kids who play sports and instruments and study to go to college. The only arena in which violence is still in style is the media, where every sort of stored-up violence against self, others, and society is on display.

The contemporary campaign against domestic abuse is a good example of how society has legislated against acts of violence. Not only have state laws and administrative weight been brought to bear on the problem, but also, according to a Marshall lawyer, recent federal statutes bar the possession of handguns by individuals convicted of domestic assault.[20] The lawyer noted that this expanding concern for domestic assault drives a revitalized vigor in the prosecution of public assault, whose perpetrators are identified as potential domestic assailants.

Civilization has determined that it must battle against anger for the sake of right and order. However, it never escapes the paradox that its trials, punishments, damages, compensations, and settlements cause frustrations, humiliations, and alienation that fuel the anger its laws seek to quench. Though civilization has successfully legislated against acts of violence, society must still cope with the subterranean rage associated with "problem" individuals who are frustrated, lack self-esteem, perhaps are addicted to alcohol or other substances, and who frequently turn their energies against themselves, their families, and their communities. Treating these "untamed" people requires considerable public investment. Whole complexes of psychologists, lawyers, judges, and probation officers (whose history and effects merit study) constantly strive to pump aggression out of the human heart and into safer channels.

Nevertheless, they often are not successful. In rural Minnesota, domestic beatings and child abuse continue, although they are cloaked in confidentiality. Now and then they break forth in mayhem or murder. Suicide, another complex phenomenon hidden in confidentiality but meriting study, still shocks. Bar fights, though infrequent, attract attention, especially if they have racial overtones, like one in Marshall a few years ago that pitted black college athletes against locals over a disputed pool game. High rates of violence among certain recent immigrant groups could be expected, given the number of single males without family or established community. Leaving aside the problem of gangs and guns, the behavior of these new immigrants, as historians should examine, seems on the surface to resemble that of the first and second generations of European immigrants.

THE ANGER OF PREJUDICE

Just as immigrants, disproportionately composed in the first years of their arrival of single males, are often engaged in more acts of violence than are established groups, they are also more often the objects of violence based on prejudice. Yet immigrants do not make the easy targets they once did. Rural society—to announce a thesis worthy of elaboration—is not as confident in its hate as it once was. *Tolerance* has become the watchword, although this does not deny that recent immigrants to the region do experience low-grade racism in housing and everyday transactions.[21]

In the past, anti-immigrant and anti-Catholic sentiments directed popular hostilities in rural Minnesota—as local historians could document. In the 1920s, the Ku Klux Klan formed chapters in southern Minnesota.[22] Antiurban, antimonopoly, anti–Wall Street, and anti-Semitic feelings were inherent in rural Populism, while antiforeigner sentiment climaxed during the First World War. Watchdog societies across the state targeted not just Germans and German communities but all foreign-language communities. They also hassled people who were opposed to intervention, the draft, and the war, and those who didn't buy their fair share of war bonds.[23] Nevertheless, lynching and large-scale anti-German riots—both of which occurred in other regions and deserve careful study—did not occur in southwestern Minnesota during either the First or the Second World War. In fact, relationships between residents and German war prisoners held in the region resulted, in many instances, in lasting friendships. Even provocative anti–Vietnam War protests, which after one demonstration in Marshall landed more than 160 protesters in jail, did not result in a violent collision with the local American Legion.[24] In the heart of the farm crisis of the 1980s, the John Birch Society's tirades against international bankers and grain cartels largely fell on deaf ears. The recent distribution of anti-Semitic literature in Marshall and nearby towns won its outside distributors only rebuff. The politics of aggression and hate have not found fertile ground here.

Nowadays there is no doubt that the sheriff, the police, and the courts are in control. The old fighters and fighting clans have largely faded away, taken to riding their Harleys on Sunday, or gone for counseling. Society both tames and explains away the violence that does occur. Yet however much we impose order on the human spirit, it still eddies and quarrels, churns and turns, with complaint, frustration, and resentment. Anger still remains a way of reacting to a world with which we are not satisfied.

THE JUDGE AND THE LAWYER

A thorough inquiry into the topic of anger involves oral history, which is one of the necessities and delights of writing local and regional history. Two people in particular shared their reflections with me during the writing of this book. One was a lawyer, about forty years old, and the other a judge, about sixty. Both are lifelong residents of Yellow Medicine County, whose county seat is Granite Falls. Yankees formed the town's original downtown business class, while Scandinavian farmers filled the surrounding countryside and marked it with a radical farm tradition.

The lawyer and the judge agreed on one central point: groups and individuals in the past expressed anger more directly than people do today. They were more fervent and militant. Fistfights were more common, even among Scandinavians. Being the toughest guy in town was for many young men the next best thing to being the town's best pitcher.

Every county had a village or two where you could count on finding a good fight. Some of these hot spots were ethnic enclaves. Wilno, a Polish community in Lincoln County, staged a notorious annual Fourth of July fight every year, when two families went at each other with all but guns and knives. Six miles to the northwest of Marshall, Ghent offered the residents of Lyon County Sunday drinking and fighting between French-Canadians and Belgians, with a handful of Irish thrown in. Its notoriety for fighting, crowned by a murder in 1898, led to the town's interdiction by the bishop of St. Paul.[25] One punch in 1919 was the talk of the immediate countryside: a French-Canadian church member in Green Valley punched the local priest in the face for adding a Belgian to the church's council, tilting the voting balance.[26]

Anger, expressed and repressed, formed the emotional texture of earlier eras, my informants told me. A raging father or mother headed many a household. Spouses warred openly or filled their homes with icy silence. Scarcity primed individual, family, and community jealousy. With not much to do and less to be proud of, reasons for provocation abounded like kindling in an overgrown forest. A stray spark, especially in the tinder of an alcohol-infused wedding reception or a closely contested ball game, could erupt into a conflagration.

Language validated anger more than it does today. Everyday phrases made anger seem natural: "She got her dander up." "Her Irish is up." "He's got a mean streak, and a hair-triggered temper. It runs in the family." Gestures testified to the larger place anger once occupied on the landscape. Anger was expressed by spitting, turning up one's nose, showing one's back, massaging one's fist in one's hand, rolling up one's sleeves, taking off one's glasses, throwing one's hat on the ground, looking out of the corner of one's eye, or in so many other ways the local historian could document.[27]

Despite the civilizing forces of the nineteenth century, anger, it seems, had a larger and more demonstrative repertoire into the twentieth—stomping, slamming doors, crumpling paper, ripping clothes, gnashing teeth, biting lips, spitting, hissing. In contemporary society these expressive gestures appear comic in their exaggeration. With wide variations, of course, country people in the past seemed more likely to say what was on their minds and to accompany their words with a stronger show of feelings. Like their fields and waters, their interiors had not yet been as fully tamed and mellowed as they are today. Likewise, emotional surfaces were not yet under control.

It is not a contradiction, however, to hypothesize that country people in the past (and the present) bottled up a lot of anger. They lived amid frustrating circumstances. Husbands and wives commonly lived with each other years after they had quit speaking to and sleeping with one another. Every village and township had—as some still do—family members or neighbors who did not speak to one another for decades.

Often silence protected people from their feelings. Speaking "the truth," whose frequent confession the contemporary world cherishes as it seeks to colonize the human heart, was understood to be dangerous. Silence, in a more explosive environment, was appreciated for its ability to bring about short-term peace and long-term survival. In one poignant example from the 1940s, reported to me by a friend, a young local Ghent girl unexpectedly returned home to the farm from a nunnery. For the remainder of their lives, neither she nor her parents ever discussed her failed calling.

Anger isn't what it used to be in the countryside. Increased mobility means that emotions are less abiding in a community. As people come and go, they take their memories with them. They undo the emotional quilts of old. As farmsteads are torn down, long-standing grudges vanish. As farms get larger and less labor-intensive and farmers grow fewer in number and more urban in perspective, local emotions dissipate. In rural towns, staid business classes and their hierarchical orders of snobbery and resentment disappear as people move away or vacation elsewhere, or as women who work outside the home focus their interests beyond local disputes. In the last three decades of the twentieth century, the emotional fabric of the rural world, and the peoples, memories, and objects it supported, unraveled, leaving only threads for migrating birds to weave into their nests.

CHAPTER 6

The Clandestine

Society constantly perceives or imagines transgressions, and these violations are a component of its collective memory. As the many possible forms and expressions of anger, complaint, and resentment show, the mind is a multidimensional and dark chamber. Much of what men and women do is hidden from the outer world and, at the same time, buried in the recesses of the mind. It is those realms, so terrifying and tantalizing, that create what I call the clandestine. Forever forming the hidden yet captivating side of human experience, the clandestine, in its many and mutable forms, must intrigue the local historian if he or she is to write of the events and subjects that so engage audiences everywhere.

LOCATING THE CLANDESTINE

Although spanning a significant and mutable spectrum, reaching from the bizarre to the dreadful, the clandestine signals threatening and violative objects, thoughts, people, and places. These can threaten by their ambiguity and amorphousness as much as by the actual danger they pose to person and community. Metaphorically, the clandestine is associated with things sneaky, sly, shifty, stealthy, covert, concealed, furtive, and sinister. No wonder the stranger, the drifter, and the interloper, who at least traditionally were suspected of being out of place and up to no good, evoke the clandestine.

The clandestine resides in caches and niches, hideouts and hideaways, corners and crannies. It inhabits attics, cellars, closets, and other dark places. Associated with human structures such as dugouts, tunnels, sanctuaries, keeps, castles, and of course, tombs, in nature it belongs to holes, dens, caves, canyons, deep, dark woods, and all the other places of fear and trepidation. Certain places, plants, and animals radiate an ominous power.[1] The wild and the savage also register the sense of the hidden, secretive, and forbidden. Every place has its own clandestine map.

The clandestine lurks below the surface like a depth charge. Whether it be the suspected infanticide, the unproved murder, the unreported suicide, the surmised adultery, or the crime being planned, the clandestine threatens the world as known, ordered, and safe. It has the power of revelation. It arrives with the confession of the seventy-year-old man who for the first time reveals that his brother had abused him when he was eight. It offers the inside and therefore true story of things. It dispels ordinary life and the common order of things.

Gossip continually sniffs out the clandestine, as suspicion scans the borders of the community and conscience the trespasses of self. With a clouded moon of its own, each mind scans others for lies and deception. "The heart of another," wrote Willa Cather, "is a dark forest, always, no matter how close it has been to one's own."[2] As the popularity of the endless, droning country music heard in rural areas testifies, cheating hearts abound.

Communities, whose purpose is to make wholes out of parts, seek to knit the many into one. But despite their efforts to use the laws of nature and religion to produce order, communities find themselves surrounded by subversion. The bodies and minds of their members jump with defiant urges. With myriad hearts murmuring dissent, law firmly teaches the vigilance and the punishment that create much of the sense of the clandestine.

Every community lives under a canopy of mutual suspicion, and the illicit takes many forms. Hidden sins may be associated with people who live amid filth or, conversely, who display effeminate dandyism. Sins can be repressed, the very mention of certain transgressions being taken as testimony to the prurient quality of one's own mind. Or they can be as public as the local newspaper editor's constant drumming on the wrongs of drinking or the subjects of all the gossip that eddies and swirls up Main Street, from barbershop and post office to the coffee shop and local courthouse.

Matters of money and property, which are covert by nature, raise rumors of secret family fortunes and tax evasion. Religious beliefs and practices that require solitude give rise to suspicion of satanism or perversion. Serious crimes always have a secret side; they involve conspiring and plotting. The whole story of a crime is never truly told. Local historians worth their salt must search these dark corners, ever facing the paradox that a place's most powerful stories often do—indeed, often must—go untold.

Social, religious, and ethnic factors shape local suspicions. Gender and generation also sculpt different senses of the clandestine. If young men were tantalized by the house of ill repute, young women paid more attention to the clandestine abortionist. The teenage imagination almost requires the telling of grisly tales (or at least it did before the thrills of today's computer games), like the one popular in the 1960s and 1970s of the Wisconsin farmer who made lampshades of human skin.

Our fate is suspicion. People suspect one another of every sin they can imagine. Never fully present to one another, we conjure hidden antics and machinations behind every closed door, curtained window, and unexplained trip. Local historians must recognize an invisible city, threatening and submerged, in every town. Populated with the sins of bribery, betrayal, envy, fraud, hypocrisy, perjury, and sedition, it conceals a hidden and forbidden history whose tales, told or only suspected, exceed in evil, treachery, and pettiness the historian's ordinary fare.

DARK STORIES IN EVERY TOWN

My wife clips out "almost crimes" from the Marshall newspaper, the *Independent,* and sends them along to our children. "Someone," it is reported, "suspiciously entered a garage, but nothing was taken." "A fight," it is noted, "ended up on the street with two fellows spraying each other with shaving cream." "A resident on Sixth Street reported that a child is throwing garbage into her yard every day." "A woman living on Locust Drive reported [that] someone was leaving love letters on her car." Every locale accumulates bizarre stories, and the history of the bizarre is adjacent to and at points overlaps the history of the clandestine, deserving a reflection of its own.

As a fan of Dostoyevsky, I am a collector of dark tales. For years I've kept newspaper articles that reveal the irrational and threatening side of the southwestern Minnesota region. They convince me that senses and revelations of the clandestine form distinct communities. Clandestine stories, once leaked, catch people's attention. When I first came to Marshall, students exaggerated a report of cattle mutilations forty miles north of town and embellished the rumored sighting of a nightgown-clad ghost of a jilted lover that appeared along the highway to Worthington. Recently attracting much attention, the local paper reported that a man "exposed himself [to a child] in the children's area of the Marshall library."[3] A seventy-two-year-old man in Canby, thirty miles northwest of Marshall, abused four of his granddaughters, and a Willmar man shook his four-month-old niece to death because she wouldn't stop crying.[4] Today I read that "police believe the deaths of a thirty-four-year-old Worthington man found hanging in a tree and the corpse of a twenty-five-year-old woman found in an apartment are related."[5] Stories like these tug at the mind and demand a complete telling.

Crimes can leave indelible tracings. They create sinuous interior pathways that shape distinct topographies.[6] In the lot of Marshall's principal grain elevator, an estranged husband stabbed his wife to death while onlookers watched helplessly from an adjacent road. Because of the crime committed there, that lot is now not easily forgotten. The blood still flows in certain local minds.

Of all the illicit stories that identify a locale, it might be said that sexual transgressions form the nucleus of a place. They are particularly potent when they violate the taboos erected between humans and animals, among family members, and between old and young. Nathaniel Hawthorne's *Scarlet Letter* and Gustave Flaubert's *Madame Bovary* have shown the potential for turning illicit sex into art; popular magazines and television shows illustrate the enduring interest of sexual violations.[7]

Stories of sexual transgression are plentiful in southwestern Minnesota. In the early 1980s, in Lake Balaton, a town fifteen miles southwest of Marshall, a photographer took pornographic films of his unsuspecting clients' children and sold them to a California pornography ring. At Lake Wilson, in Murray County, an eighty-year-old man killed his wife's sixty-five-year-old lover. North of Marshall, a woman killed two of her lovers and was sentenced to prison not for murder, but for illegally collecting the social security payments of one of the deceased's mothers. Stories mesmerize a town—and in certain instances daze and enthrall an entire region—as they attest to the hidden presence of a dark and menacing side to the human spirit.

Although sex is more openly acknowledged these days, it still titillates and captivates. Common sexual acts are never quite ordinary.

They excite, as the local historian cannot ignore, the taboo side of everyday life. No amount of the commercialization of sex or therapy can naturalize sex. Despite preachment that all is natural and fair in love, each individual, couple, and generation, as well as priest, minister, and counselor, is compelled to draw lines with words about what people may and may not do in intimacy. (A twenty-year annual survey of university students suggests, as one might expect, that in sexual beliefs and practices, the young in the countryside in aggregate follow—at delayed rates—national tendencies.)[8]

Local historians must grasp—as many great writers such as Shakespeare and Chaucer certainly did—that sex will always have a dark side and constitute a matter of curiosity. Fulfilling and distorting lives, building and destroying families and friendships, sex has always confronted human beings with the bewildering task of putting borders around it. Aside from bringing pleasure and expressing devotion, it produces shame, humiliation, and illegitimacy.

Perhaps the place of sexuality in the contemporary rural mind, surely an enticing but challenging subject for local historians, has to be taken against a recent attempt to remove sex from the realm of the clandestine. During the past several decades, the secrets of the bedroom and closet have been paraded on street and screen. Sex has been promoted by market and media as appealing to all ages. At the same time, it has been taught in schools, and from liberal and tolerant pulpits, to be essentially natural and normal. In effect, the sexual revolution has arrived in the countryside.

A SHORT AND SORDID TOUR

Enthusiastically embracing my thesis that every town has a clandestine history, a friend from north of Marshall offered to take me on a seamy tour of his hometown and I accepted. We began in the surrounding countryside, the peripheries of settlements having been identified historically with the clandestine. First, my friend pointed out the tin roof of a bachelor's home, on which the man sunbathed nude on the hottest afternoons to "bake the devil out of him." He pointed out another bachelor's place, an unheated house without running water, where the occupant purportedly lived and had sex with his animals. Whether or not that was true, the man's eccentricity was publicly displayed when, because of a bad experience at the local gas station, he refused to fill up his tank there. Rather, he parked a long way off and hauled gas, gallon by gallon, from the station to his car. His story formed only part of the large swath the irrational and clandestine cut across this countryside.

My guide, Virgil to the Inferno of his own hometown, pointed out a house to which a man frequently returned drunk, asking as he crossed the threshold, "Who am I going to beat up tonight?" His wife sent their children scurrying into the cornfield to hide. At another house, a father was rumored to have sodomized all his sons. On a nearby farmstead, there once lived a woman in her thirties who sought sex with teenage boys; she would establish an affinity for a particular boy and then pursue him. As an aside, my guide mentioned a baseball coach who fondled his players and led them in group masturbation.

My friend remarked that the smartest family in town lived in a shack with a floor covered by feces. He also noted the residence of a new, unmarried teacher, a white woman who had given birth to black twins. He directed my attention to other houses in which all the residents were permanently drunk.

At the end of my tour, wearied of dark stories, I set off for home. As night fell on the landscape, it seemed to swarm with evil.

SUSPICION OF STRANGERS

The clandestine in any region has a long history. Perhaps the easiest way for local historians to grasp this notion is to view the past as a succession of threatening strangers, for whatever is strange always feeds suspicion.

During the settlement period in southwest Minnesota, Indians were for the settlers clandestine people, and so they remained for two generations after the failed Dakota uprising of 1862. After the Indians, armed and solitary horsemen provided the foundation for shivery tales of bank robbers and lawless men. Local legend has it that the Jesse James gang passed through southwestern Minnesota one night in 1876, fleeing after robbing a bank in Northfield, fifty miles south of the Twin Cities. Even less auspicious drifters were seen as potential transgressors. Midwesterner Hamlin Garland, who wrote of the difficult 1890s, remarked when traveling the roads of rural New England, "The natural antagonism of the well-to-do toward the tramp appalled me."[9]

Newcomers who simply passed through, their origins obscure and their purposes unknown, were bad enough. But new neighbors, who were here to stay, threatened unimaginable bad things. They might be papists, as were the freshly arriving Poles who so intimidated their Icelandic neighbors in Lincoln County.[10] Indeed, newcomers might corrupt a place before it had even formed into a community and established its covenant.

From the beginning of the First World War, newspapers identified suspect populations. The spotlight of patriotism shined brightly on every nook and cranny in the countryside. Editors of larger town papers rallied the home front against a list of dangerous fifth-column foreigners, who included pacifists, draft resisters, Germans and their schools and associations, and other ethnic groups who clung to their language, such as the Dutch of Edgerton.[11]

Patriotic mobilization continued even after the war. Clandestine groups and the fear of them multiplied in the 1920s as the culture of white, Protestant America solidified. Patriotism reached to matters of style. The length of one's hair could condemn one as deviant. In many areas, Catholics were seen as the scheming agents of Rome. Chapters of the Ku Klux Klan appeared. With their announced tenets of "protection of pure womanhood," "closer relationship of Pure Americanism," and "preventing unwarranted strikes by foreign labor agitators," they targeted feminists, Catholics, labor activists, and foreigners.[12]

Prohibition—the most rigidly moral crusade of all—appeared after the war. Born out of the nineteenth-century temperance movements and the Anti-Saloon League, the Volstead Act prohibited the manufacture, sale, and import of alcoholic beverages throughout the nation. (Andrew Volstead was a United States congressman from Redwood Falls.) With the drop of a gavel, alcohol and its users became clandestine. Everything and everyone associated with it was judged criminal. Imagination helped fill out an unsavory cast of gun-toting, free-living, fun-loving bootleggers against whom a few righteously labored and many conspired. But dissenters abounded. In one town, the pharmacist filled illicit prescriptions; in the Belgian-settled village of Ghent, which eventually voted sixty-six to none to repeal Prohibition, the milkman delivered beer.

The depression forced a national redefinition of clandestine society. Bank robbers abounded, and with popular support in the countryside, militant farmers took the law into their own hands. The depression also unleashed legions of strangers in the countryside. Indistinguishable from one another, hoboes, panhandlers, and the unemployed gathered along railroad tracks, particularly down under the trestles, and in camps on the edges of towns, and circulated many a dusty road in search of work. What some perceived as threatening armies intent on subverting the republic, others judged to be masses down on their luck.

The Second World War again shifted the axis of the clandestine. Draft evasion focused suspicion on neighbors, especially when fathers conveniently retired from the family farm just in time to allow their eldest sons to claim farm deferment. As quotas were imposed and scarcity feared, the sinister machinations of the black market swelled in certain minds.

The postwar period continued the spiritual unity elicited by the war effort. With nation and locale again one, vigilant eyes turned their attention to Communists. Judged by many to be the sum of all things corrupt, communism was said to be bent on subverting the American way of life. The pursuit of the Mafia, conducted by a range of congressional inquiries, superimposed another national grid of fear. However, neither one, it seems, penetrated the minds of the countryside. Only a long stretch of imagination could locate Communists or mobsters in rural areas. These faces of the clandestine were located among the corrupt masses of the metropolis.

THE CLANDESTINE EXPLODES

Imagine the surprise of southwestern Minnesotans when in 1967 the first class of the new college in Marshall brought local people face-to-face with what they had seen on television—and feared. Subversion arrived in the form of the contemporary student. Wearing long hair, dressed to insult and provoke, living communally, smoking marijuana, affiliating with blacks, and hatching antiwar protests, students on the east end of town, especially in the trailer courts shared by young men and women, were undermining all that America stood for.[13] At least, that's how it seemed to older citizens shocked by their first experience with a college community, especially one caught up in protest.

Incidents at the college undermined the town's pride in its new institution and fed the perception that college people were alien spirits in the service of perverse forces. After a night of campus race riots, an arsonist, never discovered, burned down the temporary student center. A university professor's wife, a mother of two, hanged herself in the family garage. Most bizarre of all, a business professor—with a law degree from the University of Notre Dame—and one of his students kidnapped a student from Purdue University and brought her back to Marshall in a black box. They hoped that by sensory deprivation they could make her their love slave. She escaped, and the professor was sentenced to a long prison term.

The Vietnam War washed directly onto the town's shores. In nearby Cottonwood, resident college professors, myself among them, provoked a mini–cultural war by objecting to the local American Legion outpost's decision to install a memorial cannon in a roadside park.[14] The professors, newcomers to the area and outsiders in almost every sense, had violated the taboo on contradicting legionnaires about the near-sacral meaning of their fallen comrades' sacrifice.

At the college itself, subjects that had once been considered forbidden were shouted from podiums. Professors enunciated subversive and rebellious ideas—and threw in the "F" word to authenticate them. Militant and vocal black students and professors gathered around the "black power" movement. Down Main Street came war protesters from the campus shouting, "One! Two! Three! Four! We don't want your fuckin' war!" Students repeatedly poked the local population in its righteous eye. Again and again, they challenged the moral unity of locale and nation—and acted out the illicit and declared its worth on their T-shirts.

The farm crisis of the 1980s predisposed local imagination to seeking other hidden and dark worlds during what was felt to be an ominous time. In western Lincoln County, one of Minnesota's poorest counties, it was rumored that farmers were living off roadkill. The actions of a father and son who lured, ambushed, and shot to death two Ruthton bankers on their former homestead were said to augur the threatening and violent course of the emerging crisis.[15] In the minds of some observers, these bad times promised an imminent revolt.

The crisis also gave rise to the kind of desperation that sprouts illusions like weeds and draws confidence men like bees to honey. Scams, each worthy of study, flooded the countryside. In the early 1980s, Marshall headquartered the greatest horticultural scam in the nation's history, when American Energy Farm Systems set up shop there and sold $30 million worth of Jerusalem artichokes, considered mainly a weed, throughout the Midwest and in Canada.[16] Other swindles induced farmers to grow mushrooms and worms in Ivanhoe (in Lincoln County), and Jasper, ten miles south of Pipestone. Thirty miles south of Marshall, in the Slayton area, citizens invested in oil drilling. To the north, in Boyd, a con man from England (who claimed an ancient and glorious patrimony) offered to restore the town's failed bank. He left town in a flurry of bad checks, making fools of many. Gullible country folk had been taken to the cleaners once again by a city slicker. A history of how farmers were cheated in the twentieth century is yet to be written.[17]

In the late 1980s and early 1990s, the clandestine again shifted. Newcomers from Texas, Mexico, Somalia, and Southeast Asia who poured into the region to fill the jobs created by an expanded meat-processing industry became, for many, the object of fear and suspicion.[18] The clandestine was associated with the newcomers in part because they were strange and foreign and in part because they worked in the unknown, foul, and threatening innards of local meat-processing plants. Suspicion trailed the veiled and long-gowned Somali women who walked the streets of Marshall. It rode along with the Virgin Mary on the dashboard of the pickup truck with Texas plates that crisscrossed the whole region. Danger and intrigue seemed to emanate from these strangers' rented apartments and to cluster, especially in the late hours, in the laundromats where they gathered.

Diffuse suspicions of wrongdoing were concentrated and expanded as newcomers came to be identified with a dramatic increase in felony crimes. Hmong youths broke into the Marshall sporting-goods store and stole a small arsenal of guns. Just to the east, a patron allegedly held several farmworkers in bondage. A chain fight occurred on the streets of downtown Marshall. Nearby Tracy had the first two reported murders in its entire history. Single Latino males, as court registers from the early and mid-1990s make clear, principally accounted for an unprecedented rise in murders, rapes, gang fights, brawls, and drug dealing in Marshall, Tracy, St. James, Worthington, and other towns in the region. Individual incidents fed fear and suspicions.[19]

During the 1980s, the clandestine "newcomers" in the countryside also included young men who, in the terminal stages of AIDS, had returned home to die. (They deserve to be studied, perhaps as part of an examination of hospice care, death and dying, aging, and changing medical care in the countryside.) Objects of true compassion or harsh judgment, these dying young men evoked multiple clandestine images and feelings. They spurred imaginations to conceive images of long, painful deaths; the sinister work of the most cunning viruses; the seamy culture of sex and drugs in the innards of filthy cities; and the taboo practices of oral and anal sex. They reinforced for many rural people, at least initially, the notion that their conduct had earned them the wages of sin. In some sense, these young men—at least for a brief historical moment, until new drugs slowed death and diminished its agonies—filled the ranks of clandestine people.

As they have since the 1960s, drug users and dealers fill the ranks of the clandestine today. They are joined, because of the renewed vigilance of social services, by those who abuse their wives or children. In the wake of the revolution in state- and Indian-sponsored gaming, addiction to gambling has become a matter of public concern and has aroused considerable community suspicion about who gambles secretly and destructively. In May 2001, a dead newborn baby was found in the women's bathroom of Marshall's largest supermarket. There seems little doubt that people's capacity to injure themselves and those closest to them will continue to fuel communal fear and suspicion about the private side of life.

TAMING THE ILLICIT

From the beginning of European settlement, the fledgling nation, the army, and then individual states and the law defined the illicit. Courts served as the crossroads of human relations. Sheriffs and state and local police constituted far-reaching and uniform, if not always effective and penetrating, monitors of wrongdoing. In a parallel fashion, churches, civic associations, and clubs staked out civilization's advancing boundaries of heresy and taboo.

As civilization spread to the countryside, initial forms of the clandestine, identified with wilderness and frontier, were pushed into the deeper recesses of the human mind.[20] Sheer horror and fright, religious awe, and a sense of the ominous lived a truncated life on the prairie. Although there is need of careful folkloric study, superstitions themselves seem to have dramatically receded from the countryside as settlers took the region's lands and waters in hand. This trend occurred not just because of the speed and extent of settlement but because the wilderness had largely been tamed on the landscape and in the hearts of many settlers before they left the eastern United States and northern Europe to come to southwest Minnesota.

The state, imitating the progressive East, had been quick to clean up its act. Duels and vendettas had no legal place on the prairie. Outlaws and bandits never abounded, although bank robbers remained common until the 1940s. The insane were taken into custody relatively quickly. Almost from the start, much of the elemental stuff that forms the clandestine was denied a full local rooting in mind and place. Mass violence, cannibalism, savagery, and other examples of the darkest human experiences and thoughts were driven into remote regions of the mind and to literature's distant and exotic places.

Nevertheless, thefts, rapes, robberies, and arsons, along with infanticides, parricides, suicides, and bestiality, occupied a place in the darkest corners of the landscape. Scuffles and brawls of every sort took place. There were far more murders and attempted murders than were ever recorded, and they were carried out with the technology of the era, from the refined poison, pillow, and revolver to the more basic rifle, knife, ax, or simply boot, stick, and fist. Disease prowled at will in the early decades of settlement, proving that cruel fate and divine vengeance were far from finished with humanity and its sins. Smallpox, typhoid, and other sinister illnesses caused multiple deaths and provoked quarantines. Bestiality, sodomy, and incest, along with cruel, bizarre, and irrational deeds, filled the newspapers of earlier periods. It falls to local historians to quantify and assess the significance of all these elements. Michael Lesy's *Wisconsin Death Trip* succeeds in showing the degree to which horrible and clandestine matters occupied people's minds at the end of the nineteenth century.[21]

Compared to the denizens of old rural Europe, however, settlers arrived on the prairie largely tamed. Although historians should search out contradictory evidence, there were no recorded incidents of collective cannibalism, witch hunts, armies of enraged peasants torching the countryside, pitched battles between poachers and police, or full-scale wars between villages. No wild men were captured in the region's wetlands. No appearances of werewolves or human monsters were reported, at least as far as my research indicates. Native American tribes were defeated and deported en masse to reservations, although they lingered in settlers' fearful imaginations.

Settlement quickly took firm hold of the landscape. Electricity lit up the farmyard, chasing away ghosts, ogres, and other fearsome nocturnal creatures. More abundant use of glass and new materials such as cellophane and plastic produced a brighter, clearer world with fewer nooks and crannies to harbor trouble. Basements and attics were no longer habitats for conspiring ghosts. Imaginary creatures lost footing in the minds of people living in a controlled landscape. At the same time, technology added instruments to the arsenal of human weapons. The handgun replaced the axe, and the pill became more fashionable for suicide than the rafter and the rope. People began to observe death and violence from a greater distance.

DISPERSING LOCAL GHOSTS AND TRANSPORTING LOCAL MINDS

Once settlement had firmly taken hold and cleaned up the rural environment, other forces effectively appropriated clandestine experience from local control and imagination. The media, for example, removed the clandestine from regional landscapes and focused on it only in a nationally contrived framework. Novels elaborated and generalized clandestine images. A more literate population could get its mystery from whodunits. The radio allowed people to turn on shows that expressed their innermost fears. Film created a nationally shared horror show—and suggested there was no reason to be scared of a local person dressed in black when the real Transylvanian Dracula, right from Hollywood, could be seen for twenty-five cents or less.

Beginning in the 1950s, films started to populate the countryside with images of aliens from outer space, psychotic murderers, and other sinister types. They concentrated the clandestine in the dark but safe environment of the movie house and took up places in the brain where once local creatures had resided. Unraveling a plot with a succession of tantalizing images (far more suspenseful and engaging than grandpa's snake and ghost stories), radio, film, and then television created a standardized experience of the clandestine. People in the countryside came to share not just the songs and loves, but also the horrors and thrills of the nation.

Records (especially the ones that allegedly voiced satanic messages when played backward) authenticated parents' suspicions of an evil national conspiracy against innocence. Board games such as the secretive, role-playing Dungeons and Dragons provoked similar accusations about satanic conspiracies. More recently, videos, video games, entire television channels, and endless Web sites have further quarried violence, sex, and evil—the clandestine in one form or another—for commercial interests. What once wasn't available in small towns or on the farm is suddenly only one click away.

Today, artificial electronic worlds abound. They contribute to the displacement of the clandestine from local places to homogenized national venues. Artificially constructed and individually chosen, the clandestine now has its origins and principal manifestations outside the community. The rural world lives off derived experience; what it does and what happens to it occur in greater measure at the hands of nonlocal agents. Any given rural place is plugged in to city and nation at large.

Cultural fashions have accelerated this trend. Secular culture, authenticated by technological control and medical progress and underwritten by hedonism, challenges traditional notions of right and wrong. With origins antithetical to traditional morals, it dismisses hell, the devil, and evil. It reduces sin to something absolved through therapy, sex to a basic force of nature, and abortion to an inalienable right. Worthy of local historians' detailed attention, secular laws (initiated and supported by such organizations as the American Civil Liberties Union and Planned Parenthood) provoked reaction and ignited what remains a constant and shifting war in the countryside. These debates cleave the rural mind, whose mooring is largely conservative.

In both the countryside and city, recent history is interpreted in conservative quarters as an assault against the values of family, community, and God. Progressive political ideologies are seen as destabilizing the fundamental borders of right and wrong. These ideologies transform people long assumed to be sinners and criminals into victims. They view advocates of the sins of free sexuality and homosexuality proudly, even tauntingly, as they are paraded before the nation's eyes. For conservatives, taboo subjects of the past have become the favorite causes of today's political agendas. Advocates of these new ideologies even try to rewrite history, seeking, often successfully, to portray traditional communities and values as immoral victimizers.[22]

The clandestine furnishes consumable material for a society of leisure. Sinners, criminals, and people of unusual persuasions provide titillating subject matter for television talk shows, documentaries, and dramas. Hit men and even hit women proffer their true stories. Tell-all confession, unexhausted by two hundred years of literature since Romanticism, never grows dull. No border is left untransgressed, all in the name of art, audience, or money. Society consumes the illicit and conjures the clandestine for cheap thrills and big profits.

Old-fashioned crimes that once thrilled, and which local historians still must enumerate—horse rustling, arsenic poisoning, poker playing, dice rolling, whiskey drinking, and even fistfights—have grown quaint. Increasingly, the clandestine subject has a psychological quality. I remember my father bemoaning the loss of the straightforward old cowboy movie, where good and bad guys could be discerned easily.

What was hidden has been made manifest, and what was taken to be eerily dangerous has been judged therapeutically curable. For example, alcoholism and gambling addictions call for treatment and open discussion. Shame, guilt, and the taboo, once the moral arbiters of the local community, have been significantly weakened in the countryside, as I believe local historians might show. Addictions of all stripes, and homosexuality, have lost much of their power to shock and no longer attract quick, harsh, and universal judgment.

Conservative rural communities would condemn—that is, make clandestine—much of what the outside world brings them if they had the power to do so. Yet as they have declined in population and autonomy they have lost this power. They no longer can define the experience of their members as they once did. And what is imported electronically, in and through the air, is not regulated the way alcohol and strangers once were. In both a literal and figurative sense, rural people have moved indoors for their lives and work. Main Street is no longer the primary axis of their encounters or the arbiter of polite and respectable living. They have evacuated local grids of experience, obligation, curiosity, and emotions. Their minds are elsewhere.

The distance between village and metropolis has contracted. Professional lives increasingly march to distant drummers. Concrete relationships of the past have been replaced by the remote and specialized relationships of an increasingly legal society. The axis of law migrates away from localities toward metropolitan centers, as sums of money become greater and legal issues more complex. (The Schwan family, Marshall's most powerful, settled the contested will of its founder in Sioux Falls, South Dakota. Schwan's Sales Enterprises settled a lawsuit regarding food contamination in the Twin Cities.) Power and the clandestine senses it evokes have emigrated from the countryside.

The clandestine will not entirely vanish from the rural landscape, however. Death—the great secret keeper—will always shadow human experience. Evil will always well up in life and imagination. Temptations will always lead people into forbidden realms. Transgressions will be suspected. Crimes of passion and cunning will excite the sense of the clandestine—and newspapers will never satisfactorily tell all. Sex still will elicit the taboo. Men and women still will keep their addictions secret. Legislation will not abolish the sinister sides of gambling. So the hidden world will always shadow the manifest one—and a nose for the prurient will always push the media and its audience to uncover secrets and raise suspicions.

Local historians must be aware of the history behind the clandestine. They must find ways to measure and describe the impact of prohibitions, taboos, and daydreams. They must recognize that the clandestine changes, that curiosity and temptation, guilt and shame, are tilting the axes on which people are taught to fit their bodies and minds. The most memorable battles of life (as all of adolescence testifies) are associated with the galls of culture's harness. Even though technology has in some measure tamed the environment, wildness exists within us. And even when therapy and drugs have subdued our most savage parts, and commercial interests have homogenized much of what remains, there will still lurk among human beings a fear of secret dangers. Madness will still stalk everyday life—and despite the contemporary commandment to take possession of this garden, country people, like Dostoyevsky's underground man, will continue to swim in clandestine rivers of pride, spite, shame, and humiliation. And these hushed rivers will course more powerfully through community and mind than will history's normal fare.

CHAPTER 7

Madness

Madness pervades lives. It defines much of what individuals and communities take to be secretive, hidden, and threatening. No one escapes it. It is the groundwater of human existence. It belies the illusion of reason's control and civilization's dominance. As it engulfs individuals and communities, we all, at times, may fear ourselves to be mad, and our neighbors as well.

Everyday language testifies to the ubiquitous presence of madness in human experience, especially when conflated, as it often is, with retardation. Besides such words as *nuts, goofy, daffy, balmy, wacky, screwy, crazy,* and *bonkers,* slang offers such phrases as "missing one's buttons," "having a bee in one's bonnet," "nutty as a fruitcake," and being "one brick shy of a load." Our inability to localize madness shows up in the common use of such words as *lunatic, idiot, moron,* and *schizophrenic,* which have crossed back and forth between diagnostic and popular language. These words demonstrate that madness is a vast kingdom with imprecise and changing borders.

Ever changing in form, madness manifests here as stone silence, there as uncontrollable convulsions. It may appear as frenzied mania or slothful melancholia. It whispers fears and suspicions; it is a mill of grand delusions. It has been the mumbling companion of the peasant in his field; it has taken hold of the tongues of kings. Panic, hysteria, and myriad passions actually separate historical periods from one another. Madness furnishes religion, law, and psychology with much of their content and importance. In its many forms, it accounts for the passions of nations, the vacillations of markets, and the successions of mutating fashions. It makes afresh a stale and dreary world. In pursuit of madness, Freud followed the stairway of dreams, random behavior, and slips of the tongue into inner chambers of darkness, only to discover that Dostoyevsky had paid his own nocturnal visits to some of these dark rooms a generation before.

Like anger and the clandestine, madness also has an indisputable historicity, an uncontestable specificity. As an individual's fate, a family's abiding condition, or a transitory pandemic condition, madness is always embodied somehow. It appears at a given place, at a certain time, in a particular society and culture. It inhabits bodies and minds that have an age, physiology, and experience. Never free from an assemblage of thoughts and relationships, madness is social and cultural as well as psychological. Its diagnosis and treatment cannot be divorced from the ideas, institutions, and politics of a given era. In this sense, madness is a sound and fury of individual making.

Although the sheer scale and complexity of madness might overwhelm local historians, they cannot avoid studying and writing of it. We live in an era in which psychological and pseudo-psychological systems prevail as explanations for human intentions and behavior. Aside from its entertainment and commercial value, attested by endless talk shows and self-help books, psychology serves every newfangled therapy. It responds to individual cases of eating disorders and depression and secondary victims of airplane crashes and school murders, while offering health and liberation for even the most self-absorbed hedonists. As the irrational, defiant, neurotic, and perverse found cultural legitimacy in the nineteenth century through Romanticism, so psychology—both used and abused—in this democratic and electronic age enables the individual to normalize conflicts between traditional beliefs and expanding desires. Psychology, which arguably has taken religion and law in tow, offers as an ideal the happy and fulfilled self, which is doubtless a goal that turns us toward a conquest of the mind.

Clearly, the public turns toward the irrational. As I wrote this chapter, the president of the United States, Bill Clinton, stood publicly exposed in adultery and perversity, while one of his predecessors, Ronald Reagan, faded (though discreetly) into senility, and his last contender, Bob Dole, was speaking in advertisements for the campaign against prostate cancer, telling his fellow men to face up to their deepest fears about erectile dysfunction. Confession of everything—though not truthfulness about it—has become public. At the same time, school and workplace mass murderers fill the slots and corridors of the national mind. Also as I wrote this section, the U.S. surgeon general announced that in any one year, one-fifth of all Americans have serious psychological problems, and less than half of them seek help. Imagine the pertinence of that to any study of local history.

Local historians cannot surrender their interest in the irrational and insane without rendering their own stories irrelevant. They must recognize that a history without the facts of madness is no history at all. For example, genealogy, to take what in many instances is local historians' first source, transpires largely on the ground of the irrational. Family histories are chock-full of suicides, bizarre behavior, men who ran off with other women, women who were admitted to insane asylums, and more. Obviously, rains and rivers of this scale gather and rush through the past and present of every place.

THE BUILDING MATERIALS OF PLACE

Madness furnishes the building materials of a place. Eccentric persons and odd happenings mark the histories of farms and villages. Lunacy threads itself in and out of the history of a locale. In nearby Cottonwood there lived an eighty-five-year-old World War I veteran and clever inventor, who, when his wife died, took down the curtains and installed a lathe in his front room, flirted with the young girls at the Dairy Queen, rode his three-wheeler around town, wrote venomous letters about city garbage collection being a communist plot, and ended many conversations with an angry burst of ill-tempered words. Madness—in gentle and violent, degrading and eccentric forms—breaks the tethers of conformity, normality, and legality, and gives every place a physiognomy of its own, which should be of interest to its local historians.

Although local history narratives might omit the abiding town fool or even the rare bizarre crime, they cannot escape certain defining events that reveal unfathomable madness. Such events constitute a locale's and even a region's most memorable occurrences. They impose themselves on any story. They even bid to define the very historical epoch in which they occurred.

In *When Father and Son Conspire* (briefly discussed in chapter 5), I wrote of yet a darker and deadlier madness that more than any other captured southwestern Minnesota's mind. My subject was a father, never a long-term or successful farmer, and son, infatuated with guns, who murdered two bankers. Their three-day flight from the law ended in Paducah, Texas, where the son turned himself in; the father was found dead at a nearby farm. The son remained stone silent in the face of interrogation, trial, and years in prison, leaving in doubt who had killed the bankers and why, and how the father had died. The son finally confessed to the shooting in September 2000 before the cameras of a national television show on the eve of consideration of his release from prison.

Just as people all over the United States can recall where they were the day John F. Kennedy was assassinated, everyone within a sixty-mile radius of this crime remembers distinctly where they were when they first heard of the shooting. It was a captivating story that drew the whole locale into madness. More than a thin story about striking back against the exploitation of rural people (as the national press, left-wing ideologists, and local farm organizers would have it), it was a story of the deeply irrational—of a failed family, an angry and self-defeating hypochondriac father, and a son who had transformed himself into a hardened soldier of his own angry imagination.

Although the motives for the murders and the subsequent death of the father can be interpreted according to individual hates and confusions about one's own plight and stereotypes about bankers spawned by an emerging farm crisis, the final explanation must be found in the conspiracy of a lost father and a solitary and hateful son who believed being a soldier was the only way he—whose physical condition precluded military service—could be a man. Together a father who imagined himself to be a successful parent and farmer, and a son who imagined himself a soldier, were lost in each other's anger and madness.

These stories make the point that local historians cannot evade madness, and that madness presents itself to them in concrete incidents and specific historical forms. Historians have no choice but to seek to penetrate individual tales of madness to their intimate depths in order to pinpoint their historicity. These stories cannot be whisked away by generalization and quantitative treatment, unless historians choose to abandon the path of individuality and detail that constitutes the first and final requirement of writing local history.

CASES OF INSANITY

Insanity is one of the many faces of madness that historians overlook, even though it intrudes into their own lives and is embodied in local deeds, such as one painful story that occurred in Marshall in 1968. On the northern outskirts of town, a young man who had just turned twenty entered an elderly widow's house and took a bath in her tub. Why this young man—a native of the area, a high school graduate of marginal abilities and no employment—did this, no one knows. The widow returned home from a bridge game to discover him drying himself off. He responded by stabbing her repeatedly. As she telephoned for help, he killed her, later telling the police he did so "to put her out of her misery."

Uncertain whether he was competent to stand trial, the court sent the defendant to the Willmar Regional Treatment Center for assessment. Authorities there treated him with electroshock therapy, which destroyed his memory. The asylum returned him to the court, declaring that he was now competent to stand trial. The court, in turn, judged him not guilty of the crime by reason of insanity and placed him in the custody of the Willmar treatment center. He has remained there for more than twenty-five years, manifesting erratic behavior while receiving various treatments.[1]

Few cases reach the celebrity and unparalleled ambiguity of this case. Commitment records, of course, do not even mention legions of others whose lives were affected by insanity. They don't count those people who had private breakdowns, suffered secret addictions and compulsions, were assumed to be harmlessly crazy, or from time to time had difficult moods and manias. And they don't register all those who ran away or ended up in prison or another state institution and got their therapy and subsistence on a county poor farm, which housed the poor, elderly, and medically and psychologically infirm.

With the establishment of public asylums in the second half of the nineteenth century, families had a new choice for coping with a mentally disturbed child, parent, or sibling. The possibility of committing individuals to an asylum staked out limits of what the family would tolerate at home on the one hand and hopes for a cure on the other. This was equally true for the county and state facilities.

Formal commitments alone—of which I estimate there were twelve hundred in Lyon County between 1883 and 1950—suggest the tremendous toll madness took on individuals, families, and small communities.[2] What, for instance, did it mean in 1915 for a German immigrant father to commit his twenty-five-year-old son, "who threatens to kill his mother and says if he dressed up like an Indian he would get money from the state"? What pain lay behind the behavior of a forty-two-year-old mother of two who was described in 1897 as "charitable and a great reader of stories" but was also said to be "suspicious of others, is in fear of cyclones, and talks of electricity, and has visions"?

A summary of the Lyon County commitments from 1897 through 1899 (a period in which the records appeared thorough and particularly rich in symptoms and diagnoses) provides a cross section of cases in which the community deemed the person in question insane and chose institutionalization. The cases—which involved an initial complaint, a medical review, a hearing, and a commitment charge, were sent to the Minnesota Hospital for the Insane at St. Peter, established in 1866.[3] In crucial state legislation of 1893, the term *insane* did "not include idiocy or imbecility." The law asserted that no person was to be committed unless "(1) he has perpetrated acts dangerous to himself or to others, or to property; or (2) it is reasonably certain, by his threats or otherwise, that he has dangerous tendencies or uncontrollable propensities towards crime; or (3) he wanders about exposed to want of food or shelter, or to accidents; or (4) he is ill-treated by relatives or friends; or (5) his disease is of such a nature, or in such a stage, as to require for his recovery, care and treatments while under legal restraint." Reflecting one of the most progressive concerns of the era, the law determined that no allegedly insane person would be arrested and taken into custody, except in the first two instances. And it added, "It shall not be lawful to confine him in the same room with any charged with or convicted of any crime."[4]

The physician who certified the condition of the person committed was required to be of "reputable character," a graduate of a certified college, and to have practiced medicine for at least one year. A county judge informed of a possible insanity case was required to appoint "two examiners in lunacy to examine the alleged insane person and certify . . . the result of their examination, with their recommendation." In turn, to be committed, the insane person had to be informed of the proceedings and the county attorney had to act on his or her behalf. If the judge was satisfied that there was sufficient reason for commitment, he or she was instructed to "commit said person to the custody of the superintendent of the proper state hospital for the insane, or to the superintendent or keeper of any private licensed institution for the care of the insane."

The certificate of insanity included the name, age, birth, marital status, residence, family, occupation, and church membership of the patient. Also, inquiries were made into the first and previous attacks and treatments, symptoms, progression of the illness, intervals of the attack, and rational intervals between episodes. There were questions regarding manifestation of the derangement, its threat to others, and suicide attempts. In phrases revealing the moral focus of the era, inquiries were made into the person's "filthy habits and destruction of clothing," along with "inheritance of insanity [or] any dominant passions or religious impressions."

CASES AND COMMENTS, 1897–1899

In this section, I present in summary the majority of Lyon County insanity cases for the short but well-documented period of 1897 through 1899. Beyond what the record states and imagination conjures, each case embodies a historical period by malady, diagnosis, and treatment. These cases provide significant quantifiable dimensions of insanity, hinting at patterns that in turn shed light on local and regional history in southwestern Minnesota.

William Erickson, former director and historian of the St. Peter asylum, has also studied these cases and arrived at conclusions similar to my own. His work provides insight and background information helpful when examining these cases. In asylum admissions and retrievals, Erickson counts differences by gender, ethnicity, religion, and residency in town or on a farm.[5] Stressing the theme that immigration resulted in mental dislocation, Erickson determined that insanity among Norwegian immigrants in Minnesota was three times the rate documented in Norway.[6] Arguing that communal solidity meant fewer commitments, more rapid recoveries, and more retrievals of patients by family, Erickson offered data showing that better-established Germans were far more likely to retrieve their committed mothers than the less settled Irish were to retrieve theirs. Cases also show that men's insanity was usually attributed to external factors (especially blows to the head), whereas women were generally thought to degenerate from internal diseases.

At the opposite pole from quantification, insanity can seem merely a scientific—or quasi-scientific—variety of temporal constructs carved out of species madness. For this reason, it invites historical discussions of circumstances, conditions, culture, and public policy. Concerns over land, sexuality, religion, and scarcity were common causes for insanity identified by medical examiners. Treatments often prescribed physical remedies for moral ailments.

I purposely break the homogeneity of the text to confront the reader with the stark heterogeneity of individual cases of insanity. I hope that each commitment record described here conveys the powerful presence of the irrational in everyday life.

A forty-four-year-old married male, father of six, from Tracy, machinist and a foreman at the roundhouse, a Presbyterian, in hospital in Twin Cities for a while, has "anxiety over support of his family and his ability to retain his position. . . . Insomnia." (He made excessive displays of anger or near inertia more or less constantly.)

A sixty-year-old unidentified male is depressed and "impassive to everything that is happening. . . . He wanders about and is exposed to want of food and shelter and to accident."

Twenty-year-old male from Tracy, a father, originally from New York; hospitalized in St. Peter's one and three years before. "Restless. Incoherent conversation." Preoccupied with religion. For treatment, they gave him a few hot baths. (Hydrotherapy was a standard treatment of the insane at the time.)

A thirty-eight-year-old Bohemian, single, male farmer. Admitted to St. Peter's in 1893–94. Supposed cause of disease: "He is a masturbator. Threatens to shoot his neighbors and is suspicious of them and they are constantly aiming to do him harm. . . . He has dangerous tendencies and uncontrollable propensities towards crime."

A sixty-year-old male, with six children, born in Norway, a resident of Cottonwood. He can read and write. A violent temper and suspicious of his family. "Has taken an ax and made threats."

A thirty-one-year-old Dane, from Racine, Wisconsin, a single farmer. "Sits around in a depressed manner and masturbates daily." Talks at times about suicide. "He has had one week of treatment with bromides with some success. . . . Admits masturbation and says he does not wish to stop it."

A forty-four-year-old mother of two from Amiret, Canadian of Scottish extraction, married to a Presbyterian farmer. Previously institutionalized, she displays insomnia, restlessness, and "a desire to leave home." She tried to commit suicide by "strychnine and hanging." She "confesses to a suicidal impulse."

A forty-year-old Lutheran widow from Norway, previously admitted to St. Peter's. "Becomes violent. . . . Talks of cyclones and fires." "She talks a great deal on religious subjects—is very excitable. . . . Result of fright during cyclone."

A fifty-nine-year-old Baptist widow from New York, living in Tracy with two children. She displayed her first symptoms three years earlier. "Patient imagines that her grandchildren are being starved to death. She hears voices and at night she imagines that she hears the children calling to her for something to eat."

A thirty-five-year-old father of three, born in Bermuda. He "threatens to shoot himself." He "has a wild and quarrelsome disposition." He had measles the previous spring, and also suffered sunstroke sometime in the past.

A forty-eight-year-old Baptist farm wife from Tracy, mother of two, parents from New York and Pennsylvania. She spent four months in the state hospital in 1896. Brought to authorities by her husband, she is "discontent. Desires to leave home. Unkind things being said about her. . . . Has burnt her clothing."

A forty-four-year-old bachelor farmer, born in Iowa, parents from New York. Confined for a year, with successful treatment in the past. He started to seed land that didn't belong to him. "Imaginary claims he was not insane before, and that he was confined in order to be robbed of his property." Cause: "Probably masturbation."

A twenty-five-year-old single woman from Norway whose father was a farmer. She had typhoid fever in May 1899. She "continues to hallucinate. . . . She sees people killed around her. Also sees people hung and falling out of windows. . . . Thought to be a little odd and peculiar before having typhoid. . . . Pupils widely dilated, eyes staring, talks incessantly about people being killed around her, and breaks down and cries."

A fifty-one-year-old Swedish woman, Baptist, wife of a farmer. The request for commitment was "probably brought by husband. . . . About latter part of March or first part of April, [she] wanders away from home and makes indecent proposals to small boys. . . . [It] is most noticeable in the summer. . . . Sexual matters as a part of her religious beliefs: thinks it is correct to have intercourse with boys, with or without their consent, including her own adopted son, aged 8 years old. . . . [She] has exposed her person. . . . Her father was intemperate. Sound in every other way. . . . Expression lacks intelligence when not questioned; she is much interested in sexual matters; lacking proper modesty describing her habits."

A twenty-three-year-old Fairview Township man, a common laborer. His parents were from New York. "He has expressed symptoms during last eight years since kicked in face by a horse. . . . [He] thinks he is a great pugilist, uses horses without permission, roams about. . . . Talks at random; is not truthful."

A thirteen-year-old male, born in Iowa, parents from Pennsylvania and New York. "Three prior occurrences, sleepless, rambles on about no particular subject." Cause: "Novel reading."

A thirty-five-year-old Swedish bachelor and blacksmith from Balaton, a Methodist. "Became suspicious of his neighbors. . . . Afraid of being poisoned. . . . Hears voices. . . . says people are plotting against him. . . . [He] talks about saloon class being after him." He also "imagines that he is castrated." Cause: "Overwork and worry."

An eighty-year-old Irish housewife from Balaton, a widow. "Last fall—begging when she [had] everything [she needed] in the house and stealing from the neighbors." She was first removed to the county farm.

A twenty-one-year-old Swedish farmer from Westerheim Township. "He preaches and sings. . . . No one knows much about him except this, and he had his head covered with a red handkerchief, and reads and expounds from Scripture."

A twenty-one-year-old male from Wisconsin doubts paternity and maternity of father and mother. "Indifferent in manner and refuses to work or take any interest in business matters."

A twenty-five-year-old Catholic male of Polish-German descent, a laborer from Minneota. Became "violent and made threats to shoot self and others." Only filthy habit: "Masturbation." Subject of his disarrangement: "Infatuation for a married woman." Treated with bromides.

A fifty-year-old divorced French-Canadian. "Talks of family troubles, religious matters and says he is going to see the Pope; thinks father tried to kill him." Contributing to his condition were family troubles and sunstroke.

A thirty-nine-year-old Catholic woman, married, no children. "Believes spirits are after her—much excited and prays a great deal." Cause: "Probably uterine disease." Treatment was sedatives, hypnotics, and tonics.

A sixty-one-year-old Irish male with five children, from Balaton. "[He] thought he was conversing with the angels, imagined he saw the handwriting on the wall. . . . He thinks that he had great wealth, that he owns the United States, is going to build churches and hotels. . . . [He] talks to President McKinley daily over the phone." Possible cause: "He had an injury to one of his eyes three years ago."

ST. PETER'S

The people described in the previous section were sent to the Minnesota Hospital for the Insane at St. Peter, commonly referred to simply as "St. Peter's," an asylum situated on the banks of the Minnesota River, just above where it turns north on its way to Minneapolis and St. Paul. Minnesota's first mental hospital (it opened in 1866 and is still open), it gathered the insane of southwestern Minnesota.[7] A study of St. Peter's affords a larger perspective on the individual insanity cases listed in the last section and the place of insanity in regional history.

Although they were diverse and incompatible by classification, and heterogeneous by class and culture, the insane shared a common plight.[8] While the violently disturbed were confined to "the back wards," and special efforts were made to separate the feeble-minded, idiotic, and the senile, "the young, aged, depressed, inebriate, maniac, and criminally insane were crowded together."[9] "Patients," in the concluding words of Ellen Dwire's *Homes for the Mad,* "all lived together in institutions which served as surrogate families, refuges, prisons, and hospitals."[10] Patients experienced the ambiguous conditions of being placed in an asylum that was idealistically dedicated to curing the mentally ill and practically involved in warehousing the chronically untreatable.

Hidden away, patients underwent cycles of good and bad treatment. Medical ideas followed historical fashions. Superintendents brought different philosophies and regimens to the institution, leaving patients subject to the vagaries of administrative passion and eccentricity. The fluctuating availability and quality of staff also determined the common lot. Good staff members were hard to attain, given the low wages that they were paid and the requirement that they live with the patients. Frequently, a polyglot staff encountered polyglot patients.

Psychiatry was a nascent science. Aimed at treating the subtlest of human elements, the mind, it constituted a clumsy jumble of moral prescriptions and conventional practices. It oscillated between treating the diseased brain and treating the defective character. Prior to Freud and depth psychology on the one hand and the entire range of medical specialties associated with physiology and pathology on the other, psychiatry lacked systematic integrity and a practical language for distinguishing and treating its subjects.

Patients suffered from overcrowding at St. Peter's almost from its beginning. Overcrowding necessitated mechanical constraints such as bed straps, muffs, mittens, straitjackets, and cribs, which were in use until the second half of the twentieth century.[11] People who should have been kept at arm's length from one another ended up elbow to elbow. Dormitories that held as many as forty patients overflowed into the corridors. Until the start of the twentieth century, the absence of running water and sewage disposal exposed patients to one another's filth, infections, and dirty habits. The catastrophic fire of 1880, which burned ferociously thanks to the institution's recently waxed floors, made a holocaust of St. Peter's insane.

Nevertheless, some people were cured at St. Peter's. William Erickson estimates on the basis of his statistical review that approximately 40 percent were judged cured and released in the 1870s. Of course, some of those released returned for treatment, while others wandered off never to be heard from again. Handfuls stayed on as asylum workers, having found at St. Peter's the security the outside world had denied them.

Many others died in the institution. Those who were incurable, never properly diagnosed, or misdiagnosed (as epileptics frequently were in the early period) simply lived there until they died of old age. Like other public wards, they were buried anonymously (a numbered marker alone indicated their graves), sparing the surviving members of the family the ignominy of their relatives dying in the keep of the state.[12]

ONE PATIENT, EVERY PATIENT

Once inside St. Peter's, patients led their lives in a surprisingly normal way. Friendships occurred. Young men and women became romantically involved. Women became pregnant. Some patients worked hard and conformed, others committed crimes, and others committed suicide.

On admission, individual lives also were swept up in the collective history of St. Peter's, which, when it opened in 1866, met the burgeoning need of a new society to care for and house its temporarily and permanently insane. Government, having defined the nation's borders and defeated the troublesome native peoples, sought a lawful and healthy society. It set its institutional seines across the rivers of peoples pouring into the state, with the rough goal of ensnaring and removing criminals, disobedient adolescents, inebriates, and the insane. While it is not easy, and in some cases impossible, to distinguish the catch (especially between the insane and inebriate), government sought to do what family, locale, and county could not.

One aspect of the mission of St. Peter's could be understood to have had its origin in the idealism of a progressive state. Its inspiration came from eastern reformers such as Dorothea Dix and Horace Mann, who spearheaded the attack against the indiscriminate mixing of criminals and the insane. The other, less benign, part of its mission was to incarcerate those whom society could not dare or bear to have around.[13]

Unable any longer to export its growing population of the insane, Minnesota, starting with legislation in 1866, began to build its own asylums, which promptly filled up.[14] Refusing to foot the mounting bill of St. Peter's, the state of Minnesota in 1877 returned 125 cases to counties that did not pay to support the institution. Patients were allowed some creativity in their responses to the overcrowded conditions: they were permitted to build shacks at the back of the asylum's grounds. (They called the community they had formed "The Camp of the Fourth Horseman," by which they meant death, which alone would free them from this spot.)[15]

As patients were classified at admission, so they remained for purposes of the annual census thereafter. They were sorted according to the period's primitive psychological structures, which merged prejudices, morality, philosophy, and the new science of psychology in odd combinations. Erickson wrote: "Each case was diagnosed as to the form of insanity and its cause. The diagnoses . . . included only mania, melancholy, and dementia. Any patient presenting with agitation was said to have mania, regardless of evident cause. Diagnoses were assigned at admission and were never changed, regardless of any new information."[16]

Diagnoses, historically determined, were often mistaken. Doctors frequently misdiagnosed delirium tremens, "a transitory psychotic state induced by drinking," for other illnesses. They also misdiagnosed acute delirium caused by typhoid fever, and paresis—characterized by irregular pupils, stammering speech, lack of balance, and grandiose delusions. A case-by-case analysis of all the patients admitted during 1871 shows that 11 percent had severe epilepsy, although only half of them were diagnosed as epileptic on admission.[17]

Explanations for patients' conditions and behaviors (not yet always easily distinguished) were as erroneous as diagnosis was limited and imprecise.[18] Everything and anything was utilized to explain patients' conditions. Cited causes were distant and proximate, of mind and of body. They were the things patients did or things that were done to them. A disease or a vice, an event or a general set of circumstances provided explanations. Doubtless, any single diagnosis depended on the individual doctor and ruling medical conventions and fantasies.

Diagnoses also followed gender. On the basis of a complete census of the first 448 cases existing up to 1874 in St. Peter's records, women's problems can be seen as commonly attributed to their bodies—menstruation, pregnancy, prolonged lactation, and menopause. The death of children, marital problems, and desertion disproportionately affected them. Two were diagnosed as nymphomaniacs, while only six were judged masturbators, in contrast to thirty-two males found in the sample of 560 from the same period.[19]

The proximity of the seriously disturbed and those who manifested chronic symptoms was always a handicap to treating others. Problems of care were further exacerbated by the tendency to convert the hospital for the insane into the insane asylum. Treatment, in fact, never amounted to much more than rest and food—with confinement for the violent and work, necessary to maintain the institution, for all those who were able. Medication's purpose was to quiet the agitated, to anesthetize the delusional, or to sedate the insomniac. Hot baths also played a role. A dark room on the top floor was used in the early period to frighten violent individuals into obedience. Electroshock therapy came into vogue in the late 1930s and disappeared in the 1960s, only to stage a modest comeback in the 1990s.

Several common treatments of yesteryear would be considered cruel today. The first superintendent, who suffered a great aversion to masturbation (he referred to it as "the vicious habit"), blistered the penis to stop it.[20] A subsequent treatment for masturbation was equally horrifying: a wire was strung through the foreskin of the penis.

Surely the concept of insanity has undergone several revisions in the past two centuries, including such watershed periods as the early 1960s, when truly effective medications and the availability of federal funds made deinstitutionalization possible for some patients. This revolution reduced the St. Peter's daily census to 550 by 1990, making it a quarter of its size in 1960. But it returned many of the insane and addicted back into the community. With patients medicated or institutionalized in halfway houses, the place of madness has been transformed. The very name "insane asylum" came to resonate from an older time, when society grappled with what it did not understand.

TOWARD RATIONAL ENLIGHTENMENT

In recent decades, diagnosis has become keener. Medications have cured and improved the treatment of troubled souls. They have proven effective against depression and mania and made progress in the treatment of schizophrenia. Supervised living for the mentally impaired, the old, the troubled adolescent, has provided safer and kinder environments. As much as mental illness still haunts individuals, families, communities, and the nation, its manifestations are less grotesque, and madness is no longer the great wilderness it once was.

Yet madness still shadows human experience. Anyone who has raised children, visited older relatives at the nursing home, or even knows him- or herself well recognizes how frail the mind's balance is, how delicate its perch on the body. The fate of a recent director of St. Peter's, known for his strict and even prying regimen, shows how vulnerable the mind can be. An employee telephoned this man's wife to invite her to a social event. The director answered and replied that he had no wife. But, he added, there was a woman sleeping in his home. Suspicions were raised in the caller's mind, and a visit to the house revealed that the wife had been dead for three days. He who had shepherded a whole institution of wandering minds had lost his own.

Shared fears and hopes mean shared madness. Individuals project their madness into the world and find it reflected back at them. Even though the roots of madness lie deep in the chemistry of the body and the workings of the mind, they take on the prevalent forms of the time. Collective sensibilities and imagination mold both healthy and ill minds. The people of the countryside learn to hallucinate, to experience addiction, to suffer eating disorders, and to kill and commit suicide as the outside world teaches them.

Madness forms local mental geographies. Its deeds write local memories and often shape the most remembered landscapes. Stories of madness are essential to the local historian's full understanding of his or her subject. It is the historian's responsibility to acknowledge the power of these stories in defining a place and to connect them to a class, an ethnicity, an era, a nation, and even the development of a whole civilization. Yet the local historian must concede that madness forms rivers we will forever navigate without ever fathoming them.

CHAPTER 8

Madame Bovary and a Lilac Shirt

Literature and Local History

"No place is a place until the things that happened in it are remembered in history, ballads, yarns, legends, or monuments," wrote Wallace Stegner in *Where the Bluebird Sings to the Lemonade Springs.*[1] So we are brought to the matter of literature, that great friend and certain enemy of imagination, which gives form to reality with evocative metaphor and moving sentiment, so often cheating us of the precise and ordinary truth of things. Literature can make wonderful wholes of pieces, and yet it can so facilely reduce the past to present conjuring.

Novelists and poets can serve as true guides to local historians. As historians rarely do, they penetrate the inner, more subtle and sensual sides of human experience. With marvelous concoctions of detail and metaphor, novelists and poets assemble home and heart and embrace them as historians—for want of evidence and art—cannot. When successful, poets and novelists make the particular—the hallmark of the local—beautiful and universal, far more attractive to an audience than the clubfooted stories of fact- and argument-bound historians.

Literature's genesis can be found in the pursuit of the secret, hidden away, unexpressed experiences. Literature rejoices—indeed, takes flight—when it makes contact with the unspoken sides of life and purposes of mind. It follows the subtlest inner waters, seeking to articulate and bring forth what lies below every human surface. It pursues subjects into realms that history seldom enters and within which history never comfortably establishes itself. When successful, literature locates powerful patches amid fields of repetitious occurrences and ordinary things.

Literature explores the objects and experiences that permeate the senses and awakens keen memories. It notes how a suspicion or hope can captivate a single person or a whole community. Literature deciphers mixes of emotions and consuming passions, dwelling on unresolved ambiguities and contradictions. It is drawn, if we make the Russian giants Dostoyevsky, Gogol, and Chekhov the measure, toward the depths of mind. Pride, resentment, spite, shame, guilt, and humiliation, along with love and forgiveness, stake out literature's territory

Although local historians can be repelled by literature and its misrepresentations and distortions of people and places, they surely can make exceptions for the beautifully crafted historical novels of Willa Cather. They might admire embodied fiction like Charles Frazier's *Cold Mountain,* or yet prefer single personal memoirs cast in the guise of fiction, such as Emile Guillaumin's *Life of a Simple Man,* to academic dissertations on similar subjects. They must concede that literature at its best evokes what history cannot. Indeed, historians must learn from literature. In southwest Minnesota, they must learn to write, see, and compose from such strong prairie writers as Mark Twain, Willa Cather, O. E. Rölvaag, Hamlin Garland, Sherwood Anderson, and Meridel Le Sueur, as well as Frederick Manfred, from Luverne, Minnesota, who more than any other writer showed us how our region opens west to the Great Plains.[2] They can also learn from such contemporary regional writers as William Kloefforn, Linda Hasselstrom, Jim Heynen, Norbert Blei, and Kent Meyer. In regional literature, local historians can follow deep currents coursing through the most ordinary experience. Whole worlds will take shape in the small places they love, and they will ponder how only by creating the past can they preserve it.

REPRESENTATION AND REALITY

Leaving aside the historical truism that most literature is bad literature—the blind entertaining the blind—literature also can mislead and delude by pretending to give form to what cannot be embodied. Its enchantment frequently depends on distortion of the places and people it claims to represent. The interest of its practitioners often is anything but depicting place or time, which serve only as backdrops against which their characters function, and they vie for fame, propagating prevailing styles and sensibilities. Literature, at its worst, can be accused of cluttering the past with silly thoughts, counterfeit insights, tedious moralizing, and flagrant exhibitionism.

Literature is never free of quarrels. For the last two centuries, the subject of the countryside—its peasants and farmers, its small towns and provincial centers—has been the battleground of warring writers. Romantic novelists and short-story writers have idealized and even venerated the countryside as a place where humanity is natural, innocent, intimate, and—to note a long-standing American antiurban theme—independent. Conversely, realists have found the countryside boorish, backward, and without culture of any sort.

Rural Minnesota, lucky enough to have its own writers and literature, also has its own quarrels and competing interpretations.[3] Garrison Keillor has invented a sentimentalized countryside in *Lake Wobegon Days* and radio monologues that are dappled with occasional dark religious problems. Essayist Carol Bly, forever moralizing, has chided the countryside for its narrow-mindedness. Naturalist and writer Paul Gruchow, who has lamented the loss of the region's ecological diversity, has also bemoaned the loss of the family farm as a distinct spiritual inheritance. Bill Holm, beguiling as a writer and performer and blustering and tedious as a social critic, has enchanted us with his artful portraits of eccentric and ruckus-raising individuals from his hometown, Minneota. Humorist Howard Mohr, in *How to Talk Minnesotan,* keenly delineated and attributed a set of unique traits, customs, and mores to Minnesota even though they belonged to the larger Midwest and indeed to all of rural America. Novelist Tim O'Brien left Worthington concluding, to the horror of every local historian, that "the essential thing about the prairie, I learned, was that one part of it is like any other part."[4]

Beyond entangling historians in the sensibilities and polemics of the hour, literary depictions of the past can dupe their readers as well as their creators into mistaking the past for a temporal composite of errant insights, clichés, stereotypes, stale political traditions, and fashionable moral campaigns. They can specifically confuse the local historian by superimposing the experience of one region on another, making the lives and ways of one ethnic group those of another, or anachronistically attributing the life of a recent era to that of an earlier one.

Even when historians penetrate the historical errors of a work of fiction, they still find themselves enchained in their own distorting premises and unable to assemble a coherent view of place. They lack metaphor, narrative, and subject to provide a compelling and memorable work for a public that in majority prefers a fresh book of fiction, however false, to a stale book of history, however factual.

The popular mind tends to see the world as writers have cast it. No matter what local history writes of regions and peoples, both are often captives of what novelists make of them. To suggest by example, the essence of native peoples' spirituality, no matter what scholarship might show to the contrary, conforms to the literary crafting of John Neihardt's *Black Elk Speaks;* white settlers, regardless of what paths they trod, invariably followed the literary trails sketched by O. E. Rölvaag in *Giants in the Earth* or Vilhelm Moberg in *Emigrants* and *Unto a Good Land.* A popular work (however scintillating or dull, deep or shallow, dedicated to establishing or dispensing with historical context) becomes real. And once it becomes an idol of the marketplace, it impedes competition for alternative views. The literature that yesterday taught us to imagine the past prohibits us from exploring and explaining it today.

Literature, as conscious and articulate representation, betrays reality. To a degree, it must, for the past is ever more than we can enumerate, fathom, or represent. The past never was one; it was made of many fleeting elements of place and mind. Consciousness cannot take it in whole; it forever will be cut out of a fabric that was both inherited and anticipated. However rich historical documents are and however clever imagination can be, the past can be evoked and constructed only in a present whose own coherence and singularity is equally illusory.

Local historians' use and abuse of literature can be taken up more concretely with reference to the contemporary local poet Leo Dangel and the famous regional novelist Sinclair Lewis. Dangel, recently retired from teaching English at Southwest State University, was brought up on a farm in South Dakota. Lewis was a native-born Minnesotan who won the Nobel Prize for literature. Admittedly to twist tails, I argue that Dangel's poetry provides an example of how literature can excite historians' desire to write of fresh subjects, whereas Lewis—or, more important, the legacy of Lewis's classic novel *Main Street*—creates a false tradition for understanding the Midwestern small town.

LILAC SHIRTS AND BALING WIRE

Now collected in a single volume, Dangel's poetry invites the reader to inhabit a different world.[5] His voice of the old order is Old Man Brunner, who, if he were God, would use baling wire, once ubiquitous, to hold everything together.

> If Old Man Brunner had made
> the world, baling wire coils
> would spark the lightning
> in the clouds. Baling wire
> would keep the continents
> from sinking . . .
> . . . .
> Old Man Brunner's universe
> would be a rusty paradise
> where anything could be fixed
> with a pair of pliers.[6]

Dangel enters us into a world not only of different materials from the ones we're accustomed to, but also one in which tools and the motions made using them were different. Old Man Brunner carried his pliers everywhere he went. He speared carp with a pitchfork and trimmed his toenails with tin shears, perhaps at one time the only clippers available to many people. Tools, which abound in county and agricultural museums, were not just the givens of work and experience; they formed the metaphors with which we once hewed out our place in the universe.

Old Man Brunner's baling wire and iron tin shears prompt us to ask which materials and technology have vanished from the landscape. Obviously, there is more to this than the disappearance of the blacksmith, along with the fire, metal, rust, and the pounding we associated with the forge. There is also the question of the appearance and even disappearance of softer and lighter materials—the arrival of new alloys, of plastics, of all sorts of translucent, bright, and impervious surfaces—and the continual emergence of gasoline-driven and electric tools. A man in an automobile, equipped with portable power and tools and materials of every sort, is not the same as a walking man who lives by the strength of body. Nor is the labor of the contemporary farm wife, surrounded by appliances and fresh surfaces, the same as that of her foremothers.

Old Man Brunner's generation lived closer to the earth. They were mired in dust and manure. In "The Return of Spring," we read,

> I walk across the cattle yard,
> looking over the mud
> at the trees. My boot sticks
> and I pull my foot out.[7]

Roads, we can extrapolate, were unpaved. Horse and cow manure accumulated, and farms were without lawns. The question arises: When did farms get lawns? What prompted farmers to create them: imitation of better-off folks in the city, the arrival of tools efficient for mowing them, or wives eager to be free of dust one season and muck the next? In the poem "A Farm Boy Remembers," we learn how much closer the country once stood to dirt, manure, and their offspring, muck:

> Saturday was cleaning barns,
> forking out tons of manure.
> There are more significant ways
> to spend a Saturday, when the snow
> is melting, but this was ours.
> Throw out the shit
> and put down the clean straw.
> Renewal has never since been so simple.[8]

The proximity of manure distinguished the farmer's inferiority, but occasionally it meant revenge against the country's enduring rival, the city slicker.

> when I am spreading the last load
> and see a black Cadillac approach
> the coated stretch of road
> and slow way down (its driver
> probably wishing his luxurious car
> had the option of flight),
>
> and when I see the splatter
> cover his wheels and fenders,
> with a barnyard smell he'll carry
> into the city, his car stinking for weeks
> from the manure baked on his muffler
> and catalytic converter,
>
> then I breathe deeply the spring air
> and think how good life is on earth.[9]

Surely, rivalries real and imagined are topics worthy of the local historian's attention. They weren't confined to the baseball diamond, the predictable fight at the end of the dance, or to country versus city. They dealt with language, images, manners, gestures, and associations in schools, stores, and churches. Also worthy of tracing for any locale would be the changes that brought together town and country, township and township, class and ethnic group.

As the barriers were lowered, so change intruded on the world of Old Man Brunner. Things seen and picked up at the store, small and seemingly insignificant, can, bit by bit, transform self-images and dreams. "One September Afternoon" conjures a history of rural consumption:

Home from town
the two of them sit
looking over what they have bought
spread out on the kitchen table
like gifts to themselves.
She holds a card of buttons
against the new dress material
and asks if they match.
The hay is dry enough to rake,
but he watches her
empty the grocery bag.
He reads the label
on a grape jelly glass
and tries on
the new straw hat again.[10]

Around Old Man Brunner's place, a fresh order of things assembles itself. It is not just a new straw hat but the car in which the family drives to church, where the minister tries out a brand-new public address system. In "Country Church Technology," Dangel writes:

Old Man Brunner, who hasn't slept
through a sermon since they hung
those speakers on the walls,
sits stony faced, with his arms
crossed, and after church, he says
the cows in Harley's pasture
across the road will stop giving milk.
He talks about how sweet
it used to be, on a spring morning
when windows were open, to hear
the song of a meadowlark in church.[11]

Over time, Old Man Brunner and his children changed in mind and body. They even walked differently as they got out of their boots and muck and learned to slide and glide their feet on the smooth surfaces of town places. In fact, walking itself seemed out of place—something one did only on the way to mounting or dismounting from a tractor, strolling out on the dance floor for a swing, or lingering on Main Street. Dangel instructs readers on "How to Take a Walk" in the countryside without appearing odd:

This is farm country.
The neighbors will believe
you are crazy
if you take a walk
just to think and be alone.
So carry a shotgun
and walk the fence line.
Pretend you are hunting.[12]

The same Old Man Brunner who knows how to walk also proved he knows how to handle a wedding dance:

Brown pants, blue blazer,
green shirt, purple tie.
His cracked shoes are smeared
with Esquire liquid polish
right over the cow manure.
. . . .
Still the old buzzard can waltz.[13]

Old Man Brunner's progeny couldn't escape the mounting urge toward self-beautification. It came right along with democracy, literacy, and the Sears catalogue. In "Farming in a Lilac Shirt," Dangel suggests an awful lot about the interior roads rural people traveled on the way to joining consumer society and to becoming self-respecting citizens.

I opened the Sears Catalog.
It was hard to decide—dress shirts
were all white the last time
I bought one, for Emma's funeral.
I picked out a color called *plum,*
but when the shirt arrived
it seemed more the color of lilacs.
Still, it was beautiful.
No one I knew had a shirt like this . . .

In spring I began wearing the shirt
for everyday, when I was sure
no one would stop by. I wore the shirt
when I milked the cows and in the field
when I planted oats—it fits perfectly.
As I steered the John Deere,
And I looked over my shoulder and saw
lilac against a blue sky
filled with white seagulls
following the tractor, and not once
did I wipe my nose on my sleeve.[14]

There is much more in Dangel's work for local and regional historians. There are stories of hidden emotions, jokes, children's play, and first kisses, including one daring girl who kissed a freshly caught carp. There are hints and clues for writing a rich and distinct history of past minds, senses, and communities. A poet like Dangel helps us imagine and know ourselves better.

AN AMERICAN IN SAUK CENTRE

Despite the temptation, historians must not fall in love with every lilac shirt the poet presents. They must use literature cautiously. The first and most obvious reason stems from the simple fact that most writers do not provide original observations and penetrating understanding but rather repeat clichés and stereotypes they have learned from other books—often about other places.

At their best, novelists and poets capture only a portion of the prairie experience. As a matter of necessity, they must reduce it to background (large or small) for the particular narrative they wish to construct. Even the best fiction writers shape the prairie to fit their own prejudices, sensibilities, and ambitions.

The strongest novelists and poets impose their metaphors and styles on the weaker writers, who, in turn, disseminate the words and images they have learned. In this way, better works—often diligently and intelligently crafted over decades—become the opium of writers and readers alike. In this way literature, which can form the sole, precious pathways into human experience, frequently proves a bridge from one literary conception to another without the interruption of either observation or thought. Novelists and poets then end up not taking people to reality but providing shortcuts through and around it. Sparing the reader the need to weigh local words and things, they seduce readers into believing that they need only take up the book at hand and they will know the truth of home, place, and locale. Bibliomancy of old is alive and well in contemporary hands. The near century-long recitation of Sinclair Lewis' *Main Street* as the true representation of small-town life illustrates how long words and images endure even though they are free of fresh observation and thought.

Along with a group of literary critics of the 1920s, I believe that Lewis's ultimate inspiration for Carol Kennicott, the central character of *Main Street,* was Flaubert's tragic *Madame Bovary,* and that Kennicott should be known, as a Lewis biographer had it, as the "Madame Bovary of the wheat elevators."[15] In *Main Street,* Lewis followed Edgar Lee Masters's 1915 *Spoon River Anthology* in indicting "the midwestern country towns for their spiritual and cultural poverty" or, in Carol's terms, their smallness, unrelieved dust and dirt, and, least forgivable, boredom. Receiving far more acclaim than Masters's work, *Main Street*—didactic and simply written—became the standard interpretation of "sterile towns and despondent heroines."[16]

In *Main Street,* the story Lewis tells of the fictional town of Gopher Prairie (and here the historian should pay careful attention) is essentially that of the successful old-guard Yankee ruling class of Sauk Centre. The group he focuses on—without much sociological precision—is his own: the Easterners who came west to capture the land and opportunities of the prairie frontier around the time of the Civil War. His Yankee ancestors (originally English, Scottish, and Welsh) were the first to establish the village and countless other towns across the upper Midwest and northern prairie. They were families who came to explore business opportunities, careers, and real estate in the West. Protestants, Masons, and Republicans, they identified with the sacrifices and victory of the Union Army.

The importance of Union officers in the settling and development of prairie towns deserves a study. By virtue of having served the victorious national cause, they brought enhanced moral claims to their powers and presumptions. As John Radzilowski suggests in *Prairie Town,* while buying available Midwestern land, founding cities, and making money, they also could present themselves as models of what was best in the nation.[17] They simultaneously took up the roles of representatives of the nation, embodiments of the civic ideal, leaders of commerce, and pioneers of the future.

Save their own immense household chores, their wives, as Lewis pointed out, shared their husbands' cast of mind. From it flowed and commingled senses of cultural, civic, and economic preeminence. Though an outsider, Carol Kennicott is a duty-bound member of this elite. It shows in her unceasing restlessness for improvement, her reflex to keep up with the styles of the East, her presumption to judge as inferior the local libraries, books, and drama, and her contempt for the dusty and short streets without sidewalks.

Carol attends two clubs: the Jolly Seventeen, which plans entertainments, and the Thanatopsis group (Lewis's mocking title refers to the contemplation of death), which surveys world literature by leaps and bounds. These memberships alone place her, in contrast to the other three thousand town inhabitants, at the icy social peaks of Gopher Prairie society. Gratuitously empathic, with sufficient time on her hands to bestow her empathy on those she encounters, Carol concedes that the masses show great courage in toiling through mighty boredom.

Like Carol, the Yankee women of the era saw it as their responsibility to domesticate their husbands, children, and town. They had to make sure their husbands' love of hunting and fishing did not cause them to lose all consciousness of the finer things. In turn, the women themselves had to develop an appreciation of the finer things. They had to prepare true urban amenities in the towns to which their husbands sought to lure money and manufacturing. They had to transform their small towns into thriving metropolises. They put a good face on their towns, which, despite their efforts, became stagnant within a decade or two of settlement.

Similar to Carol, these good Yankee wives were charged with the duty of taming and polishing their practical, commercially minded, and unaesthetic menfolk. They turned up across a wide horizon of activities in the last decades of the nineteenth century and the first decades of the twentieth. They formed reading clubs, undertook drives for libraries and schools, showed aesthetic concern for architecture, and sponsored a variety of fashionable events and historical pageants. In addition to keeping up with city styles, especially in dress and shoes, women like Carol soon took up new activities such as swimming, bicycling, and even automobile driving—all of which make potentially fine subjects for local and regional histories.[18] Also, the most forward-looking women put in their two cents on matters of sanitation and vaccination, and more than their two cents on women's suffrage and Prohibition. Back from her yearlong experiment of living without her husband in wartime Washington, Carol returns to town with her reformist ideas. She even volunteers to clean the public rest room, the new addition that proved how progressive Gopher Prairie was.

Righteousness did not free Yankee women or their husbands from certain dilemmas. They had to ask, as do members of any second and third generation of a founding group, who exactly their true heirs would be, with the age of heroism over and the age of consolidation at hand. Underlying these questions were others more painful and thus less frequently asked, expressing a common dissatisfaction itself worthy of historical examination. Why did their town not become the city-republic they had imagined and boosted, the thriving and autonomous community that is the highest measure of success? Why did their hour of glory never come, and why had their chance to achieve it already passed them by? Why, they had to ask, if their little town was so good, did everyone, including themselves, look elsewhere for newer things, better ideas, and more fun and power?

Although obviously they could gloss over these questions with rhetoric about neighborliness, what gave this problem a particular rub—and makes it worth studying—is that the Yankee fathers and their families abandoned the towns they founded. Some of them never took root, a few were liars and confidence men, and others quietly went broke. Many, sniffing opportunity elsewhere, sold off their businesses, land, and farms and headed down the road. These people lived at a time of extraordinary expansion. Separated from family and community over two or three generations as they pursued their activities, they became, like Carol, restless and dissatisfied to the core.

Also chafing at their parents' local loyalties, the most ambitious of their own children left home. They went away for an education and never came back. An analysis of changing rates of emigration and return from different types of hamlets, burgs, villages, and towns would make a valuable addition to understanding continuity and discontinuity in prairie communities. Laura Ingalls Wilder's father is a classic example of prairie restlessness: He couldn't stay put. Distant pastures always seemed greener to him. Perhaps this left Main Street with only one answer—to make village and nation one. National patriotism united them despite the economic, cultural, and moral factors that mismatched them.

Local historians are put on guard right from the start of *Main Street,* when Lewis writes, "Gopher Prairie, Minnesota, is the continuation of Main Streets everywhere. The story would be the same in Ohio or Montana, in Kansas or Kentucky or Illinois, and not very different in Upstate New York or in the Carolina hills. Main Street is the climax of civilization." And they may be equally wary when they grasp that the story will essentially be narrated through and around the subjectivity of its protagonist.

By claiming that his *Main Street* represented all Main Streets, Lewis disregarded, as perhaps writers must, differences he knew existed, or at least with a moment's thought he would have grasped. His principal character herself contradicts him with her awareness that there are growing towns and there are dying towns. (At her time, Sauk Centre had added only one manufacturer in several decades, and it went broke.) As Lewis knew, some towns are county seats and others are not. Different religions, singularly and in varied proportions, differentiated towns, as did hunting and fishing opportunities and winning civic traditions and baseball teams.

Some towns, like Sauk Centre, were stationed along transportation routes and had existed as settlements before the coming of the railroad. Another type of town, which deserves attention, comprises those that functioned as ethnic enclaves, or—and this merits a case study or two—in the early decades, as the Yankees left, became defined by ethnic groups who had entirely different interests, assumptions, and consciences.

Melrose, a town less than twenty miles east of Sauk Centre, illustrates how short a distance Lewis's generalization accurately traveled and how much it ignored the changing patterns of ethnicity in the formation of prairie settlements. In Melrose, German Catholics dominated. They not only superseded the town's Yankee founders and their Episcopal and Presbyterian churches, they also far outnumbered their fellow Catholics, the Irish settlers. They accounted for the bishop's attempt to move the bishopric from St. Cloud (seat of Stearns County) to Melrose. This town's enduring strength lies with the members of its cohesive German farming community and its determination to prosper and build a church, schools, and a distinctive culture.

Lewis missed the ethnic story not only in Melrose but also in his own Sauk Centre. *Main Street* remains the truncated story of its Yankee shopkeepers and their wives—and more precisely the agonizing sensibility and limited perspective of his heroine. Lewis had no interest in the cultures of the Germans, who "crowded saloons, bellowing pidgin German or trolling out dirty songs—vice gone feeble and unenterprising and dull."[19] The ethnic peoples who composed Sauk Centre remain the hidden side of *Main Street.* In the novel the Germans are described only stereotypically; we learn virtually nothing about the Swedes, who live in Swede Hollow; and the Irish and French-Canadians go unmentioned.

What Lewis and his kind might have learned about the Germans was hidden behind a screen of muck and manure, the prejudices of American nativism and anti-German sentiment generated by the First World War. Even though a local German priest taught Lewis German and a little Greek, Lewis was not disposed to think about the ethnic German Catholics at all. He didn't grasp what caused the Germans to stick to the land. Neither they nor any other ethnic group lived within the ken of his literary interests and his class sensibility. He and his kind pursued careers and meaning elsewhere. His work thus demonstrates the danger of taking literature for history.

Lewis's primary question is why Carol—restless in spirit and sexually frigid—cannot make herself at home. Unanchored in body or community, her mind has a thousand doors through which every fashion revolved. Free of the discipline of work and the burdens of home (as her husband constantly reminds her when they fight), she is perpetually vulnerable—as Lewis himself was—to the merry-go-round of changing ideas and imagined possibilities. She embodies that old question asked of soldiers returning from World War I, albeit paraphrased, "How are you going to keep them in the small town, once they have thought of Gay Paree?"

In contrast to the obdurate, vulgar, yet practical Main Streeters, Carol, like Madame Bovary, belongs to the family of the spiritually rootless. She is not one with herself in her feelings, home, or the community where she has landed. She wishes—even feels it her duty—to shape this piece of prairie to her tastes. She would have home become her idealization of it. Having inhaled the fumes of suffragette and early feminist discontent, socialism, and the demands and complaints of labor unions, she wants to reform all she sees. She places the era's urban expectations and demands on this little, dirty, dusty, and comparatively boring place.

Despite her failures, Carol will not admit defeat. She declares that her final vindication will be to raise her son to fit an idealized future. Carol's final words to her husband and her last line in the book constitute her closing attempt at self-justification: "I do not admit that Main Street is as beautiful as it should be! I do not admit that Gopher Prairie is greater or more generous than Europe. I do not admit that dishwashing is enough to satisfy all women! I may not have fought the good fight, but I have still kept the faith."[20]

Lewis was raised in a small town. A whole lifetime was not enough to shake its dust off his feet. As a high school student, he eyed finer things and distant places. As a young man he read literature that disposed him to see small towns as tedious and banal. Lewis found within himself the clash between the prairie's Main Street and the East's Beacon Street. According to his biographer, "The ambition to find in the East what is not available in the Midwest is usually exposed as false and fruitless, as in *Main Street;* and when the East is pushed on to mean Europe, later novels arrive at the same conclusion."[21]

Sinclair Lewis belonged to the waves of nineteenth-century intellectuals and poets, many of them European, who turned the rejection of home into art. He disliked the isolation, boredom, and smugness of the tradition that had bred him. He railed against Main Street—its men, women, buildings—much as if he were a member of Paris's bohemia, which since the 1840s had been attacking the bourgeoisie as vulgar, materialistic, narrow, and boring. Lewis aspired to rise beyond his origins through art. His aspiration to be a writer added another province to the spiritual hegemony of the city and gives local historians reason to be suspicious of artists' depictions of home. Local historians must indeed embrace literature, but keep one eye peeled. To paraphrase Stegner, they must look carefully at the songs, stories, pageants, ballads, yarns, legends, and monuments that create a place.

CHAPTER 9

The Red Rock

Inventing Peoples and Towns

The local historian, as envisioned here, deals with much that is intangible and even imperceptible. He or she will write histories of the senses, emotions, the clandestine, and even madness. At the same time, he or she will recognize how much of the history of the countryside—its environment, society, peoples, and development—is inseparable from ideas, concepts, and literary sentiments and conventions. The local historian will forever confront the notion that the countryside, its places, its landscapes, and its communities are invented—that is, consciously fashioned, argued, and made a tradition. I attempt to show this in the following case study of Pipestone, illustrating how its native peoples, its settlers, and the town itself were created out of interpretations of the meaning of its red rock.

Some places are described by the whole of their surrounding landscape. Others are defined by individual features that capture the eye, excite curiosity, hold memory, or give rise to legends. Local names testify to the hold landscape has on place. Plains and hills, caves and gullies, and rivers, creeks, and marshes give places their names. Up and down any river of significant length, one might discover a plethora of names derived from crossings, falls, and overlooks, and would probably encounter at least one *butte des morts*—a cliff from which legendary Indian lovers threw themselves to their deaths to avoid a life without each other.

Yet of all natural claimants to the naming of places, rocks, I believe, predominate. As imposing mountains, they define whole regions across ages; as eroded ridges and slopes, they are the solitary survivors of distant kingdoms.[1] Rocks define what is hard and immovable. They arise from the depths of the earth and stand firm against time, begrudgingly yielding to erosion over millennia. As single megaliths, fields of boulders, or frozen rivers of lava, rocks rule innumerable localities. They define children's initial encounters with place and senses of home. This is true not only in Sicily and Sardinia, but also at points on the vast, open, and flat tallgrass prairie.

PRAIRIE ROCK

In southwest Minnesota, granite surfaces found in the Granite Falls area provide geologists with an interesting text. It relates the story of how, several billion years ago, tectonic plates pushed up mountains as high as the Himalayas. These remnants of the oldest North American mountains were succeeded by a fresher range of mountains, composed of the metamorphosed materials of an ancient sea. They too were worn down by wind and water and scoured and buried by a million years of glacial advances and retreats. The sources of this region's distinctive red rock, these mountains now lie buried under a great glacial moraine called the Coteau des Prairies (see Map 2).

Flowing off the moraine from west to east, the tributaries of the Minnesota River also remind us of glacial times. Fed by four rivers descending from the Coteau, the Minnesota itself follows the oversize river valley of the Glacial River Warren, which emptied the vast, ancient, inland Lake Agassiz. The rocks and stones that push themselves up every spring in the region's farm fields originated in this ancient era of scouring and piling glaciers.

To this day, the Minnesota River makes for perilous navigation. One must heed not just the snags created by fallen cottonwoods but also submerged boulders the size of cars. At some points, the river offers what geologist J. A. Grant characterizes as "a tantalizing window into the Canadian Shield . . . because of the high grade of metamorphism, [and] especially because of the antiquity of the rocks."[2] At Granite Falls there are Precambrian protoliths of gneiss—unmetamorphosed parent rock—3 to 3.6 billion years old, placing it among the oldest rock found on the North American continent.[3]

A younger red rock, Sioux quartzite, marks the Late Precambrian period. Deposited an estimated 1.4 billion years ago as a coastline sediment, this hard, metamorphosed rock traverses southwestern Minnesota like a great red serpent.[4] Starting in eastern South Dakota—on display at Sioux

Falls's Palisades Park—it snakes east, where it surfaces in Minnesota at Pipestone, Jasper, and Blue Mound State Park. The red rock surfaces again, fifty miles or so farther to the east, in the Storden-Jeffers area. There, it lays itself out as a great red slate, furnishing a leisurely bed on which prehistoric residents (a thousand or more years ago) incised their turtles, spears, and thunderbirds. The petroglyphs signal this land's claim to the great West, where red rock stands out clearly and speaks boldly to the blue skies.

Nowhere did the rock play a greater role in human experience than in upland Pipestone and Rock Counties. Buried beds there are a mile and a half thick, and the pink, brick red, and even purplish surfaces of quartzite beds make beautiful intrusions on the landscape. They form waterfalls, gorges, and palisades. They furnished cliffs off which, legend has it, Indian hunters drove buffalo to their deaths. They thwarted even the greediest plows and offered captivating building materials out of which magical towns were erected.

PIPESTONE QUARRY

In no place did the rock's beauty so beguile as much as at the Pipestone quarry, now a national monument.[5] Containing an accessible intercalated layer of soft and workable clay (a sedimentary bay material of similar composition to the metamorphosed quartzite), the quarry for hundreds of years was the primary source for the red stone used by Native Americans to fashion ceremonial pipes. A large collection of petroglyphs indicates the frequent visits of early peoples to the Pipestone quarry. According to one recent researcher, proto-Mandan peoples did not use the pipestone, but "the first quarrying here was probably done by people associated with the Oneota.[6] By 1700, with the Dakota in control of the adjacent Coteau des Prairies, pipestone was commonly extracted and became an important trade item.[7] Pipes made of this red stone have been found across much of the North American continent, testifying to the extensive trade networks of native peoples.

Writings by white explorers such as artist George Catlin, who visited the quarry in 1836, and Joseph Nicollet and John Frémont, who were there in 1838, put the quarry on the cultural map of the young republic.[8] Local fur trader Joseph Laframboise led both the Catlin and Nicollet parties to the Pipestone quarry from his settlement at the Great Oasis, a lake thirty miles south of present-day Marshall.[9] Laframboise himself already sold pipes to supplement his fur trading income.

By 1858 the quarry's ownership had received its preliminary legal definition. In an 1851 treaty, the eastern Sisseton and Wahpeton bands of the Dakota had relinquished their rights to southwestern Minnesota. The Yankton Dakota, however, claimed that the Sisseton and Wahpeton had sold land that wasn't theirs. In an 1858 treaty, the Yankton secured compensation from the federal government and negotiated a clause assuring "their free and unrestricted use of the Red Pipestone Quarry."[10] The government additionally agreed to survey the land in and around the quarry and permit the Indians to visit the site and procure pipestone.

In the wake of the 1862 Minnesota Uprising, a violent conflict between the Dakota Indians and white settlers in the Minnesota River Valley, the land and the quarry were opened to full commercial exploitation. Feeling it unsafe to have his men work at the quarry unprotected, an early entrepreneur and army supply contractor named James Boyd Hubbell hauled large quantities of the stone to abandoned settlers' cabins on Lake Shetek, in nearby Murray County, and mass manufactured pipes there. Ultimately, the army did not use the five thousand pipes for treaties, as originally planned, but peddled them to Indians up and down the Missouri River. The pipes, for which the army had paid five dollars apiece, were each traded for "a well dressed buffalo robe or its equivalent in skins."[11]

In 1874, settlers, coming principally from Iowa, moved onto the less fertile and elevated lands of Pipestone County. In 1876, the town site of Pipestone was platted, and settlers intruded onto quarry land. This gave rise to a long, litigious process characterized by white intrusion, Indian complaint, and government inaction. In 1887, in the face of flagrant treaty violations, the army removed white settlers from the contested lands, and in 1891 the Yankton were compensated for railroad rights-of-way, settling a first order of conflicts surrounding the quarry.

Quarreling at the quarry was far from over, however. A complex legal and legislative zigzag lasted another two generations. Contesting words and laws placed the fate of the red rock in the pages of court filings and briefs, as whites and Indians took their claims to court and lobbied local governments. Quarry lands were appropriated by the federal government without compensation to Indian claimants for the new Pipestone Indian Industrial School, opened in 1893. The school's headmaster became the quarry's master. In 1926, the Supreme Court confirmed that the U.S. government had taken possession and control of the 648 acres of quarry tract in violation of the earlier treaty, and that the Yanktons deserved just compensation. After further calculations completed in 1929, each member of the tribe received $150.[12]

With the question of title now settled, the quarry could at long last be transformed into a public park that would recognize the town's inheritance and serve its commerce. After a variety of aborted proposals for a state and then a national park by the local Pipestone Shrine Association, in 1937 President Franklin Roosevelt signed legislation to create Pipestone National Monument. Laying the foundation for future conflicts, quarrying rights were reserved not just for the Yankton, but for all Native Americans.[13]

The quarry itself had been dramatically transformed since white settlement. It had been extensively quarried for quartzite and pipestone. A railroad now cut across the landscape. A small lake and swimming beach had been built, fulfilling the city's desire to have a park on the site. In 1912, school officials had blasted away the higher eastern rim of the Winnewissa Falls, on Pipestone Creek, in order to drain eighteen acres of farmland for the sake of Indian agricultural instruction.[14] Upstream neighbors had taken advantage of the increased gradient, further altering Pipestone Creek for drainage purposes. With the burns the Indians had once applied to the prairie brought to an end, and the planting of a hundred white elms, woody plants began to invade the area.[15] A place once defined by a stark cliff of red quartzite was increasingly coming to resemble an arboreal grotto. It now seemed to host different gods.

Today, paved roads entering the monument lead to a large parking area surrounded by grassy lawns. Inside the visitor center, a museum offers a history of the region, the quarry, and the use of the ceremonial pipes. Native artisans work on pipes and effigies, offered for sale at the far end of a hall, where their wares are displayed on walls and in glass cases.

Visitors walk a thousand feet from the center to the artificial lake, called Hiawatha. They proceed another seven hundred feet, past a major site of Indian quarrying, before glimpsing through the trees the quartzite ledge of Winnewissa Falls, the rock holding the Nicollet Expedition Marker, and the perilous Leaping Rock, from which, legend has it, braves jumped to prove their love. Government, commerce, and traditional sentiment all make different claims to the quarry. This place, though of contested memory, has also become a consumable artifact, even though it still hosts traditional rituals such as sweat lodges and sun dances.

THE PIPE AND NATIVE SPIRITUALITY

Throughout the ages, people have shaped their words on the anvil of the Pipestone red rock. Cultures have spiritualized and told stories of the quarry and its stone. Traditional uses and tribal claims, commercial enterprises, lawsuits, and legislation all have contributed to our image of the rock.

For indigenous peoples, the quarry and the stone held precious elements of self-definition as they were engulfed by an alien world. As they lost control over their environment and their lives, the quarry and the red rock became touchstones, part of their cultural subsistence. Their beliefs, rituals, and special powers were invested in both.

The pipe served North American peoples in many ways. It provided the pleasure of smoking. It offered occasions of sociability, especially for the men. Aside from its varied medical uses, it expressed hospitality, confirmed understanding, and sealed peace agreements. The long-stemmed pipe, which was draped and decorated with meaningful objects, served the highest ceremonial and religious purposes.[16]

Perhaps the smoking of the pipe held even more cultural significance as native peoples came under the pressure of encroaching European cultures and American civilization. Like the sweat lodge and the sun dance, the pipe was embedded in foundational native ceremony and myths. It resonated with special powers among the Dakota. As Dakota leader Looking Horse tells the story, White Buffalo Calf Woman, a holy messenger, came to teach the Dakota the pipe's importance and use. The Great Spirit appeared at the quarry, and the stream that issued from him formed waterfalls. Tearing a chunk of red rock from the quarry, the Great Spirit fashioned an immense pipe. Lighting it, he called together all the tribes, instructing them that the pipe was the flesh of their ancestors and that on this ground amity among them must be preserved.[17]

Dakota thinker and wise man Black Elk confirmed the centrality of the pipe to Dakota culture and was an important contributor to the renewal of Indian spirituality. In *Black Elk Speaks* (first published in 1932), poet John Neihardt artistically introduced Black Elk, a seventy-year-old cousin of Crazy Horse, as a prophet. Academically preoccupied with the "twilight of Sioux culture," Neihardt found a living link to it in Black Elk, who believed that as a youth he had received visions of his people's tragic fate and his responsibility for their restoration.

Neihardt's *Black Elk Speaks* became the Bible of Indian spirituality—what Vine Deloria, Jr., described as "a North American Bible of all tribes."[18] Republished in 1961 and multiple times thereafter, the book appealed to Indians and whites who dissented from the prevailing European culture and conceived a spiritual wholeness in the traditional Indian way.

In 1947 Joseph Epes Brown tracked down Black Elk. Now approaching ninety years old, the elder looked back on a long life in which he had known Sitting Bull and Red Cloud and had fought against the whites at Little Big Horn (even scalping a soldier). He had traveled with Buffalo Bill's Wild West show to Italy, France, and England, where he had danced for Queen Victoria, and, upon his return to South Dakota, survived the 1890 massacre at Wounded Knee. From extensive interviews with Black Elk, Brown derived a sacramental theology of the pipe.

In *The Sacred Pipe: Black Elk's Account of the Seven Rites of the Oglala Sioux* (first published by the University of Oklahoma Press in 1953), Brown describes the pipe as purifying, consecrating, and carrying the people's wishes to heaven. The pipe keeps dead souls in the great circle of the people and releases them from the bounds of this earth. It keeps people on the true way, or to use the Dakota expression, "the true red way." It conveys lamentation and offers a way to vision. In rituals, the pipe itself is substantially transformed: it becomes man and the four directions of the earth. Brown quotes Black Elk on the red pipe's power: "The whole universe was placed in the pipe and then, turning to the people, the keeper of the pipe says: 'Since we have done all this correctly, the soul shall have a good journey, and it will help our people to increase and to walk the sacred path in a manner pleasing to *Wakan-Tanka* [the Great Spirit].'"[19]

Neihardt's and Brown's approaches transformed Black Elk into a literary spiritual leader. In elevating him to the status of prophet, they reduced him to fit their own cultural agenda. They disregarded his awesome capacity to adapt his mind and serve his people over eighty years of monumental change. His biography—as is often the case—made Oglala Sioux religion into a straightforward alternative to the Catholicism that Black Elk himself had formerly taught. It struck a one-to-one correspondence between crucifix and pipe, Christ and White Buffalo Calf Woman, producing an easy transfer of allegiance from Christianity to the Indian religion.[20]

Neihardt and Brown did not discuss the Black Elk who had converted to Catholicism, was a great friend of priests, and had served more than thirty years as an effective Catholic catechist. They didn't distinguish between what he had inherited and how he had reshaped and formulated this inheritance in light of Catholic theology. Michael Steltenkamp, who makes much of Black Elk's career as a catechist, remarks, "His life is not a profile of syncretism but is, rather, an example of reflexive adjustment to new cultural landscapes that had not been previously explored."[21]

However the genesis and use of Black Elk's teachings are interpreted, the greater truth is that the present requires all peoples to reformulate their past—particularly Indian peoples. Confronted by Christian and European cultures and overwhelmed by their people, economy, and governments, native peoples had to articulate a sustaining vision if they were to exist at all. Beyond their own enmities, they had to forge out of place and legend, artifacts and ceremony, a continuity that events had denied them. They had to invent a tradition that would gather in spirit a people dispersed in mind and body.[22]

Black Elk, the pipe, and the Pipestone quarry constitute for native and white peoples alike a cultural response to engulfing and homogenizing national and commercial culture. The red rock symbolized the buffalo hunter, whose spilled blood tinted the rock. The pipe's rising smoke promised restoration. And because it did, it was inevitable that some Indian leaders would seek to save the pipe, the rock, and the quarry from trespass and commercialization. As the Yankton protested the quarrying and the selling of the rock by whites at the end of the nineteenth century, so AIM—the American Indian Movement—protested quarrying and disrupted the city of Pipestone's Hiawatha Pageant in 1970.[23]

THE LITERARY APPROPRIATION OF THE ROCK

In keeping with the cultural invention of landscape, Europeans and Americans symbolically transformed the Pipestone quarry and the pipe itself into legend, story, and metaphor. The story of their idealization spans more than a century and a half. It extends from George Catlin's Romantic travel narrative, published in the 1840s, to the establishment of the city of Pipestone in the 1870s. It reaches from the adaptation of Henry Wadsworth Longfellow's 1855 *Song of Hiawatha* by the Pipestone Federal Indian School as a play in 1932 to its incorporation into a city pageant in 1949 amid mounting talk of closing the Indian school, which in fact occurred in 1953.

Longfellow captivated whites and Indians alike with his Romantic narrative poem *Hiawatha*. He spun it from the writings of two fellow Romantic travelers, George Catlin and Henry Rowe Schoolcraft. Pennsylvania-born artist George Catlin brought much attention to the Indian peoples of the trans-Mississippi West and the Pipestone quarry. His painterly eye sought out the richness and variety of indigenous peoples—their bodies, dress, and mannerisms. His interest in the actual conditions of Indian life and his curiosity about natural landforms added to his works' irreplaceable value for understanding American Indian life. Based on his extensive trips to the Missouri River and to the Northwest between 1832 and 1839, his 1844 book *Manners, Customs, and Conditions of North American Indians* offers a panorama of vanquished peoples.[24]

A moral passion supplemented Catlin's curiosity. He was caught up in the Romantic era's expanding sympathy and pity. He consciously bore witness to what he saw as the elimination of the Indian, whom he took to be mortally afflicted, suffering from smallpox, the effects of forced relocation, the voracious commerce of the frontier, alcoholism, and other deleterious effects of a one-sided encounter with a more powerful civilization. Catlin concluded his work by calling on Christians and philanthropists to acknowledge that "there is an unrequited account of sin and injustice that sooner or later will call for national retribution."[25]

Catlin's trip to the quarry took him to the heart of the people and frontier about which he moralized. The West to which he went was not "the simple West—the vast and vacant wilds which lie between the trodden haunts of present savage and civil life—the great and almost boundless garden-spot of earth."[26] This land, so recently fought over, was for the moment a vast "neutral ground" on which "Nature's men are rapidly vanishing" and "civilized man advances, filled with joy and gladness."[27] Awe filled the poetic Catlin as he entered the "sublime" Coteau des Prairies and saw the majestic Pipestone quarry for the first time. Here, along the high ridge where the waters part for the Missouri and the Minnesota rivers, Catlin wrote, "The Great Spirit called the Indian nations together, broke from its wall a piece, and made a huge pipe [and] . . . told them that this stone was red—that it was their flesh—and that they must use it for their pipes of peace."[28]

The native people he encountered did not want Catlin to enter the sacred land. They believed that he and his party were government agents seeking to assess the value of the rock and that their entrance would involve setting white hands on their red rock flesh. But Catlin gained admission, and he noted each identifying quarry spot and recorded the Indian legends associated with it. He noted how profits to be made from commerce had led the Dakota to take exclusive control of the quarry and took samples of the rock himself for analysis. As a result, the scientific name granted to Pipestone rock is catlinite.

Henry Rowe Schoolcraft's collections of North American Indian stories—especially his two-volume *Algic Researches,* published in 1839—were the other quarries out of which Longfellow hewed his *Song of Hiawatha.*[29] Widely read in contemporary European and French literature, Schoolcraft also belonged to the literary sensibility of the Romantic era. He trod the same paths as the wandering Rousseau and the literary voyager François-René de Chateaubriand, whose books took poetic voyages to the Holy Land, Italy, and America (and places in them he never actually visited). In 1855 Schoolcraft romantically wrote:

> Within a beauteous basin, fair outspread
> Hesperian woodlands of the western sky,
> As if, in Indian myths, a truth there could be read,
> And these were tears, indeed, by fair Itasca shed.[30]

However, Schoolcraft's travels served a higher purpose. In the tradition of the broad naturalism shaped by the German baron Alexander von Humboldt, Schoolcraft's undertakings belonged to the emerging fields of natural and ethnographic science. Inspired by American statesman and explorer Lewis Cass, Schoolcraft viewed his travels as a quest for knowledge. Their results included his discovery of the headwaters of the Mississippi River at Lake Itasca, in Minnesota.[31] Covering thousands of miles of the upper Great Lakes region, his travels entailed intensive contact with native peoples. The fruit of his long labors as Indian agent of the tribes of the Lake Superior region, with headquarters at Sault Ste. Marie, Michigan, resulted in the first truly extensive collections of Indian ways and stories.

Longfellow used Schoolcraft's stories to produce *Hiawatha.* His admiring biographer, Chase Osborn (a former governor of Michigan) glowingly wrote of Longfellow's intellectual development: "It was not all an expansion of his brain. His heart grew, and his soul, and he became a humanist of a deepest conviction. No demonstration of woe and sorrow failed to affect him. His poetic temperament was marching through his entire being to a great future. He said his whole soul burned ardently for improvement."[32]

With adroit poetic skills and the beat of the Finnish national epic, the *Kalevala,* humming in his brain, Longfellow romantically transformed Schoolcraft's stories. For the primary content of his Indian tale, Longfellow took an Indian of mythic birth—be he known as Michabou, Chiabo, or Manabozho—who was sent among his people to enhance their lives and teach them the arts of peace. Into this tradition, Longfellow said, "I have woven other curious Indian legends, drawn chiefly from the various and valuable writings of Mr. Schoolcraft."[33] Even though he drew his hero from the Ojibway hero Manabozho and set his tale "by the shore of Gitche-Gumee" (Lake Superior), Longfellow used as its introduction a creation story from Pipestone as found in Catlin's *Manners, Customs, and Conditions of North American Indians*. He opens his poem thus:

On the Mountains of the Prairie
On the great Red Pipe-stone Quarry,
Gitche Manito, the mighty,
He the Master of Life, descending,
On the red crags of the quarry
Stood erect, and called the nations
Called the tribes of men together.[34]

Longfellow lacked Schoolcraft's sense of ethnography and Catlin's keen eye for distinction and the tragic sense about the Indians' plight. His poem sanitized the violence and sexuality found in Schoolcraft's stories. It overlooked the tragic and devastating aspects of the encounters between Indians and whites. Instead, Longfellow offered a sonorous palliative, using fashionable Indian motifs to evoke his audience's curiosity. *Hiawatha* appealed to those who considered themselves possessed of benign feelings and sympathetic disposition toward the Indians.

Ye whose hearts are fresh and simple
Who have faith in God and Nature,
Who believe, that in all ages
Every human heart is human,
That in even savage bosoms
There are longings, yearnings, strivings,
For the good they comprehend not,
. . . .
Listen to this simple story.[35]

The substance and plot of *Hiawatha* turn on a beneficent Indian chief who learned the wonders of nature from his grandmother. He excels in all contests and even kills the god Mondamin, from whose grave springs corn to feed his people. He seeks his wife in the "distant land" of the Dakota, taking Minnehaha, daughter of an old arrow maker, for his bride. Then, tragedy strikes. A famine settles on his people, and he returns from his failed search for food to find his beloved Minnehaha dying of a fever. After her death he spends a long, solitary winter in mourning, then returns to his people with an empty heart.

Hiawatha's experience confirms the great traveler Iagoo's tale: "Bearded white faces" will come from the east, "where morning, lightning, and storms arise." They will cross "a sea much broader than Gitche Gumee." "Wheresoe'er they tread, beneath them / Springs a flower unknown among us, / Springs the White-man's Foot in blossom."[36]

> They come as crowded nations until
> All the land was full of people,
> Restless, struggling, toiling, striving,
> Speaking many tongues, yet feeling
> But one heart-beat in their bosoms,
> In the woodlands rang their axes,
> Smoke their towns in all the valleys,
> Over all the lakes and rivers
> Rushed their great canoes of thunder.[37]

And a darker vision of expropriation follows:

> I beheld our nations scattered,
> All forgetful of counsels,
> Weakened, warring with each other,
> Saw remnants of our people
> Sweeping westward, wild and woeful,
> Like the cloud-rack of a tempest,
> Like the wither leaves of Autumn![38]

To satisfy the command that this vision of dissolution brings, Hiawatha welcomes a black robe, a Christian missionary. The latter offers Hiawatha solace with stories of Abraham, Moses, Mary, and Christ. Hiawatha accepts them as a gift of a prophet sent by "the Master of Life." And, as if their very hearing somehow lifts from Hiawatha the burden of responsibility for his people, he suddenly and inexplicably bids them farewell. He starts out on a long, solitary, and vague journey west, ever west, to the hereafter:

> Thus departed Hiawatha,
> Hiawatha the Beloved,
> In the glory of the sunset,
> In the purple mists of evening,
> To the regions of the home-wind,
> Of the North-west wind, Keewaydin,

Of the islands of the Blessed,
To the kingdom of Ponemah,
To the land of the Hereafter![39]

Striking romantic chords of love, mourning, and solitude, the poem appealed to people securely removed from the frontier. Perhaps it offered the respect granted the vanishing; that is, as we glorify hunting when we no longer need the food it yields, so humans venerate the peoples they have defeated and domesticated. Surely, the poem gloves the fist of custodianship with sympathy. The new nation relieves Hiawatha of his responsibility. It turns him and his kind into legends. It affirms that agriculture, literacy, and Christianity offer a superior fate—leaving an illustrious chief with nothing else to do but beat a solitary retreat to the great beyond. It is a noble thing for the most noble of the noble savages to do.

Hiawatha secured Longfellow's lifelong fame. Considerable criticism did not deter impressive sales on both sides of the Atlantic. And not everyone was critical. Walt Whitman, whose *Leaves of Grass* appeared the same year, pronounced Longfellow a poet of all sympathetic gentleness, a "universal poet of women and young people."[40] Schoolcraft himself, perhaps seeking to cash in on *Hiawatha*'s popularity, appropriated the name for his own *Myth of Hiawatha,* which he published a year after the publication of Longfellow's poem.[41]

Hiawatha's popularity took many forms. People dressed up in Indian costumes and recited the poem. It was set to music. Drinks, steamships, and streets were named Hiawatha and Minnehaha. In 1868, when Longfellow visited Europe, he was welcome everywhere he went, and he received honorary degrees from Cambridge and Oxford.[42] Longfellow clubs and associations sprang up. In London a regular *Hiawatha* pageant was enacted. In the vicinity of Minnehaha Falls, in Minneapolis, Longfellow Gardens was built during the 1910s, containing a replica of Longfellow's Boston childhood home.[43] In 1900, the Ojibway living along the northern shore of Lake Huron invited Longfellow's daughters to see them perform their father's play. On their birch-bark invitation they wrote, "Ladies: We loved your father. The memory of our people will never die as long as your father's song lives, and that will live forever."[44]

Longfellow became a legend in his own lifetime. His poetic tale quickly spread to the frontier of which he wrote. Soon both white prairie settlers and Indians looked to the New England writer and his poem to understand who they were.

A NEW TOWN OF THIS ROCK

One person who could not separate his love of the quarry and its rock from the writings of Longfellow was Charles Bennett, the founder of the town of Pipestone. A settler and pharmacist in the newly founded town of Le Mars, in northwestern Iowa, Bennett set out in 1873 to examine the land around the quarry as a prospective site for settlement. He was filled with the era's passion to settle, build, and profit. It was bred in his bones. Born in 1846 in Union, Michigan, he belonged to a restless and ambitious family. His father, Isaiah Bennett, as local tradition has it, had founded several towns in Michigan. After serving in the Civil War in an Illinois artillery unit, the young Bennett followed his Yankee family's tradition of going west in search of opportunity.

In moving to and taking up a role in settling the new railroad towns of southwestern Minnesota and the prairie, Bennett joined legions of Civil War officers who went west and made themselves the builders and founders of the Main Streets of the new prairie towns. Local historian Christopher Roelfsema-Hummel estimates that one out of three of Pipestone's businessmen at the time were Civil War veterans, and they played an important role in the Masons and other civic organizations and churches.[45]

Bennett was particularly drawn to the Pipestone quarry. The red rock fascinated him, he had read Catlin and Nicollet, and he was infatuated with Longfellow.[46] Visions of real estate prospects accompanied him on his journey north to the quarry. Not even the deaths of his wife and child that year deterred his intention to build a new town on the red rock. He brought with him a handful of his fellow citizens, including Daniel Sweet, D. C. Whitehead, and John Lowry, all of whom were *Hiawatha* fans as well. With a passion equal to Bennett's, Lowry and Sweet spent the winter of 1874 on the future site of Pipestone in small houses they had built. They were fifteen miles from their nearest neighbors in Flandreau, South Dakota, and twenty-five miles from Luverne, Minnesota, the nearest railroad station, which would later serve as the principal portal of Pipestone's supplies and immigrants.[47] Bennett himself took up residence in Pipestone in 1875.

The fledgling town struggled during its first years.[48] The rock proved no fortress against drought or the 1876 grasshopper plague. Success depended wholly on the decision of the railroad companies—if the train came through Pipestone, the town would thrive; if it didn't, Bennett and his followers would have to leave. Bennett thus donated land to the railroads to entice them into coming.

The town's prosperity also hinged on selling the rock. The local newspaper, the *Pipestone County Star,* which was founded in 1879 by I. L. Hart and remained in the family until 1958, praised the quality of available farmland and called for increased exploitation of the nearby quarries. In a special written salute to the railroad, Hart opined, "The day is not far distant . . . when those quarries must be worked to their fullest capacity in order to supply demand, and this will mean much to our little city—the investment of more capital, the installing of more and heavier machines . . . and the building of more railway side-tracks to handle the shipments and employment of scores of workers in and around the quarries."[49]

In 1879, not one but two railroads arrived in the county. The Southern Minnesota line (later the Chicago, Milwaukee, and St. Paul) reached Pipestone, and the competing Sioux City and St. Paul made it to the nearby village of Woodstock. In that year Pipestone was declared the county seat. Real estate filings skyrocketed (forty thousand acres changed hands between May and December that year), and contracts for the purchase of land for pending railroad development escalated.[50] Pipestone boomed.

In 1883, the four Close brothers, English entrepreneurs, arrived in Pipestone, persuaded by Bennett's promises of compensation in town property if they would join development efforts.[51] "They had a reputation for doing big things," wrote county historian Arthur P. Rose, "and promised a boom for Pipestone County."[52] They retained business addresses in Le Mars and Chicago, and from their office in London they sold farms to British buyers.[53] With ever scarcer land to sell, and flying in the updraft of a favorable economic decade in the 1880s, the Close brothers demonstrated the power of salesmanship. They promoted Pipestone up and down the tracks and overseas.

In one pamphlet they identified "THE GREAT PIPESTONE QUARRIES" less by their economic potential than by "the site's natural beauty and its place in North American poetry and Native American religious tradition."[54] They devoted another pamphlet to the place's legends. It featured pieces by Longfellow and local poets, possibly including Bennett's second wife, Adelaide.[55] The Close brothers also distributed pipestone as advertisement. They sent bountiful specimens to their English partner, who attached pipestone trinkets to the promotional flyers he disseminated throughout Europe.[56] On one occasion, almost depleting Bennett's own collection, the Close brothers' agent turned a giant sale of artifacts into a Pipestone real estate advertisement. He tagged each piece (some specially made for the sale by the era's most talented Indian pipe maker, "Big Charlie") with a description of land for sale.[57]

Pipestone flourished as a consequence of the Close brothers' activity. In 1884 three more railroad lines arrived. The number of stores nearly doubled, from 53 in 1880 to 102 in 1885, which left Pipestone with two jewelers, three book and stationery stores, three druggists, and a level of retail specialization expected only in larger towns.[58] In the same period, the population grew from approximately two hundred to eleven hundred. Thanks to a Close brothers connection, British capital endowed one local bank, allowing it to advertise five hundred thousand dollars available for loans.[59] Other British investors were drawn to the county as well. One sought to establish a Scottish colony in Pipestone and adjacent Murray Counties, purchasing some thirty-five thousand acres in the vicinity of Woodstock.[60]

Construction dramatically increased.[61] By 1887, the year illegal white squatters were evicted from the nearby Yankton reservation, Pipestone had started building itself out of its own native rock. The Pipestone County Bank, a high school, the Syndicate Block, Bennett's Drug Store, and the Commerce Block all shone bright and red in the setting sun. Plans were simultaneously under way to build an immense courthouse and expand the city's hotel, the Calumet, which was later advertised as the finest hotel between Minneapolis and Denver.[62]

Quartzite became the medium of architectural self-definition. Pipestone's most important buildings were made of it. The railroad provided the means of selling the rock to the world. "The quarrying industry was worth thousands of dollars to the county in the late 1880s," historian Christopher Roelfsema-Hummel wrote, "and Hart promised it would eventually be worth millions."[63]

With the arrival of the railroads, Pipestone's leaders had extended the town's direct interests far beyond the city limits. In 1888 a new round of exploitation began with the opening of the private Poorbaugh quarry, adjacent to the Yankton reservation, igniting visions of worldwide profitable commerce in the stone. Demand for the hard and nearly indestructible quartzite—harder than granite and capable of withstanding a pressure of twenty-five hundred pounds per square inch—grew dramatically. In one short year, the quarrying industry came to dwarf all other area industries and further fueled the imperial commercial vision of the town.[64]

Pipestone businessman J. M. Poorbaugh espied yet more opportunity at nearby Jasper, and purchased Jasper's quarry from its developers, the Rae brothers. It quickly proved itself a more productive quarry than even that of Pipestone. Soon its quartzite was being hauled by the thousands of tons all over the world for building materials. It was shipped east and north to St. Paul, Minneapolis, and Duluth, south and east to Cedar Rapids and Kansas City, and south and west to Watertown, Sioux City, Omaha, and beyond.[65] With its distinctive red color and its enduring strength, pipestone gave lasting form to some of the era's most attractive architecture worldwide.

OF ROCK AND IDENTITY

Charles Bennett cleaved to the rock from the moment he arrived in Pipestone. It occupied him body and soul. He built his life, his business, and his town around and out of it. His passion for the stone won him a second wife, a New Hampshire poet named Adelaide George, who wrote to the Pipestone postmaster for information about the area and requested a sample of the stone made famous by Longfellow's poem. Bennett replied to her letter. A correspondence resulted, then a romance took shape, and finally the two married in the autumn of 1877. The newlyweds visited an aging Longfellow on their honeymoon.[66]

Bennett never separated idealization of the rock from its exploitation. If aesthetic sensibilities aroused by Longfellow's sentimental poetry led him to appreciate things Indian, his passions enrolled him in the ranks of both whites and Indians who had commercialized the stone since the start of the century. As early as the 1830s, merchants, including Joseph Laframboise, had perceived the significant economic value of pipestone. From 1864 to 1871, exploiters had mounted several sizable quarrying ventures. Between 1865 and 1868, the Northwest Fur Company made two thousand pipes, and by the eve of the First World War, pipes made mainly by whites already had begun to appear in museums throughout the world.[67]

Bennett joined in the fevered exploitation of the red rock. By 1880 an advertisement claimed that Bennett's Drug Store had "the largest and finest variety of Indian Pipes, Sleeve Buttons, Match Boxes, and other trinkets manufactured from Pipestone by whites and Indians."[68] (The town newspaper's bookstore also sold pipestone goods.) The period from 1880 to 1887 witnessed an expansion of the pipestone handicraft industry. By 1892 Bennett estimated that 99 percent or more of the pipes in circulation had been made by whites.[69] Promoting and exploiting the rock formed a matrix with personal gain and civic reputation in Bennett's mind. He thrived within the comfortable pews of a faith that seamlessly fused the idealization and commercialization of the rock.

By 1890, Indians had disappeared from Pipestone and the vicinity. From their nearby reservation in eastern South Dakota they continued to pursue their principal lawsuit over the land taken from them by the federal government, until it was finally settled in 1927. In 1891 the railroad compensated the Indians for a right-of-way across their Pipestone reservation, although no Indian resided there. (The Yankton received $1,740 for the trespass, which amounted to 99 cents for each tribal member.) In the same year, the 648-acre reservation in toto was appropriated by federal legislation for building the Pipestone Indian Industrial School, though the Indians retained visiting and quarrying rights.[70]

In 1892 the federal government began constructing the Indian school out of stone taken from the quarry, awarding the contract to J. M. Poorbaugh.[71] With its 1893 completion, the school fulfilled a sixteen-year-old dream of Pipestone's founders, realized largely through legislative lobbying sweetened by the selective distribution of pipestone souvenirs. The school's purpose was to teach a large range of applied practical arts, such as printing, nursing, and tailoring. Its 1914 catalogue declared that the students, drawn from the surrounding states, found themselves in a "rarely equaled and certainly unexcelled" school. "Its fine buildings of red stone" occupy "one of the highest and most commanding points not only in the locality but the state." Existing "within a mile of Pipestone, with its four busy railway lines, . . . the choice of the site is all that could be desired 'On the mountains of the prairie, / By the great red pipestone quarry.'"[72]

The school was first conceived as a moneymaker for the town: many of its buildings would be made of local stone, and the school, once completed, would bring many new residents to the town. Also, the school may have salved consciences about the plight of the vanished Indians. Surely it evoked a custodial formula familiar to that era: the Indians may have lost title to the land, but it had been put to a higher purpose, one that served them well.

Pipestone, by the 1890s, was ready to show the fruits of its rapid progress to the whole world. Identifying itself with the red rock, Pipestone put itself on display at the 1893 Chicago World's Fair. Known as the Columbian Exposition, the fair celebrated, though a year late, the four-hundred-year anniversary of Columbus's arrival in the New World.

Pipestone clubs, churches, individuals, and companies sent quartzite to the exposition by the ton, as well as its best Indian arrowheads, handicrafts, curios, and catlinite artifacts. The Pipestone and Jasper mantel, covered by glass, was accorded prominent display in the ladies' waiting room on the second floor of the Minnesota State Building. Bennett put his immense collection of curios up for sale at the base of the grand staircase. One visitor reported, "The raw pipestone [Bennett had] taken intact from the quarries with overlaying of Jasper and sod [was placed] in Minnesota's collective exhibit on the east aisle of [the] Mining Building, [with] a duplicate section in the Anthropological Building directly in front of the main building."[73]

Pipestone leaders found no incongruity between identifying their city with quarry rock and Indian symbols and at the same time insisting that it embodied the essence of the advancing nation. To the contrary, they took themselves to be the true children of Columbus.

On the eve of the fair, Charles Bennett posed for a photograph at his backyard fence, along which stood the Indian petroglyphs he had removed from the reservation. Bennett said he had done this to save them from vandalism. He labeled himself a "preservationist." Over a number of years, artifacts slowly disappeared from the reservation, only to reappear in his drug store. They supported his advertisement, which declared that he had "the largest collection of pipestone relics in the world."[74]

Although many of the petroglyphs Bennett had in his possession before the fair ended up missing, charges of stealing never smudged Bennett's reputation as a good citizen and merchant. What he had taken—at least in the eyes of those who had power and who set the era's standards—was minuscule in relation to what he had built. After all, Bennett had built out of rock a unique Midwestern town, which in the aftermath of the fair filled itself out in red and pink quartzite. It added in red stone a Presbyterian church, a new city hall, and an entire downtown block, the Moore Block, named after a talented sculptor who had decorated its corners with medieval-inspired gargoyles.[75] The opera house was finished in 1898; a new quartzite county courthouse was constructed in 1901; and nearby, in 1903, the pink quartzite Carnegie Library—a small gem of architecture—was erected.

Bennett's acts and beliefs had coincided perfectly with the times and thus were never summoned to judgment or even subjected to suspicion. He had proved a faithful member of the Republican Party, the party of the winners of the Civil War. He had served Pipestone as first county attorney, first town clerk, one of the first city councilmen, and chairman of the board of county commissioners, as well as the first clerk of court, a justice of the peace, and mayor. He was a charter member and officer of the Old Settlers Historical Society, the predecessor of the present Pipestone County Historical Society, which gave him the advantage of writing and celebrating his own deeds. He was also on the board of the Presbyterian church. He belonged to the local chapter of the Masons and to the Grand Army of the Republic, both of which, as elsewhere in the Midwest, provided the informal community links between those who ran the town's politics and those who ran its businesses.[76]

Bennett's ethnic identity also perfectly matched the ruling profile. He was of Yankee-Protestant heritage. His affiliation with English immigrants derived from the Close brothers and the English settlers they'd brought to Pipestone.[77] It also stemmed from his ties to Le Mars, which accounted for so much travel from London that at one point, as historian Lee Olson noted, "British steamship lines listed Le Mars above New York City on their timetable postings of arrival and departures."[78] All this made Bennett as "truly American" as one could be at the time. Bennett could share the nativist views that mixed senses of superiority with those of fear toward the arriving hordes of immigrants from eastern and southern Europe. During World War I, Bennett could unreservedly champion the cause as its fervor spread from east to west, city to countryside.

ROCK OF RIGHTEOUSNESS

In fusing locale and nation, business and politics, tradition and manifest destiny, Bennett's faith was the orthodoxy of many Midwestern Main Streets. Like Bennett, Pipestone's leaders found no gap between religion and ethnicity, commerce and civilization, Pipestone and the United States of America. By every star, they could claim that they were destined to rule the nation in the twentieth century.

In that spirit, one can understand how the politicians and press of Pipestone expressed the prerogatives of the county seat and the county's most important town, but they also spoke for the future of the nation. Beyond the wonderful quartzite buildings that lined its downtown and glowed so warmly at sunset, Pipestone, with its Masonic lodge and chapter of the Grand Army of the Republic, presumed itself to be the moral leader of the countryside.

Pipestone took to the Great War with verve. On April 10, 1917, a banner on the front page of the *Pipestone County Star* read: "PIPESTONE

PEOPLE JOIN IN GREAT PATRIOTIC GATHERING." Patriotic fervor greeted the public meetings held at the courthouse and at the Presbyterian church, which together held an overflow crowd of nearly eight hundred. Charles Bennett presided over the meeting at the courthouse. The Indian School Band gave a stirring performance. Speeches that addressed "the starry flag" received considerable applause. The newspaper described how, over the past few days, schools had engaged in patriotic exercises, homes had been decorated, and flags had been flown throughout town. The editor wrote, "A large flag is suspended over the intersection of Olive and Hiawatha and is illuminated at night by a powerful flashlight on the roof of the Moore Block. And," he added, "it is soon to be replaced by a larger one." His conclusion left no doubt: "The people of this community willingly and loyally assume whatever burdens and sacrifices the war may impose upon them."[79]

A little more than a month later, the banner on the paper alerted its readers to the cash needs of a nation at war. "EVERY LOYAL CITIZEN OF THE UNITED STATES is expected to render some service in the war against the Imperial German Government. $2,000,000,000 is now required and the people of this nation are expected to subscribe liberally to this bond issue. Liberty bonds will be issued in small amounts so that we can all show our patriotism in harmony with our incomes."[80]

Its presumed role as conscience of the county led Pipestone to campaign to defeat drink, to defeat Germany, and to sell war bonds. Coercion aside, it succeeded admirably in the case of the latter. The town boasted that Pipestone and adjacent Murray and Worthington Counties were three of the top four per capita bond sellers in the state.[81] Pipestone bragged: "Sixty-nine and nine-tenths per cent of Pipestone County's population purchased Liberty Bonds. . . . Pipestone County led the nation in per capita sales." The U.S. Navy recognized these efforts by christening one of its ships the *Pipestone County*.[82]

Pipestone also abided by the broad surveillance charge of the Minnesota Commission of Public Safety (CPS). The charge, as vague as it was sweeping, included watching labor unions, members of the Non-Partisan League, the state's liquor industry, and the loyalty of members of a society filled with immigrants, noninterventionists, and Germans.[83] The Pipestone Commission of Public Safety proved itself particularly vigilant and noisome to its neighbors. It sought out the seditious foreign elements in its midst and was particularly watchful of the recently arrived Dutch-speaking immigrants, who in 1917 had just established their own school, the Edgerton Christian School. Suspicion focused on the school's use of foreign languages. Resentment against the school also brewed because in calling itself a "Christian" school, it implied that the public school wasn't "Christian."

Like other Yankee-owned and pro-war rural newspapers, the *Pipestone County Star* printed extensive lists of those who volunteered for military service, joined the Red Cross, or subscribed for liberty bonds. Carrying it a step further, the *County Star* also began to print the names of those who *didn't* buy liberty bonds. Nearby Lyon County made a fuss over "war bond slackers" as well. A group of Marshall citizens painted a Kaiser mustache on the face of a Ruthton slacker after his public refusal before the County War Board to buy his share of bonds.[84] Pipestone's Presbyterian minister, E. N. Prentice, a certified CPS speaker, contended that one should economically support the war or leave the country. Pipestone's CPS enumerator, keeping tabs on aliens, took special interest in the Dutch, who in addition to sending their children to their own, private school, bought so few bonds and claimed military exemptions based on their alien status.[85] When the Edgerton paper did not support the painting yellow of a Ruthton citizen who had made disloyal statements, Reverend Prentice took the paper to task at a public address at Pipestone's opera house. The high point of his aria, besides denouncing the nearby Trosky saloon, took aim at the Edgerton Christian School as un-American and undemocratic.[86]

The small village of Trosky, in south central Pipestone County, surely was a burr under the saddle of righteous Pipestone, which had battled saloons and saloon keepers from at least the late 1880s on.[87] Trosky's first recognized business was a " blind pig" in the service of railroad men. While Pipestone went dry early, Trosky stayed wet, and persisted in allowing alcohol sales even as adjacent counties dried up. The young men of Pipestone found their pleasures—drinking, gambling, and whoring—by driving their cars or taking the local train from Jasper (affectionately named the Boozer) to Trosky, where traveling tents of women found profitable encampments.

So sin thrived in what should have been a righteous kingdom. Pipestone was not alone in trying to use the Commission of Public Safety against Trosky, whose saloon hired fifteen bartenders in a town of 250. When the bars were limited to an eight-hour day by the CPS Order Ten, the *Pipestone Leader* expressed considerable pleasure and used the new rule as an occasion to decry the "brutal and disgusting nature concerning the frequenters of these 'thirst resorts.'"[88] With the end of the war, Trosky was relieved of the burden of the Minnesota Commission of Public Safety, but its joy was short-lived, for later in the summer the entire county went dry a few months ahead of the passage of prohibition.[89]

ALWAYS THE ROCK

Yet Pipestone could not live by its high-minded morality and patriotic national reputation alone. It forever returned to the quarry and the pipestone to hew an identity and a living for itself. In the 1920s, Pipestone accelerated its campaign to turn the quarry into a national monument, an idea that had originated with the chamber of commerce in 1887. In 1937 Franklin Roosevelt signed legislation making the dream a reality.[90] After that, the town increasingly became known by the monument.

So, by name and location, Pipestone cannot separate itself from the red rock, even though the white man's quarries have been stilled for a long time. The rock still speaks to the eye of the present and the eye of memory. It forms the base of the region's roads and railroad beds. The historic buildings and tourism lock the town in an ongoing conversation with the rock. Distinct from surrounding railroad towns and ethnic villages, Pipestone dresses itself up in red rock—and Indian garb.

Buffalo, arrowheads, and tepees decorate streets and stores in town. A red pipe is the logo of the town's stationery. The annual Hiawatha pageant, in which hundreds of citizens participate, associates the town with the accreted images of Indians in general and Longfellow in particular. When it was open, the Indian school encouraged its students to look into Longfellow's poem for their own meaning and to so represent it to the community. Beginning in 1932, the Indians put on the pageant of Hiawatha to affirm that they were the noble and progressive savages Longfellow depicted. The pageant was next taken up by the Hiawatha Club, and the city took over its production in 1949.

The pageant, which still draws an audience from region, nation, and even world, is staged against the backdrop of the Three Maidens, three glacial boulders that define the northern end of the quarry for Indians and whites alike. The foreground, separating audience and actors, is the water-filled private quarry that once supplied the town with its rock. The pageant fittingly concludes, true to the poem, with Hiawatha paddling from an artificial beam of light into the jet-black darkness of night.

The Hiawatha pageant (recently rivaled, in accord with Bennett's other spiritual side, by a summer Civil War reenactment) reveals how much Pipestone is captivated by the stone and the stories told of it. However much the town might struggle for new industry, such as boat building or large pig-feeding operations, it seems frozen in time by its own history. Its own past has taken it captive.

So what conclusion remains, other than the circle of landscape and place? Stone drives feelings and thoughts. Thoughts and feelings pulverize rock. They turn it into myth and legend. The red rock was transformed into all that minds could make it—and it now lies buried by layer after layer of the sediment of human meanings. Indeed, Pipestone is the most magic and invented of all places in southwest Minnesota.

Culture shaped the stone into pipe, town, myth, artifact, and trinket. And the red stone claimed the minds—and lives—of the people who lived around it. As I concluded this essay, I received a lengthy e-mail from the grandson of an early Jasper resident. It shows the power of local stone over memory, its contribution to a sense of place and of home:

> If you are talking color of the rock, it varies considerably depending on the quarry where it was extracted. Buildings can be identified as being built of stone coming from a certain quarry. . . . The rock varies from a deeper purplish color to grayish-purple to gray to a rose pink (I think the pink is from the south quarry), purported to be the most beautiful of all. Also, there are the "moons" present in the rock. . . . These moons are buttery, cream-colored, or vellum-colored round spots in the darker stone varying from granule-sized to about the size of a quarter. These were caused by radioactive material present at the time of formation of the stone, supposedly 1.3 billion years ago.
>
> When the stone is polished, it takes on a glass-like finish, unique because of the rock's density and hardness. It is renowned for its beauty and [accounts] for the expansive city blocks of the warm pink stone, probably enhanced when backlit by a setting sun. It must have been an impression like no other obtained in Southwest Minnesota.
>
> My grandparents' beautiful home was made of Jasper rock and was built by a former quarrymaster. The south bedroom had extra large windows because the story was that the quarrymaster was trying to recover from tuberculosis when he built the house and hoped the sunlight would expedite his recovery. . . . Instead he died at 42, I think, from silicosis caused by the fine dust from the quarries, not tuberculosis. . . . It was apparently a frequent cause of death for the quarryworkers.
>
> My grandfather drove Oldsmobiles and I remember a rose or coral pink one, probably a 1958. Even as a kid, I understood that it was an unusual color, though don't remember asking about it. Now it seems that the pink car must

have been chosen to identify with the town's quartzite. . . . [T]he townspeople all laughed because my grandpa had chosen a woman's car. He was a prominent citizen, dentist there for nearly 50 years and mayor in the war-year '40s and very active in DFL politics, and he was probably showing a bit of boosterism, as well as individuality, in his choice of the pink Olds.[91]

CHAPTER 10

Business First and Always

Business history throws opens the door to the history of the prairie. Every village is an economic entity whose well-being is measured by profit and loss. The country town, however much it informs American sentiment and culture, is first and foremost about business. Importing dreams and laws as well as products and goods, business forms the principal purpose and lubricant of small towns. As reluctant as a cultural historian like me might be to admit it, business makes the whole countryside go.

Business history, however, is no simple subject. Rather, it forms a network with endless branches for local and regional historians. And, to my consolation, in the end, if business history is carefully followed, one branch of it leads back to cultural history, for making money and participating in a capitalist society are undertakings of the individual and collective mind. Scratch the smallest crystal of commerce on the prairie and we find the largest economic galaxy reflected in it. In a single southwestern prairie town—my example is Marshall, Minnesota—the historian can observe the articulation of national and international markets, the growth of specialization, and the dramatic transformation of contemporary rural life.

The twentieth-century prairie story is more about turbulence and transformation than about continuity and permanence. It can even largely be seen as the onset of irreversible and overpowering decline, as Richard Davies observes in *Main Street Blues.*[1] My argument here is that decline and growth are dramatically fused in the contemporary countryside. Disrupted by economic cycles, transformed by changing technologies, altered by contracting and expanding markets, and influenced by politics, the prairie is awhirl with change. It is no place for historians to seek fixed souls and enduring communities.

A BUSINESS OF GLOBAL IMPLICATIONS

Of course, local historians can restrict their scope to histories of individual businesses and business owners. Main Street past offers countless stories of the twists and turns of the fate of single-family businesses. Almost every region records the success story of a local son or daughter. In Marshall, for instance, a Russian Jew, Louis Weiner, and his two sons, Julius and Benjamin, founded a multimillion-dollar food industry in the 1930s and 1940s. In later decades, a young Marshall-born entrepreneur named Marvin Schwan turned a local ice cream company into a multibillion-dollar manufacturer and distributor of frozen food. Frequently, local business history mingles with the exemplary community service of local businessmen or the idealism of their wives, who, like Carol Kennicott in Lewis's *Main Street,* strive to make their village the city it should be. At times, a town's growth so turns on the shared visions of its upper class that business history seems (more to my liking) to be an appendix to cultural history.

Like a running river, business history flows into economic history, especially railroad history, which quickly enmeshes its students in competing economic visions of how to organize the world. Railroad magnates' dreams of connecting farm and city, east and west ensnared farmers, merchants, and speculators in visions of wealth. The equation that underlay the vast railroad projects linked government and business in a symbiotic partnership. Government gave the railroads vast amounts of property, which the railroads in turn sold to recover their investment. They thrived by hauling products out of the countryside and carrying goods and people back in. Towns prospered by serving as exchange points between city and countryside. As railroads moved west, with more help from European capital and the federal government (including its army), towns were founded, farms were established, native peoples were removed, and vast ecological zones were converted to agricultural lands to feed an emerging urban nation.

In this way, as suggested in chapter 3, American civilization marched west town by town in tune with European expansion. As nations and markets took control of the European countryside, the Americas were settled. As Africa was colonized and China nearly annexed, the great grasslands of Russia, Latin America, and the United States were opened for agriculture. Capitalism generalized the reign of money over land, commodities, and labor. In the smallest and newest prairie villages, people gauged their activities by the common measure of money and the success of commerce.

A century earlier, Thomas Jefferson himself—a child of the Atlantic community and the bourgeois eighteenth century—recognized the dominance of commerce in the new republic. In 1784, he wrote George Washington, another property and economic developer:

> All the world is becoming commercial. Were it practicable to keep our new empire separated from them, we might indulge ourselves in speculation whether commerce contributes to happiness of mankind. But we cannot separate ourselves from them. Our citizens have had too full a taste of the comforts furnished by the arts and manufactures to be debarred the use of them. We must, then, in our defence endeavor to share as large a portion as we can of this modern source of wealth and power.[2]

Before the West was settled, Ralph Waldo Emerson, in an article entitled "Wealth," declared on behalf of every American farmer that money counts out "the strokes of his labor, . . . so much rain, frost, and sunshine, . . . so much hoeing and threshing."[3] Money influences "all economic and social relationships," wrote noted historian Fernand Braudel.[4] It calculates both the greatest transactions and the purchase of a fish hook, a hatpin, a chew of tobacco, or a lollipop.

A PRAIRIE TOWN

Marshall, a prairie town, a county seat, and over time a regional center, lies at the intersection of two railroads, the Chicago and Northwest and the St. Peter. Every mile of track laid in the nineteenth century linked Marshall to Minneapolis, the milling center of the upper Midwest, and beyond to the great prairie metropolis, Chicago, and to New York. Through this metal umbilical cord, Marshall was connected to the flow of capital and goods and the metropolis's plans, schemes, and visions. Marshall was birthed along these tracks into an intensely competitive world. Never swaddled, it was compelled to stand on its own infant legs.

As John Radzilowski remarked in his indispensable history of Marshall, *Prairie Town,* there could be only so many "new Chicagos" on the prairie. In fact, some towns were born to an inevitable decline.[5] Boosting could not bewitch economic reality. Like its fellow prairie towns, Marshall was quickly thrown up along the tracks on the northwestern corner of the tallgrass prairie, where the Redwood River coming down off the Coteau des Prairies reaches the floodplains. Wolves were still heard howling on the town's outskirts as buildings went up slapdash to fill in the railroad's standard grid, and at least one buffalo broached the city limits. After a few years, boasting a few streets, two thousand residents, and a county seat designation, Marshall declared itself the economic hub of the region.

While the town satisfied the abiding human need for community, its raison d'être was economic. A depot dispatching crops and importing products, it provided indispensable goods and services and the amenities of advancing civilization. Doctors and dentists offered the rudiments of medicine, a theater produced frivolity and serious productions, and a general store sold fashionable hats, harmonicas, and frilled bloomers in addition to flour, brooms, and nails.

A trip along Marshall's Main Street in 1873, four years after the town's founding, would reveal to local historians that the town's primary function was commercial. In addition to a newspaper, not uniquely named the *Prairie Schooner,* there was a railroad agent, a telegraph operator, a postmaster, and a land office. Also two hotels, a livery blacksmith, a lumberyard, and a drug store. The general store was complemented by a meat market, a confectionery, a hardware store, a furniture store, and—for those who wanted to capture themselves in their new environment at a historic juncture in the nation's life—a photographer. A Masonic lodge was formed that year, and the Congregational society built a church.[6]

Like other early Midwestern towns, Marshall housed two types of businesses: retail and artisanal. The artisans, represented by the once all-important blacksmiths, cobblers, harness makers, and wagon makers, vanished over time. Suggesting how technology and markets work a continuous transformation of local business and population, they were replaced by automobile mechanics, metal-shop workers, electricians, and others in the building trades.

Retailers had to keep pace with changing and expanding markets. Their goods were brought by the railroads from the metropolis. Whether they stocked bulk foods or complex machines, the retailers' enduring burden was knowing what and how much to buy at one price and sell at another price. This universal economic law applied to the smallest commercial undertaking. Successful business activity increasingly involved acuity in calculating the volume of potential sales in relation to profit margin, and the range of products in light of customers' evolving tastes.

Two other challenges illustrate how local historians of business are increasingly required to write of the place they care about in detail with reference to the laws of economics, as opposed to the challenges that face other types of historians, who, when writing of concrete places, often are dragged into the abstract. First, the less a merchant sold of a product, the higher his or her prices had to be; and the higher the prices, the more likely customers were inclined, given the opportunity, to buy elsewhere. The mail-order catalogue became the local merchant's rival. The U.S. Postal Service had brought catalogues to every town and farmhouse by the end of the century. Be it Montgomery Ward's catalogue or that of Sears and Roebuck, the catalogue set both a range of offerings and a price against which the town merchant had to compete.[7] After a few decades of futile struggle, local retailers, whether in Minnesota, Ohio, or Montana, signaled their surrender by placing these catalogues on prominent display right next to their cash registers.

The second general law that drove local business was that the more varied a merchant's stock, the more capital he or she risked on products that might not sell or that might have to be liquidated at steeply reduced prices. Conversely, if merchants didn't expand the variety of their stock, customers found fewer reasons to patronize their stores at all. On this count, merchants often bought certain products at great risk and others with no hope of profit at all but rather out of a need to make their stores convenient and fashionable for customers who had grown accustomed to the wide range of choices offered by the mail-order catalogues of Montgomery Ward.

Individual virtues and vices and family fortunes and misfortunes add color to local business history, but the overall picture for small-town businesses, retail and artisanal alike, was uniformly poor. A hundred years of prairie business history testify to this. Markets were small, even fragile, to begin with. Not much could help them, and almost anything could injure them. A fight between farmers and the owners of the town elevator or a clash over school districting could do irrevocable damage to community cohesion, cooperation, and commerce. The orthodoxy of Main Street rested on the truth that the merchants would sing or hang together. If the town did well, so did they. If it waned, they failed.

Competition magnified with the growth of transportation and communications. Markets shrank as the farm population decreased. Profit margins diminished as big-city merchants bought and sold in volume.

Local merchants faced the puzzle of finding a balance between selling enough and offering an attractive range of fresh goods. Among the acquired tricks of the merchant's trade were keeping inventories low, starting an associated business (sellers of lumber learned to build houses, furniture merchants moonlighted as undertakers), and extending interest-free seasonal credit, which has disappeared in recent decades. (Credit, a matter of ongoing tension between retailer and customer, forms a subject of particular interest to the historians of business, as does the recent history of the growth of credit agencies.) Regardless of what small-town merchants did, they tended to go broke in one of two ways: with little or nothing to sell, or with unsold goods stacked high.

Dispelling a sentimental view of static small towns is the fact that rural business experienced change and turbulence from the beginning. Radzilowski contends that in the case of Marshall, between 1880 and 1910, businesses averaged a 45 percent turnover rate during each five-year period.[8] Across the same period, especially during the farm depression of the 1890s, farm ownership was characterized by failure, and stores' primary customers were farmers. During the decades preceding the First World War, regional centers (defined as towns of several thousand people, as distinct from the smaller prairie towns and villages) grew and expanded their business into the surrounding countryside.

THE MARRIAGE OF BUSINESS AND CULTURE

As was the case in other regional centers, Marshall's merchants played leading roles in civic affairs. Yankees—Anglo-Saxon Protestants from out east—formed the town's social elite. As fresh and comparatively wealthy immigrants from Britain, Germany, and Scandinavia joined in prairie leadership, an equation between northern European ancestry and business leadership was drawn throughout southwestern Minnesota and much of the Midwest. This tendency was reinforced, according to Radzilowski, by the railroad companies' assumption that "native-born white Protestants were the proper 'stock' for running the towns," while hardworking immigrants with large families would make better farmers.[9]

While the ambitious sons and daughters of town leaders went off to college and opportunities elsewhere, the Yankees, who dominated commerce, continued to define civic leadership. They held seats on the city council and the school and library boards. They filled the ranks and leadership of such important voluntary organizations as the Grand Army of the Republic, the Masons, and the Odd Fellows. Their wives formed and ran study circles and temperance groups that added a moral sheen to towns whose roads were just being paved and whose houses didn't yet have indoor plumbing. Membership in Episcopal, Congregational, Presbyterian, and Methodist churches added religious certitude to their economic calling. As good Christians and proud Americans, they marched into the twentieth century in stride with the nation. With prosperity beckoning, technology improving, and a holy crusade to be fought overseas, they believed that they held their fate in their own hands.

Marshall proved itself progressive after World War I as well. It succeeded in providing itself with water, sewage, electricity, and paved streets. It displayed its willingness to court commerce and support the town's economic growth by helping pay for a new Catholic church, which dwarfed the Episcopal church that stood directly behind it on Main Street. However, these efforts to commit itself to progress didn't insulate it against the forces that engulfed the nation and the world.

The late 1920s and the 1930s brought change of unprecedented magnitude. Tractor and automobile redefined farming and rural life. National financial crisis and worldwide depression followed a period of depressed farm commodity prices. Grim realities overtook Marshall. The covenant between the countryside and the advancing urban nation was broken. Yankee editors of local papers like the nearby *Cottonwood Current* vainly attempted to sustain the patriotic union of progress and nation by interpreting the depression as a crisis of morale rather than one of failed economic policies and national politics. The efforts of the editor of the *Current* fell every bit as short as those of the editor of the *Minneota Mascot,* who had advocated isolationism during the First World War. The overwhelming dimensions of the interwar crisis years explain why small-town people of the 1920s and 1930s idealized the prewar period, and especially the pioneer days, as a time of order, certitude, and stability.

Marshall, which had begun to suffer demographic stagnation in the 1920s as the national rural economy faltered and the town's children followed opportunities elsewhere, experienced a period of population growth and turmoil in the 1930s. The town population grew by more than 40 percent as people from nearby farms and hamlets came to Marshall in search of work in processing plants and New Deal programs.[10] The poverty of these immigrants becomes clear when one recognizes that even though Marshall's population increased sizably during the decade, the town's bank deposits remained constant in the same period, at only

25 percent of the total county bank deposits. (In the 1990s, deposits reached 80 percent.) The town, which had known its traveling salesmen, peddlers, tramps, and Roma (Gypsies) in the past, was now filled with transients. Renters, hired hands, drifters, and farmers leaving the land appeared in droves, defining the poverty and mobility of the era. Not easily distinguished from hoboes, newcomers in need were more numerous than Marshall's resources could support, and they testified to Richard Lingeman's observation that during the depression, the inadequacies of small-town governments became glaringly apparent.[11]

THE UNEXPECTED SIDE OF SUCCESS

If the 1930s taught fatalism, the 1950s and 1960s stimulated a nervous confidence. A look at the differences between these decades shows local historians how much their principalities are affected by the national economy and the moods it elicits. In the 1950s, as elsewhere in the nation, Marshall's population increased, housing starts multiplied, and the city took up such fundamental tasks as building a new sewage system.[12] The 1960s were a heyday for Marshall and towns like it. If Marshall ever was a self-determining community, it was then. The population tripled between 1965 and 1970. The economy thrived, with retail sales elevated to the national average of 22 percent or more between 1958 and 1963.[13] The assets of Marshall's banks are estimated to have increased by nearly 60 percent between 1961 and 1967.[14]

Yet the new wine didn't break the old wineskins. Established families and store names still held Main Street together. The old business gang, along with the head of the chamber of commerce and the superintendent of schools, still essentially ran the town. Eventually, however, a new generation of leaders composed of newcomers and sons and daughters who'd stayed in town took up the matter of Marshall's future. Perhaps it was only unwittingly that they remained loyal to the town's progressive tradition. Whatever the case, Marshall's commerce and politics continued to be ecumenical. Together in coffee shops and city government, Protestants, Catholics, and several prominent Jewish families ran the town. Collectively, they cast their lot with growth and were determined to find a way to differentiate Marshall from its regional town rivals in southwestern Minnesota.

Their ambition and dilemma were the same as those facing other regional centers. Each had to make its town grow while staving off the exodus of its brightest youth. And along with a dozen or so other communities in southwestern Minnesota, Marshall arrived at what for a moment seemed like a solution to both problems: encourage the Minnesota legislature to establish a four-year college, which southwestern Minnesota, alone of all the state's regions, lacked. The legislature approved the college, but left the decision about where the college would be located to a subsequent session.

Landing a four-year college constituted a crowning achievement of the town leaders' political efforts, who won their university against considerable odds. An incalculable and debatable combination of factors made the victory possible. It turned on Marshall's central geographic location, its new sewage system, and politics. But it also turned on the town leaders' political acumen, determination, and sacrifice.[15]

Marshall triumphed especially over its nearby rival, Redwood Falls. Its coup, never forgotten by Redwood Falls, meant that Marshall would double in population while surrounding towns of similar size remained static at five thousand or fewer. Pride filled the town's leaders. They had built a college in a cornfield.

But Southwest State College (later promoted by the mere change of name to University) proved the saying that historians write much of their text with irony. The new college, founded in 1967, wound up trampling the very hope that had created it. It did not retain Marshall's best and brightest young people, as planned. What's more, in most unanticipated fashion, the university's students and faculty soon paraded the shocking cultural changes and protests of the 1960s and early 1970s down Main Street. By 1971, the year the first class graduated, the town had discovered it had potted in its own soil an institution of strangers.

The college served up many bitter cultural potions to its hosts. Antiwar protests offered especially heavy draughts. On May 11, 1972, for example, 166 protesters were put in jail as Marshall joined the nation in criticizing Nixon's mining of the North Vietnamese ports.[16] Not since the Holiday Farmers had overrun the town some thirty-five years earlier had Marshall marched into the national headlines. With war protests, interracial conflicts, the burning of buildings, and a small but escalating drug trade, the town certainly got more than it bargained for. Liberal clothing styles and language daily rubbed salt in the wound of misunderstanding. Five years of aggressive and provocative activities by a unionizing faculty, who were intent on protecting their jobs and battling an unimaginative administration, both outraged and defied the understanding of a downtown business establishment that expected gratitude for its part in founding the college.

The college both declined and ascended during its first decade. Talk of its closing came and went, like the seasons themselves. The Twin Cities media had reported rumors of the school's closing before its buildings were even completed. All this did not undermine the fact that the college increased business revenues in Marshall, but it did damage the business leaders' sense of pride in their creation.

Meanwhile, with the university's drama keeping most eyes riveted, a small company in Marshall called Schwan's grew steadily, even stealthily. Throughout the 1970s, a multibillion-dollar food industry took shape, one that would eventually become the town's leading industry. Rooted in the conservative philosophy of its locally born owner, Marvin Schwan, and a collection of other local men he had gathered around himself, the company grew from a door-to-door seller of ice cream to a national supplier of frozen foods. Schwan's entered the frozen pizza business in 1970 and emerged at its top less than two decades later. (It includes the Tony's and Red Baron brands, with $542 million a year in sales.)

Despite the disruptive cultural changes of the era, Marshallites (who neither understood nor controlled the fate of either the university or Schwan's) had reason to be proud in the 1960s and 1970s. They appeared to have found the magic formula that served both economic growth and community strength. It rested on the progressive notion that good business and stable government (from which Marshall truly benefited) resulted in a good town. Local pride was enhanced by observations of the growing nationwide disillusionment with big-city life and a diffuse appreciation for "small is beautiful" and "back to the land" sentiments.[17] Boosters were often heard reiterating clichés about having "the best of both worlds."

DECLINE AMID PROSPERITY, PROSPERITY AMID DECLINE

In spite of some genuine successes, all was not roses with Marshall's economic progression. Growth implies that as some things are being born, others are dying. Thus, in the case of Marshall, as elsewhere, local historians are forced to tell a double-sided and more sensitive story as they approach the present. And autopsies on the living, as it were, are painful.

At an accelerating pace, Marshall in the 1960s began to enter into fuller and more direct contact with metropolitan markets. Census and state business reports illuminate these changes, which were occurring across the nation. The rate of change at work in all sectors of Marshall's economy and society make it "a community of strangers" and a servant of distant transforming forces.

The contrast in Marshall these days is between an expanding and mutating regional center and a surrounding ring of diminished farms and villages. This juxtaposition places a double burden on local historians. They are compelled to document two stories simultaneously. They must describe the declining countryside on the one hand and, on the other, characterize a regional center that, ever metamorphosed by the nearby metropolis, transforms the very countryside it claims to serve and represent. Each element of this reconstruction challenges historians to find numbers to confirm their hypotheses and words to broadcast their findings.

It fell to me, as a local and regional historian, to announce decline to the region. In two articles for the League of Minnesota Cities prior to the 1990 census and in a small book titled *The Decline of Rural Minnesota*, a colleague and I set forth the unwelcome message.[18] We contended that lead cities like Marshall (the last outposts of vitality in the countryside) were themselves perched on a melting iceberg.

The reasons for decline were manifest: between the 1950 and the 1990 census, national farming employment dropped from just under 8 million to a little over 3 million, and the number of farms dropped from 5.8 million to 2.1 million. The percentage of the rural workforce in agriculture dropped to 7.6 percent, as it correspondingly gained in manufacturing and services.[19] In Minnesota, between 1930 and 1960, the growth of the nonfarm population in unincorporated areas grew from 78,000 to 313,000, or from 5 percent to 11 percent of the total population.[20] By the 1980s, out-migration averaged 11 percent among all nonmetro counties, or those that lay beyond the ring of suburbs circling the Twin Cities, with a 17 percent loss of their eighteen-to-thirty-four-year-old population.[21]

An elemental law was at work: As farms get bigger and farm families smaller, rural population declines and rural towns shrink. As available goods, jobs, and other opportunities vanish or fail to keep pace with those available in the city, rural children go elsewhere to seek their fortunes.

Decline cannot be isolated. It jumps from farm to town, mutating as it goes. It spreads to hamlets and villages, which lose not just population but the remnants of their Main Streets. Small towns lose their banks, newspapers, and schools while retaining only bars and junk shops. They struggle to save hardware stores, coffee shops, and restaurants, the last havens of the daily news and gossip that cement a community together. Having exchanged schools for nursing homes, many towns appear to be settlements for the dying. Between 1990 and 1995, in more than a dozen counties in southwestern Minnesota, more people died than were born.[22] The old stand witness to the twilight of their towns, and local historians find themselves having to recount the death of their homes.

Decline eventually attacks regional centers, where it manifests itself in the end of the small family business and the decline of Main Street. By the 1980s, local historians of once-thriving regional centers could document by a simple stroll downtown not just the end of a way of doing business but also the end of a social class and the traditional leadership group drawn from it. The empty storefronts prompt the question of who will rule next. The answer, in Marshall, is public employees, including college teachers. These newcomers have taken the seats of lifelong locals everywhere in town—in the mayor's office, on the city council, and on school and hospital boards. Simply by recording the obvious, by announcing the changing of the guard, local historians tread on sensitive ground. Nevertheless, if my experience is any guide, many town people will appreciate the historian's candor.

In Marshall, like so many other Midwestern towns, Main Street seriously began to flounder in the 1970s. John Radzilowski offers this general assessment: "Main Street retained its viability with a cluster of public service establishments: library, post office, museum, public utility building, municipal building, and county courthouse. Specialized businesses serving small niches in the retail market no longer formed the Main Street of yesteryear with its full complement of businesses to serve every need; that has become a thing of the past."[23] The decline of Main Street coincided with the ascent of a commercial strip along East College Drive. Characterized by food services, gas stations, banks, and a variety of convenience stores, the strip steadily grew, drawing customers from the college and the growing residential areas nearby.[24] The downtown's decline was ensured by the building of a shopping mall in the 1970s at the east end of town, across East College Drive from the college.

But a grocery store, a national department store, and a discount store failed to anchor even the mall. The volume of customers simply wasn't great enough, and many shop spaces remained empty. In the early 1990s, ShopKo and Wal-Mart, which established themselves next to each other along the southern bypass of the town, superseded the mall. These chain stores—which appear to prosper by drawing from the whole region—are the assassins of small-town businesses. On close investigation, the local historian who keeps an ear cocked might find in time that the chains too might suffer insufficient volume of business when on-line commerce reaches its prime.

The roots of decline that local historians describe in southwestern Minnesota lie in the rural world at large. The volume of trade is insufficient to support the local community's multiplying wants and tastes. Since the introduction of the automobile, larger numbers of people have been traveling greater distances to fulfill expanding desires at cheaper prices. More and more of them shop and amuse themselves in Sioux Falls, Mankato, Willmar, and the Twin Cities. Consumers increasingly are shopping by mail and electronically, as the frequently circulating delivery vans make plain.

The dawning era of on-line shopping may prove more challenging to rural commerce than even catalogue shopping. The majority of people are shoppers first and citizens second: they are more sensitive to price than anything else. Franchise managers will benefit even less from loyalty than did their Main Street predecessors. Surely these revolutionary developments add lanes to the great highway of exchange between country and city. As technology invites rural people to participate in a global system of information creation and dissemination, it also permits spatial dissemination and consolidates the metropolitan control that increasingly denies local orders their autonomy.[25] Local and regional historians must assess the truth of commerce's triumph over community, culture, and politics.

The visionary and the historian, who converge by virtue of their preoccupation with the changing present, conjure a countryside with hardly a farm and towns with nary a store, except franchises of national chains serving community members and passersby equally. One need be no Cassandra to foresee a novel time in history when we have cities without an agora—a "community" without local markets in which to exchange goods, opinions, and gossip. Only a handful of random convenience stores, along with telephones, copiers, fax machines, e-mail, and video arcades, will serve local places' physical and social needs.

MORE FOR LESS, MORE WITH LESS

Marshall has not escaped this aspect of decline. Accounting in 1970 for approximately fourth-fifths of county sales revenues and slightly more than half of the county's $80 million in bank deposits, the town has been running on the treadmill of regional service. It must, if it is to survive, increasingly expand the range of its goods and services to the surrounding area.

Marshall's bankers, the commercial linchpin of the town, found they had to affiliate with banking chains to minimize the cost of operations and broaden their services to incorporate investment and other services in an increasingly competitive environment. They've had to carry their business farther afield. At the same time, they've had to strive to increase volume in a limited market. To expand business with established customers, they have to discount services.

Marshall's hospital and its physicians address similar economic factors in a corresponding way. They offer more and more medical services simply to keep pace with the profession and to satisfy a population insisting on these services. Marshall's doctors have approximately tripled in number over the past two decades. The hospital has expanded, adding a wellness facility, a residential living complex for the independent elderly, and a larger nursing home for long-term medical care giving. At the same time, health providers in Marshall have joined forces with a larger, regional medical complex, Affiliated Medical Services located in Willmar, seventy miles to the northeast of Marshall.

Lawyers and accountants, likewise marking the end of the one- and two-person office, have consolidated. They offer increased expertise in a specialized environment and find that only in consolidation can they handle the rivers of paperwork contemporary law requires, complex as it is. Law seems to be the twin of every important facet of this rapidly changing society. Wherever there is change, there is potential for dispute and the need for resolution. Defying stereotypes of the countryside as a straightforward place where "one's word and a handshake" suffices, rural areas grow lawyers. Law is a fertile field for local historians wishing to grasp the change under way, as individual practices and small, local firms wane and larger, more aggressive regional firms grow in cases, clients, and wealth, reflecting the transition from the local to regional, state, and national practice.

Government and public employees cause, and are consumed by, a growing storm of paper and regulations. Each legislative session and administrative directive fuels the emergence of a more convoluted and alien order in the countryside. The public health nurse and the social worker at the courthouse, the pollution control officer and the extension officer in the field, or the special education teacher and psychologist in the school are perpetrators and victims of the same bureaucratic order. Held accountable for an ever greater number of increasingly protected and demanding clients, they are transformed into valets for the auditors, bankers, hospital workers, and farmers. (How specialization and bureaucracy spread across a community and actually form a kind of rural environment would be a lovely study. A more moderate but worthwhile study would tell the story of the growth of public agencies in a single county courthouse.)

At the university in Marshall, the same tight-fitting pants chafe. With insufficient staffing, Southwest State University nevertheless must offer a range of programs and services identical to those of any other four-year university. It must respond to students' broadening academic and nonacademic desires, meeting expanding accreditation standards. Subject at all times to the whims of the governor and the legislature, it remains under the control of the state university system, which in the course of the past three decades has evolved from a single chancellor to an administrative staff of more than a hundred and a citizens' board that seeks to govern approximately forty institutions.[26]

As articulated in *The Decline of Rural Minnesota,* this rule of doing more with less commands the town:

> There is no end to requests for reports, evaluations, and implementations of new moral-social directives [in the college]. . . . There are emotionally exhausting and crippling budgetary about-faces, spawned by changing administrative orders, a fluctuating economy, and the vagaries of bi-annual state legislation. . . . One hears similar stories from regional businesses [especially those in road construction], law offices, medical clinics, and farms, especially at tax time. They too agonize as they try to keep up with an increasing flood of laws, demands, and specialization that engulfs their professions and their lives. Some remark that they find themselves outpaced by new technologies, increased demand for paperwork, ever-refined sensibilities. . . . Few, if any, believe that innovative and labor saving devices are doing away with old functions faster than new functions are appearing. The farmer escapes being harnessed to the plow to be chained to the pencil.[27]

The need to keep up is evident throughout Marshall's economy. Schwan's illustrates well the effect of national and international markets on rural economies. Staying abreast requires the company to participate in global markets. While hiring computer programmers from Bombay, it must sell sandwiches in Prague. Now the leading frozen pizza company in America, Schwan's must continue to develop new products.[28]

The local corn processing plant, Minnesota Corn Processors, also must deal with complex global markets. It has to find ways to turn corn into multiple products. Proving not every sea that is seen can be successfully sailed, this farmers' cooperative recently beached itself when, amid a major expansion, it guaranteed the price of a finished product without having secured the price of supplies. As a consequence, a significant part of its stock now belongs to agricultural giant Archer Daniels Midland.

Increasingly, local historians discover that national and even global realities underlie local phenomena. Telling local stories requires acknowledging distant forces. The story of finite places further joins the course of civilization itself. People, as well as limited resources, are forced to keep pace with a world whose possibilities multiply exponentially. To do more with less at breakneck speed causes frenzy. The sense of falling behind, of never quite doing enough, becomes a common feature of mental life in the idyllic countryside. Efficiency hasn't banished malingering or shoddy work any more than the sun has stopped rising and setting, and the countryside not only looks more and more like the metropolis, it feels, thinks, plays, and works that way too. To read the same outside control into our past denies us a history. Retrospectively, our entire story appears to belong to someone else—to the story of rise and control of a dominating metropolis, as John Borchert told of the Twin Cities' hegemony over almost all of Minnesota, western Wisconsin, the Dakotas, and much of Montana, and William Cronon told of Chicago's creation and dominance of a whole inland empire, reaching north to Michigan and Wisconsin, south to Kansas, and west to Iowa, southern Minnesota, and beyond.[29]

Marshall cannot do what a lead city by definition should do. Not only can it not lead; it simply can't keep up. From hospital and bank to bookstore, travel agency, and coffee shop, Marshall is not equipped to meet rising expectations. It can only scramble to keep a semblance of bringing urban civilization to the countryside. How else could it be for a medium-size depot town in a global age?

The countryside's audience is small, divided, and mixed. Aside from distinct but diminished farming neighborhoods—the ethnic victors of a century of competitive farming—the countryside has lost much of its own context and continuity. Relatives and neighbors have emigrated from weakening towns. More and more strangers, willing to travel greater distances for the sake of lower housing costs, inhabit towns depleted of the businesses, organizations, and associations they once had. Closures and mergers in town and country correspond to the weakening and vanishing of traditional rural communities and cultures associated with townships, farm groups, fair boards, and co-ops.

At the same time, accelerated economic, social, and cultural transformation deny coherence in regional centers like Marshall. Increased turnover and turbulence on every front strip them of audiences to whom local and regional historians could direct their work. In fact, insofar as Marshall is the model, a question imposes itself: Have the most vibrant and hopeful places in the declining countryside—regional centers—become for all intents and purposes communities of strangers?

Local and regional historians who have not sworn themselves to irrelevance must push toward the most controversial edges of their subjects. They must inquire into the practice of power. They must check the very pulse of power, the belief that one can make things happen, and record whether such blood flows at all in rural veins. Moreover, they must inquire whether local leaders, fatalists to the bone, have become robots of administrative directives.

This epoch imposes fresh themes and questions on local and regional historians. They are compelled to think about uncertain change, endless transformations, and incomprehensible metamorphoses. Unless local historians are to miss their hour, they must respond. They must try to measure in detail and depth the irreversible mutation dramatically upon us and still make their stories count to all who cherish the sustaining values of freedom and place.

CONCLUSION

The Plight of the Local Historian

The practice of writing local history can be viewed positively and negatively. Although I have espoused both views at times, I find neither adequate to describe what I have experienced as a practicing local historian over the last twenty years.

Positively, local historians can be seen as serving a distinct community. They can inform rural leaders about who inhabits the region, about what is happening to its institutions, emerging trends, and so on. They delineate the perimeters of the possible and impossible. They can offer protection to all but the most gullible, foolish, and desperate against preachers of rural development and sellers of Jerusalem artichokes. Furthermore, they can stimulate companies, co-ops, and towns to take action. When, for example, I announced "decline in southwestern Minnesota" at a major conference of the League of Minnesota Cities in 1988 and developed its varied implications in an ensuing publication—*The Decline of Rural Minnesota*—I spurred influential conversations in diverse political and economic quarters of the region. Aside from influencing Marshall's own civic discourse, the conversations included founders of Renville's new generation of cooperatives.

My subsequent book on the region's new immigrants, *To Call It Home,* also helped shape the region's dialogue over present and future conditions. When my colleagues and I identified the meatpacking industry and its turnover rate as the principal sources of immigrants in the region and of a range of social problems initially associated with them, we provided a basis for clear conversation about who was now among us. This information proved crucial for members of the education, housing, social work, and police communities.

From the experience of doing contemporary research—which I passionately exhort local historians to do—comes the exaltation of discovering that knowledge actually can set agendas and even break a faulty tablet or two. Different from those who promote economic development, who establish policy centers, or who coordinate rural coalitions, those who conduct, publish, and disseminate local and regional research can offer indispensable self-knowledge. And this type of knowledge (which is empirical and developed by continuous retrospective and projective inquiry and comparison) awakens a passion for understanding the compass of local action. In this way, local history serves the intelligence that frees the energy of local people to work in the dimensions of the possible. Committed to understanding the present and the changes that characterize it, local history proves a golden asset for all vital people of a place.

Local history can even impart a certain level of regional celebrity to its writers. And with that comes a degree of acceptance in a locale and a surrounding region, depending, of course, on the historians' reputation, ability to write, and use of the media. Speaking engagements become common fare, as do chicken dinners and roast beef suppers on an "eat and talk" speaking tour. At some point, local historians can constitute regional voices and be asked to represent the entire state, or even a larger area—which means larger stipends and more radio and television appearances. In time, historians might have the good fortune to begin to appear in a number of educational television documentaries and have select writings of theirs turned into documentaries. Along with all this comes an array of friends, acquaintances, and experiences, and the sense that one's work actually helps define a place.

What prestige local historians win for themselves, they may also win for any institutions with which they might be affiliated. They can even win for their home institution the reputation as a regional interpreter, which strengthens its hand politically. This was the notion I had in mind when I formed Southwest State University's Center for Rural and Regional Studies, which brings together three faculty members (focused on geography and rural and regional studies), an environmental educator, a journalist, and a handful of graduate students, and offers a rural and regional studies curriculum, a history center, a geographic-information studies laboratory, a small publisher, and an independent local and regional history society. Needless to say, once an idea takes institutional form, it gains an administrative, personnel, political, and ideational history of its own. At that point, historians have to guard their time, energy, and concentration for research and publications, forever remembering the discipline required to keep gathering and disseminating information.

Teaching also brings practitioners of local knowledge—be it history, rural studies, geography, or environmental studies—their share of bliss. Teaching means showing students how to create. One's own creations can serve as texts and illustrations of local inquiry. Students' work can be transformed into publications and conferences. In the process, students learn that their own region is worthy of study and that learning depends on getting one's own feet muddy. Beyond that, they discover that knowledge is made, and they can take pride in making it. The nearby field becomes their laboratory, making contemporary change a possible topic. And all this has the consequence of freeing students from rote textbook learning and elevating them to being creators of historical records.

Exultant surprise awaits historians who venture into the present. Aside from unexpectedly large and intense audiences, the historical perspective wins a claim to relevance in a protean age. As historians are recognized, their desire to do more work grows, and they develop a fresh concern for the implications of what they write. They identify with their subjects and find themselves, perhaps proudly, with a passion for what by almost every external measure is minuscule. Their work—be it a history of a flood, an environmental study of a county, or documentation of Civil War Veterans' or women's roles in the early years of a town—gives them a voice. Its gives them a laboratory and a community of their own.

Yet, the screw turns the other way as well. Local historians are not strangers to negative conditions, experiences, and consequences. Their commitment to the micro-landscapes in an era of macro forces leaves them always embattled as they move back and forth between the big and the small. They read the best of such generalizing regional books as historian William Cronon's *Nature's Metropolis,* geographers John Hudson's *Making the Corn Belt,* and John Borchert's *America's Northern Heartland.* They benefit from analytic regional discussions like Andrew Cayton and Peter Onuf's *The Midwest and the Nation.*[1] They learn from the explanatory power of comprehensive discussions and narratives. Nevertheless, at least as I would idealize the coming generation of local historians, they plot rebellion against the hegemonic characteristics of macro-regionalism. Generalizing sociology and the politics of rural development elicit the same reaction from them. They will not have a locale subsumed, annexed, and silenced by a region.

The new breed I imagine wants a positivism that does not and cannot add up. They want a history of the particular that finally defies systematization. They join de Tocqueville, who wrote in *Democracy in America:*

> General ideas are no proof of the strength, but rather of the insufficiency of the human intellect; for there are in nature no beings exactly alike, no things precisely identical; no rules indiscriminately and alike applicable to several objects at once. The chief merit of general ideas is that they enable the human mind to pass a rapid judgment on a great many objects at once; but on the other hand, the notions they convey are never other than incomplete, and they always cause the mind to lose as much in accuracy as it gains in comprehensiveness.[2]

My ideal local historians reject overarching explanations for microhistories, instead staying true to details, anecdotes, and peculiarities of place. They prefer case studies to academic theory. On the other hand, simultaneous with the passion to defend the integrity of the local against macro-regionalism comes the recognition that since its inception, the entire rural order has been shaped by metropolitan goods, engines, and forces they describe.

If contrariness is the occupational vice, intellectual discontent is the common condition. Pain derives from the impossibility of the local historian's position, which paradoxically may constitute the proof of its integrity. Local historians (as I idealize them) are forever conscious that they, as the writer, the politician, and the propagandist, fabricate the place they write about. Specifically, as they anguish, they are always dealing in intellectual contraband. They forever use examples, ideas, sensibilities, and ideologies from other places and times in elucidating their own locale. Their supposed home brews made from borrowed recipes render them intellectual bootleggers of a sort. (I confess to constantly adapting themes and approaches from European intellectual and cultural history in order to explore southwestern Minnesota.) They forever must ask how capricious and arbitrary is their making of a place.

Writing itself also causes discomfort. As much as the practice of local history might gain the local historian recognition, the work is lonely work. Companionship at times amounts to no more than a handful of colleagues and friends. Yet, the practice of writing local history fails to provide the benefits of monastic solitude. It lacks a common rule and communal support. It does not always find a comfortable home at a university, which contains a medley of competing programs often dependent on changing administrations and precarious and vacillating funding. The singular loyalties of local history invariably smart in the hands of power. Its practitioners do not dance easily with local commercial enterprises or ever fashionable but superficial regional developers. Local historians do not necessarily agree with the redemptive missions of many regional agencies, nor do their interests square with canons of prestigious national and cosmopolitan knowledge. Philanthropic foundations are likely to dismiss the work of local historians as insufficiently applied and therapeutic in light of their own mission to cure social and economic problems.

But these are only the external dimensions of the solitude that accompanies the local historian. The deeper loneliness arises from having a fidelity to a subject about which the ever imposing external world cares little. Local historians cherish vanishing places, and the more they cherish their subjects, the more they recognize how little others care about them and how helpless they are to preserve them from the ravages of time. Time undoes and overruns the memories of a place—the details of a childhood bedroom, the voices of celebrating neighbors, the backbreaking labor that went with putting up the hay from the first cutting of a wet spring, and all the sounds, sensations, fears, and madness of the countryside of old. Generations, their communities and landscapes, their homes and favorite places, vanish.

Local historians recognize the fragility of their subjects, which are awash in decline and transformed by turbulence—and even possibly prey to corporate interest and political ambition. Localities everywhere, they sense, are on the verge of oblivion. Only a handful of documents and one's own passionate effort stake places to a crumbling bank. Few books last the year. Local historians know that unless God shares their passion for details, time will dissolve past and historian alike. Death, as they are constantly aware, is the final enemy not just of life but of memory as well.

On out-of-the-way shores, local historians ply their craft. Their burden is giving form to little places in an era of massive forces and encircling generalizations. Like folklorists or ethnographers, they strive to keep alive in memory ways of life and habits of mind that civilization no longer countenances. And their reward for doing this is carrying out a singular duty to a singular place. Their passion for the meanings of small things forces them to deliberate not just on the fate of their beloved places, but of all things human. Their faithfulness to home is a compass in a great and shifting sea.

Although it forever moves between the ragged edge of contemporary change and the cutting blade of time, local history compensates its practitioners with the blessing of preserving other lives, places, and times. Surely, there are less worthy callings than giving fresh forms, however transitory they be, to the work and complex ways of human beings.

At times I have embraced these positive and negative views, but my mind, when more generous and reasonable, sets them aside. Then, they strike me as melodramatic. Aging, a process that local historians well know, leads one to acceptance—gratitude for lesser but more sustainable conditions. One worries with age more about feet and the ground they stand on than the cerebral thought that supposedly fills one's head. Historians, if their studies have taught them anything, know that all things have temporal and material bounds.

But there is more consolation than discouragement in the local historian's common lot. Local history brings with it a passion and mission. How can one measure the privilege of being joined in a unique conversation with passing generations? The local historian, caught up with a hundred questions and topics that need exploration and exposition, need never feel ennui. One day I imagine what a history of insects would resemble, the next I wish to consider the different types of aging that now characterize the region, and the day after that I try to encourage a local specialist in soils to imagine the possibility of a history of bacteria.

Regional narratives, born of historians' insatiable curiosity, are the very sinews of community, providing invisible sources of strength and vitality. At the Center for Rural and Regional Studies, our work almost seamlessly reaches from books and essays to hypotheses and possibilities to developing regional river maps, bicycle tours, or a travel guide organized around ecological, geological, and ethnic themes. Local historians' driving ambition is to record the manifold realities of the place one calls home.

As local historians give birth to their own regions, so they appreciate the works of others who do the same for their locales. In the summer of 2000, in Fort Benton, Montana, along the Missouri River—traveled and described by Lewis and Clark—a local journalist, Joel Overholser, transformed his enthusiasm and archives into an independent research center for a unique town that stood as a gateway north and south, east and west, for an expanding nation.[3] A few weeks later, along the Atlantic, I read naturalist Jennifer Ackerman's *Notes from the Shore*. She provided me with a rich guide to Cape Henlopen and Lewes, Delaware, and their dunes and beaches. She reminded me again of the infinity of small things, a sense local historians must develop and a sense that deepens over time. She writes that in the tiny, watery capillaries of a mere handful of sand "there is a riot of life."[4] There is equally a riot of life in every prairie town and within the walls of every individual farmhouse. Travel and reading prosper as a sense of local history abounds.

All history is local. Every place is a universe unto itself. Yet home remains the microcosm in which we learn and know all we will ever learn and know of fellow humans and the world at large. And when joy subsides, there remains a puzzling delight somewhere between the exceptions we cherish and the determining sciences we cannot ignore. To be without resolution can also satisfy.

There is no complete history, yet local historians provide a passionate attachment to concrete places in an age when home and place, locale and landscape, are in a state of great mutation. This tension provides the basis for an ever deepening conversation. It provides fresh ways of researching, thinking, writing, and disseminating knowledge. It offers a substance, integrity, and individuality that neither contemporary academic nor ideological discourse can provide. One hundred good historians committed to one hundred contemporary local subjects might inspire a renaissance in rethinking home.

Notes

INTRODUCTION

1. For a history of the American Association for State and Local History, see their commemorative *Local History, National Heritage* (Nashville, Tenn.: American Association for State and Local History, 1991). For a useful guide to writing about diverse elements of local history, see the association's publication by David Kyvig and Myron Marty, *Nearby History: Exploring the Past around You* (Nashville, Tenn.: American Association for State and Local History, 1982). Not sharing its equation of state and local history, and accenting the difference between local and state, macro-regional, and national history, I entertain a more problematic view in which facts and values, locale and nation, and history and heritage are, if not always at odds, abidingly in need of critical reflection. Representative of this perspective is Michael Kammen, *In the Past Lane: Historical Reflections on American Culture* (New York: Oxford University Press, 1997), esp. 161–212. It was most influentially articulated for me by the French regionalist Guy Thuillier and his colleague Jean Tulard in *Histoire locale et régionale* (Paris: Presses Universitaires de France, 1992). See my review of Thuillier's work in *Review of Social History* (winter 1993): 375–80.

2. For two pathbreaking works from geographers on place and landscape and their transformation in the contemporary era, see Yi-Fu Tuan, *Topophilia: A Study of Environmental Perception, Attitudes, and Values* (New York: Columbia University Press, 1974), and D. W. Meinig, ed., *The Interpretation of Ordinary Landscapes* (Oxford: Oxford University Press, 1979).

3. Paul Valéry, "Remarks on Intelligence," *Politics and Intelligence* (New York: Pantheon Books, 1962), 79. The italics are his.

4. Constance McLaughlin Green, "The Value of Local History," cited in Carol Kammen, *The Pursuit of Local History : Readings on Theory and Practice*

(Walnut Creek, Calif.: American Association for State and Local History, 1996), 90–91.

5. For an introduction to thinking about nostalgia, see Fred Davis, *Yearning for Yesterday: A Sociology of Nostalgia* (New York: The Free Press, 1979).

6. Charles Péguy, "À nos amis, à nos abonnés," *Oeuvres poétiques complètes* (Paris: Editions Gallimard, 1957), 48–49.

7. Lewis Mumford, "The Value of Local History," cited in Kammen, *Pursuit of Local History,* 88.

8. Ibid.

9. For a useful introduction to environmental history, see Dan Flores, "Place: An Argument for Bioregional History," *Environmental History Review* (winter 1994): 1–18; for additional works, see "Acknowledgments and Sources," this volume.

10. For a single example, see Carlo Ginzburg, *The Cheese and the Worms: The Cosmos of a Sixteenth-Century Miller,* trans. John and Anne Tedeschi (Baltimore: Johns Hopkins University Press, 1980); for additional works, see "Acknowledgments and Sources," this volume.

11. Joseph Amato and John Radzilowski, *Community of Strangers: Change, Turnover, Turbulence, and the Transformation of a Midwestern Country Town* (Marshall, Minn.: Crossings Press, 1999).

12. Richard Davies, *Main Street Blues: The Decline of Small-Town America* (Columbus: Ohio State University Press, 1998).

13. Valéry, "The Crisis of the Mind" (1919), in *Politics and Intelligence,* 35.

14. Thuillier and Tulard, *Histoire locale et régionale,* 119.

15. This observation is part of the force of Guy Thuillier's insight into the conditions of the local historian; see esp. Thuillier and Tulard, *Histoire locale et régionale.*

16. Valéry, "The Crisis of the Mind," 23.

17. For recent anthropological definitions of region, see Eric Wold, *Europe and the People without History* (Berkeley: University of California Press, 1982); John and Jean Comaroff, *Ethnography and Historical Imagination* (Boulder, Colo.: Westview Press, 1992); and Richard Fardon, ed., *Localizing Strategies: Regional Traditions of Ethnographic Writing* (Washington, D.C.: Smithsonian Institution Press, 1990).

18. Joseph Wood Krutch, "New England and the Desert," *The Best Nature Writings of Joseph Wood Krutch* (New York: William Morrow and Co., 1969), 93.

19. Jeremy Black's *Maps and History: Constructing Images of the Past* (New Haven: Yale University Press, 1997), Dava Sobel's *Longitude* (New York: Penguin, 1995), and Anne Marie Claire Godlewska's *Geography Unbound: French Geographic Science from Cassini to Humboldt* (Chicago: University of Chicago Press, 1999) are three recent testimonies to the notion that places are discovered, imagined, invented, and contrived by mapmakers as well as historians.

20. In addition to books listed in "Acknowledgment and Sources," an excellent example of an ecological work based on an ecology and a distinct aspect of a region is Dan Flores, *Caprock Canyonlands: Journeys into the Heart of the Southern Plains* (Austin: University of Texas Press, 1990).

21. See, for example, Donald Worster, *Under Western Skies: Nature and History in the American West* (Oxford: Oxford University Press, 1992); Patricia Limerick, *The Legacy of Conquest: The Unbroken Past of the American West* (New York: W. W. Norton, 1987); and Richard White, *A New History of the American West* (Norman: University of Oklahoma Press, 1991). Also of use to historians of the West is Walter Nugent, "Where Is the American West? Report on a Survey," *Montana* 42, no. 3 (summer 1992): 2–23.

22. In his essay "Reading the Landscape," prominent geographer D. W. Meinig shows the importance of place in the thought of two of the contrasting founders of landscape studies: the British thinker W. G. Hoskins, and the American thinker and founder of the journal *Landscape,* J. B. Jackson (*Interpretation of Ordinary Landscapes,* 195–244).

23. The role of the invention of tradition was first articulated by Eric Hobsbawm, *The Invention of Tradition* (Cambridge: Cambridge University Press, 1983). Its influence is seen in introductory pages of Witold Rybczynski, *Home: A Short History of an Idea* (New York: Viking, 1986), esp. 9–10, and Joseph Amato and Anthony Amato, "Minnesota, Real and Imagined," *Daedalus* (summer 2000): 55–80.

CHAPTER 1. A PLACE CALLED HOME

1. Throughout this essay, I have drawn on Gaston Bachelard's discussion of home in *The Poetics of Space* (Boston: Beacon Press, 1969).

2. This idea was adopted from David Sopher as he was indirectly quoted in the introduction of D. W. Meinig, ed., *The Interpretation of Ordinary Landscapes* (New York: Oxford University Press, 1979), 3.

3. This incident became the source of my book *Guilt and Gratitude: A Study of the Origins of Contemporary Conscience* (Westport, Conn.: Greenwood Press, 1982).

4. Those nineteen counties are Brown, Chippewa, Cottonwood, Jackson, Kandiyohi, Lac Qui Parle, Lincoln, Lyon, Martin, Meeker, Murray, Nobles, Pipestone, Redwood, Renville, Rock, Swift, Watonwan, and Yellow Medicine.

5. John R. Tester, *Minnesota's Natural Heritage: An Ecological Perspective* (Minneapolis: University of Minnesota Press, 1995).

6. James Malin, *History and Ecology: Studies of the Grasslands* (Lincoln: University of Nebraska Press, 1984), 220.

7. Ibid., 238.

8. Scott Anfinson, *Southwestern Minnesota Archaeology: Twelve Thousand Years in a Prairie Lake Region* (St. Paul: Minnesota Historical Society Press, 1997), 9.

9. Ibid., 13.

10. Scott Anfinson, "The Prehistory of the Prairie Lake Region in the Northeastern Plains" (Ph.D. diss., University of Minnesota, 1987).

11. For the history of the metropolis's shaping of the countryside, see John C. Hudson, *Plains Country Towns* (Minneapolis: University of Minnesota Press, 1985); John Borchert, *America's Northern Heartland: An Economic and Historical Geography of the Upper Midwest* (Minneapolis: University of Minnesota

Press, 1987); William Cronon, *Nature's Metropolis: Chicago and the Great West* (New York: W. W. Norton, 1991); and Joseph Amato and John W. Meyer, *The Decline of Rural Minnesota* (Marshall, Minn.: Crossings Press, 1993). Borchert also contains a useful discussion of different factors forming and integrating a region; see *America's Northern Heartland,* 3–23.

12. Molly Rozum, "Grasslands Grown" (Ph.D. diss., University of North Carolina, 2001).

CHAPTER 2. GRASSES, WATERS, AND MUSKRATS

1. Walter Prescott Webb made this argument in *The Great Plains* (New York: Grosset and Dunlap, 1931).

2. See Alfred Crosby, *The Columbian Exchange: The Biological Consequences of 1492* (Westport, Conn.: Greenwood Press, 1972); idem, *Ecological Imperialism: The Biological Expansion of Europe, 900–1900* (Cambridge: Cambridge University Press, 1986).

3. George Catlin, *Letters and Notes on the Manners, Customs, and Conditions of the North American Indians: Written during Eight Years' Travel (1832–1839),* vol. 2 (1844; reprint, New York: Dover Publications, 1973), 256.

4. See Joseph A. Amato, *Victims and Values: A History and a Theory of Suffering* (New York: Praeger, 1990).

5. See Patricia Limerick, *The Legacy of Conquest: The Unbroken Past of the American West* (New York: W. W. Norton, 1987), and Daniel Worster, *Under Western Skies: Nature and History in the American West* (Oxford: Oxford University Press, 1992).

6. See Daniel Worster, ed., *The Ends of the Earth* (Cambridge: Cambridge University Press, 1988); Philip Terrie, "Recent Works in Environmental History," *American Studies International* 27, no. 2 (October 1989): 42–65. Additional works on the transformation of the American landscape by native and European peoples are Dan Flores, "Bison Ecology and Bison Diplomacy: The Southern Plains from 1800 to 1850," *Journal of American History* 78 (September 1991): 465–85; James Sherow, "Working the Geodialectic: High Plains Indians and Their Horses in the Region of the Arkansas River Valley, 1800–1870," *Environmental History Review* 16 (summer 1992): 61–84; and Stephen Pyne, *Fire in America: A Cultural History of Wildland and Rural Fire* (Seattle: University of Washington Press, 1997), 66–122.

7. Southwest State University faculty and community members affiliated with the Center for Rural and Regional Studies have published an interdisciplinary study of the county immediately to the south of the university: Anthony Amato, Janet Timmerman, and Joseph Amato, eds., *Draining the Great Oasis: An Environmental History of Murray County, Minnesota* (Marshall, Minn.: Crossings Press, 2001). It comprises seventeen essays covering topics such as geology, soils, wetlands, plants, mammals, birds, native prairie, drainage roads, weeds, and barns.

For foundation work from the previous decade stressing the interaction between humans and environments, see William Cronon, *Changes in the Land: Indians, Colonists, and the Ecology of New England* (New York: Hill and Wang,

1985); Timothy Silver, *A New Face of the Countryside: Indians, Colonists, and Slaves in South Atlantic Forests, 1500–1800* (Cambridge: Cambridge University Press, 1990); and John Mack Faragher, *Sugar Creek: Life on the Illinois Prairie* (New Haven: Yale University Press, 1986).

8. See Robert Delort, *Les animaux ont une histoire* (Paris: Éditions du Seuil, 1984).

9. According to the files of Alan Woolworth, an anthropologist from the Minnesota Historical Society, it appears that before white settlement, the population of grizzly bears extended from the Rockies to the Minnesota River. A headline in the *St. Cloud Democrat* (August 25, 1864) announced, "A Great Bear Hunt: Five Bears Killed: The Days of Boone and Crockett Eclipsed." The article told of the slaughter of three cubs shot out of a tree.

10. Big game were virtually nonexistent by the time of permanent white settlement in southwestern Minnesota. One period account states that in the 1860s, buffalo could still be found after a three-hour ride to Hanley Falls (Carl and Amy Narvestad, *A History of Yellow Medicine County, Minnesota, 1872–1972* [Granite Falls, Minn.: Yellow Medicine County Historical Society, 1972], 122).

11. Ibid., 128. As late as 1921, one clam-digging crew sold twenty-eight tons of shells to the Muscatine button factory for twenty-one dollars per ton, a low price for the time. The game and fish department then banned clamming in the Minnesota River between the Lac Qui Parle and Yellow Medicine Rivers for five years to allow clam populations to recover, and I suspect it was never resumed thereafter. Turtles were also harvested, but less profitably.

12. Ibid., 125. In the years studied, the most common animal caught in traplines was the skunk. Many a farm boy was sent home from school after checking his traplines in the morning and getting bathed in the stench.

13. For a study of the grasshopper plagues in Minnesota, see Annette Atkins, *Harvest of Grief: Grasshopper Plagues and Public Assistance in Minnesota, 1873–1878* (St. Paul: Minnesota Historical Society Press, 1984).

14. Pipestone mayor Barbara Hansen, lecture at Southwest State University, Marshall, Minnesota, March 5, 1999.

15. Cited in U.S. Department of Agriculture, *Grass: The Yearbook of Agriculture, 1948* (Washington, D.C.: Government Printing Office, 1948), 6.

16. Richard Manning morally assesses what he takes to be the awful cost of substituting wheat and corn for the natural grasses of the plains in *Grassland: The History, Biology, Politics, and Promise of the American Prairie* (New York: Penguin, 1997). Representing an alternative approach is Geoff Cunfer's "Common Ground: The American Grassland, 1870–1970" (Ph.D. diss., University of Texas, 1999). Cunfer bases his work on a number of case studies from the Great Plains.

17. C. P. Barnes, "Environment of Natural Grassland," in *Grass,* 45.

18. For the soils of the region, see J. L. Anderson, D. F. Grigal, and T. H. Cooper, *Soils and Landscapes of Minnesota,* rev. ed. (St. Paul: Minnesota Extension Service, 1996). For a general discussion of soils, see Edward Hyams, *Soil and Civilization* (New York: Harper and Row, 1976); U.S. Department of Agriculture, *Soils and Men: Yearbook of Agriculture* (Washington, D.C.: Government

Printing Office, 1938); idem, *Soil: Yearbook of Agriculture* (Washington, D.C.: Government Printing Office, 1955). For a recent example of the living quality of the soils, see J. A. Sandor and N. S. Each, "Significance of Ancient Agricultural Soils for Long-Term Agronomic Studies and Sustainable Agricultural Research," *Agronomy Journal* 83, no. 1 (January–February, 1991): 29.

19. David Costello, *The Prairie World* (New York: Thomas Y. Crowell, 1969), 63.

20. John R. Tester, *Minnesota's Natural Heritage: An Ecological Perspective* (Minneapolis: University of Minnesota Press, 1995), 132.

21. Ibid., 133.

22. Allan Bogue, *From Prairie to Corn Belt: Farming on the Illinois and Iowa Prairies in the Nineteenth Century* (Chicago: University of Chicago Press, 1963), 3.

23. L. R. Moyer, "The Prairie Flora of Southwestern Minnesota," *Bulletin of the Minnesota Academy of Sciences* 3 (1910). For Moyer's life and writing, see Edmund Bray, "Surveying the Seasons on the Minnesota Prairies: L. R. Moyer of Montevideo," *Minnesota History* (summer 1982), 72–82. Moyer approached compilation of such an inventory when he divided the region's plants into the following groups: (1) the upland prairie flora; (2) the wetland and marsh flora; (3) the prairie meadow flora around marshes and between hills; (4) the alkali flora on level, saline prairies; (5) the valley flora where there is good drainage and plenty of moisture; (6) the bluff flora where the soil is dry and xerophytic plants abound; (7) the rock flora on gneiss or granitic rocks where the soil is shallow and conditions are drier; and (8) the bog flora around prairie springs. See L. R. Moyer and O. G. Dale, eds., *Chippewa and Lac Qui Parle County History* (Indianapolis: n.p., 1916), 68–86.

24. Cited in Philip Shabecoff, *A Fierce Green Fire: The American Environmental Movement* (New York: Hill and Wang, 1993), 57.

25. Cited in Mrs. Hester Lynch Piozzi (Salisbury), *Anecdotes of the Late Samuel Johnson* (1786; reprint, Cambridge: Cambridge University Press, 1925).

26. Edmund Bray and Martha Bray, eds. *Joseph N. Nicollet on the Plains and Prairies* (St. Paul: Minnesota Historical Society Press, 1976), 60.

27. Scott Anfinson, *Southwestern Minnesota Archaeology: Twelve Thousand Years in a Prairie Lake Region* (St. Paul: Minnesota Historical Society Press, 1997), 123. Also see Anfinson, *Prairie, Lakes, and People: The Archaeology of Southwestern Minnesota,* Rural and Regional Essay Series (Marshall, Minn.: Society for the Study of Local and Regional History, 1999). This work belongs to a series of booklets published by the Society for the Study of Local and Regional History in cooperation with the Center for Rural and Regional Studies at Southwest State University. The name of the series was changed in 1998 from Historical Essays on Rural Life to the Rural and Regional Essay Series.

28. Quoted in Kelly Kindscher, *Edible Wild Plants of the Prairie: An Ethnobotanical Guide* (Lawrence: University of Kansas Press, 1987), 1.

29. Bray and Bray, eds., *Joseph N. Nicollet,* 69.

30. Aldo Leopold, *A Sand County Almanac* and *Sketches Here and There* (1949; reprint, New York: Oxford University Press, 1987), 27.

31. For an introductory discussion of the uses of fire, see Pyne, *Fire in America,* 66–99, and John C. Hudson, *Making the Corn Belt: A Geographical History of Middle Western Agriculture* (Bloomington: Indiana University Press, 1994), 16–30.

32. Pyne, *Fire in America,* 84–85.

33. Joseph Amato and Janet Timmerman, eds., *At the Headwaters: The 1993 Flood in Southwestern Minnesota* (Marshall, Minn.: Minnesota Conservation Corps / Southwest State University Flood Recovery Project, 1995).

34. For a guide to wetlands, see Milton Weller, *Freshwater Marshes: Ecology and Wildlife Management* (Minneapolis: University of Minnesota Press, 1994).

35. For an introduction to the history of drainage, see David Nass, "The Rural Experience," *Minnesota in a Century of Change* (St. Paul: Minnesota Historical Society Press, 1989), esp. 130–31.

36. See Scott Anfinson, "The Prehistory of the Prairie Lake Region in the Northeastern Plains," (Ph.D. diss., University of Minnesota, 1987), esp. 3–5. On the Prairie Pothole Region, see Arnold Van Der Valk, ed., *Northern Prairie Wetlands* (Ames: Iowa State University Press, 1989), 11.

37. For a guide to aquatic plants and their seasonal variations, see Steve Eggers and Donald Reed, *Wetland Plants and Plant Communities of Minnesota and Wisconsin* (St. Paul: Army Corps of Engineers, 1987), and Harold Kantrud, John Millar, and Arnold Van Der Valk, "Vegetation of Wetlands," in *Northern Prairie Wetlands,* 132–87.

38. Paul Miller and Francis Clark, "Water and Micro-Organisms," in *Water: The Yearbook of Agriculture, 1955,* ed. Paul Miller and Francis Clark (Washington, D.C.: Government Printing Office, 1955), 32; Harry B. Humphrey, "Climate and Plant Diseases," in *Climate and Man* (Washington, D.C.: Government Printing Office, 1941), 499–502; James Hyslop, "Insects and the Weather," ibid., 503–16. For a book on the influence of climate on the resource base and the social organization of indigenous peoples, see Douglas Bamforth, *Ecology and Human Organization on the Great Plains* (New York: Plenum Press, 1988).

39. See Carl Ernst and Lee French, "Mammals of Southwestern Minnesota," *Journal of the Minnesota Academy of Science* 43 (1977): 128–33.

40. See Paul Errington, *Muskrat Populations* (Ames: Iowa State University Press, 1963).

41. Tester, *Minnesota's Natural Heritage,* 171–72.

42. In one year he shipped out nine thousand hides. See Janet Timmerman, *Draining the Great Oasis: Claiming New Agricultural Land in Murray County, 1910–1915,* Historical Essays on Rural Life (Marshall, Minn.: Society for the Study of Local and Regional History, 1993), 3.

43. George Chamberlain, "Muskrats, Politics, Religion," in *Illustrative History of Jackson County, Minnesota,* ed. A. P. Rose (Jackson: n.p., 1910), 313.

44. "The Omaha Indians, for example, were known to determine the route of their summer buffalo hunt not by where they would find buffalo, but by the location of prairie turnips and other wild food" (Kindscher, *Edible Wild Plants,* 4).

45. Forty years ago, Waldo Wedel noted in *Prehistoric Man on the Great Plains* (Norman: University of Oklahoma Press, 1961) that the Plains Indians

and their environment had not occasioned a full study (p. 293), and that essentially remains the case today. For a survey of recent literature on the buffalo and the plains environment, see Dan Flores, *The Natural West: Environmental History in the Great Plains and Rocky Mountains* (Norman: University of Oklahoma Press, 2001), 50–70, 215–22.

46. The Santee Dakota, a name commonly used to denote the Eastern Dakota, "occupied a mixed ecological zone transitional between the Woodlands and the Plains," according to Alan and Nancy Woolworth. See their indispensable article "Eastern Dakota Settlement and Subsistence Patterns Prior to 1851," *Minnesota Archaeologist* 39, no. 70 (May 1980): 71.

47. *St. Paul Pioneer Press,* October 21, 1863. Alan Woolworth of the Minnesota Historical Society graciously opened to me his rich files—composed of newspaper articles and pages from county histories—from which I draw some of the following material.

48. The complex question of who occupied the prairie, and how and when southwestern Minnesota was home to a succession of peoples who entered the prairie, is still highly controversial. W. Raymond Wood makes this clear in his review of literature, "The Plains-Lakes Connection: Reflections from a Western Perspective," *Reprints in Anthropology* 31 (Lincoln, Neb.: J & L Reprint Company, 1985), 1–8.

49. Quote from Thomas Williamson, a missionary who, in 1835, began to live among the Sisseton and Wahpeton bands of the Lac Qui Parle region, cited in Woolworth and Woolworth, "Eastern Dakota Settlement," 76. Another useful survey of historic Dakota subsistence settlement patterns, based on Samuel Pond's *The Dakotas or Sioux in Minnesota as They Were in 1834* (St. Paul: Minnesota Historical Society Press, 1908), is Mary Whelan, "Late Woodland Subsistence and Settlement Size in the Mille Lacs Area," in *The Woodland Tradition in the Western Great Lakes: Papers Presented to Elden Johnson* (Minneapolis: n.p., 1990), 55–75.

50. Thomas Williamson cited in Woolworth and Woolworth, "Eastern Dakota Settlement," 76.

51. Pond, *The Dakotas as They Were,* 27–31.

52. Cited in Kindscher, *Edible Wild Plants,* 4.

53. Narvestad, *History of Yellow Medicine County,* 33–34.

54. Amos Bruce, "Report of the Commissioner of Indian Affairs," cited in *1842 Message from the President of the United States to the Two Houses of Congress at the Commencement of the Third Session of the Twenty-seventh Congress* (Washington, D.C.: Thomas Allen, 1842), 427–28.

55. Ibid., 428.

56. Ibid., 429.

57. None of the foregoing, however, suggests that muskrats were food only for Plains Indians. I had a cousin in St. Clair Shores, Michigan, a suburb of Detroit, who in the 1930s trapped and regularly ate muskrats, or "marsh rabbits," as they are commonly called. A useful essay on the deep historical connections between the Indians of woods and prairie is Michael Michlovic, "Northern Plains-Woodland Interaction in Prehistory," in *The Woodland Tradition,* 45–54. See also Mary Whelan, "Late Woodland Subsistence," ibid., 55–75; Eric Grim,

"Chronology and Dynamics of Vegetation Change in the Prairie-Woodlands Region of Southern Minnesota, U.S.A.," *The New Phytologist* 93 (1983): 311–50.

58. Cited in A. E. Tasker, *Early History of Lincoln County* (Lake Benton, Minn.: News Print, 1936), 204.

CHAPTER 3. THE RULE OF MARKET AND THE LAW OF THE LAND

1. Daniel Worster, ed., *The Ends of the Earth: Perspectives on Modern Environmental History* (Cambridge: Cambridge University Press, 1988), 15.

2. William Cronon, *Nature's Metropolis: Chicago and the Great West* (New York: W. W. Norton, 1991); John Borchert, *America's Northern Heartland: An Economic and Historical Geography of the Upper Midwest* (Minneapolis: University of Minnesota Press, 1987). See also John Radzilowski, *Prairie Town: A History of Marshall, Minnesota, 1872–1997* (Marshall, Minn.: Lyon County Historical Society, 1997), which shows that a fair amount of southwestern Minnesota grain went directly to Chicago.

3. On the automobile in southwest Minnesota, see Randy Abbott, Jr., *The Automobile Comes to Southwest Minnesota,* Historical Essays on Rural Life (Marshall, Minn.: Society for the Study of Local and Regional History, 1993); Michael Berger, *The Devil's Wagon in God's Country* (Hamden, Conn.: Shoe String Press, 1979).

4. John C. Hudson, *Plains Country Towns* (Minneapolis: University of Minnesota Press, 1985), esp. 9–10, 70–85.

5. Almost all the towns in southwestern Minnesota were conceived on the drafting boards of remote companies. Even the existing plans of tiny pre-railroad river towns, county seats, and hamlets were dramatically transformed by the coming of the railroad. The importance of the railroad for Marshall, Pipestone, and other southwestern Minnesota towns is demonstrated by John Radzilowski, *Prairie Town,* and Alan Woolworth, *The Genesis and Construction of the Winona and St. Peter Railroad, 1858–1873,* Rural and Regional Essays Series (Marshall, Minn.: Society for the Study of Local and Regional History, 2000).

6. Hudson, *Plains Country Towns,* 146–48.

7. Hal Barron, *Mixed Harvest: The Second Great Transformation in the Rural North, 1870–1930* (Chapel Hill: University of North Carolina Press, 1997), 8.

8. Ibid., 9.

9. John C. Hudson, *Making the Corn Belt: A Geographical History of Middle Western Agriculture* (Bloomington: Indiana University Press, 1994).

10. The issue of when the farm depression actually began, in the 1920s or the 1930s, can be resolved only by local analysis. For a local analysis of the farm economy in the 1920s, see Paul VanMevern, *In Search of the 1920s Farm Depression: A Study of Rock Lake Township, Lyon County, Minnesota,* Historical Essays on Rural Life (Marshall, Minn.: Society for the Study of Local and Regional History, 1994).

11. See Deborah Fink, *Agrarian Women: Wives and Mothers in Rural Nebraska, 1880–1940* (Chapel Hill: University of North Carolina Press, 1992).

Additional works include Glenda Riley, *Frontierswomen: The Iowa Experience* (Ames: Iowa State University Press, 1981), and Rachel Ann Rosenfeld, *Farm Women: Work, Farm, and Family in the United States* (Chapel Hill: University of North Carolina Press, 1985).

12. For the recent farm crisis, see the *Pioneer Press,* St. Paul, Minn., June 27, 1999, special sections A and B.

13. See Joseph Amato and John Radzilowski, *Community of Strangers: Change, Turnover, Turbulence, and the Transformation of a Midwestern Country Town* (Marshall, Minn.: Crossings Press, 1999). Also see Amato et al., *To Call It Home: The New Immigrants of Southwestern Minnesota* (Marshall, Minn.: Crossings Press, 1996).

14. For a single example of varied reactions to market conditions in southwestern Minnesota, see Jeffrey Kolnick, "A Producer's Commonwealth: Populism and the Knights of Labor in Blue Earth County, Minnesota, 1880–1892" (Ph.D. diss., University of California, Davis, 1996).

15. For general guides to agricultural history, see Morton Rothstein, *Writing American Agricultural History,* Historical Essays on Rural Life (Marshall, Minn.: Society for the Study of Local and Regional History, 1996); R. Douglas Hurt, *American Agriculture: A Brief History* (Ames: Iowa State University Press, 1994); Willard Cochrane, *The Development of American Agriculture,* 2d ed. (Minneapolis: University of Minnesota Press, 1993); Lou Ferleger, ed., *Agriculture and National Development: Views on the Nineteenth Century* (Ames: Iowa State University Press, 1990); and David Danbom, *Born in the Country: A History of Rural America* (Baltimore: Johns Hopkins University Press, 1995).

16. David Nass, "The Rural Experience," in *Minnesota in a Century of Change: The State and Its People since 1900,* ed. Clifford Clark (St. Paul: Minnesota Historical Society Press, 1989), 142.

17. Especially useful for illustrating this in a single locale in southern Minnesota is Kolnick, "Producer's Commonwealth," 66–119.

18. See VanMevern, *The 1920s Farm Depression.*

19. Ibid., 150.

20. For an outline of what farming's decline means for the contemporary countryside, see Joseph Amato and John Meyer, *The Decline of Rural Minnesota* (Marshall, Minn.: Crossings Press, 1993).

21. On ethnicity on the prairie and in the Midwest, see Allen Noble, ed., *To Build in a New Land: Ethnic Landscapes in North America* (Baltimore: Johns Hopkins University Press, 1992); Frederick C. Luebke, ed., *Ethnicity on the Great Plains* (Lincoln: University of Nebraska Press, 1980); June Drenning Holmquist, ed., *They Chose Minnesota: A Survey of the State's Ethnic Groups* (St. Paul: Minnesota Historical Society Press, 1981); and Robert Ostergren, *A Community Transplanted: The Trans-Atlantic Experience of a Swedish Immigrant Settlement in the Upper Middle West, 1835–1915* (Madison: University of Wisconsin Press, 1988). For ethnicity in southwestern Minnesota, see Joseph Amato, *Servants of the Land: God, Family, and Farm, the Trinity of Belgian Economic Folkways in Southwestern Minnesota* (Marshall, Minn.: Crossings Press, 1990); John Radzilowski, *Out on the Wind: Poles and Danes in Lincoln County, Minnesota, 1880–1905* (Marshall, Minn.: Crossings Press, 1992); and idem, "Family Labor

and Immigrant Success in a Polish-American Rural Community," *Polish American Studies* 51, no. 2 (autumn 1994): 49–66. Also of interest are Odd Lovoll, *Norwegians on the Land,* Historical Essays on Rural Life (Marshall, Minn.: Society for the Study of Local and Regional History, 1992), and Robert Swierenga, *The Dutch Transplanting in the Upper Middle West,* Historical Essays on Rural Life (Marshall, Minn.: Society for the Study of Local and Regional History, 1991).

22. James Shanon, *Catholic Colonization of the Western Frontier* (New Haven: Yale University Press, 1957).

23. Carl Pansaerts, "Big Barns and Little Houses: A Study of Flemish Belgians in Rural Minnesota, Lyon County, 1880s to 1940" (master's thesis, University of Minnesota, 1987).

24. Edgar Anderson, *Plants, Man, and Life* (Berkeley: University of California Press, 1967); Herman Viola and Carolyn Margolis, eds., *Seeds of Change* (Washington, D.C.: Smithsonian Institution, 1991); Charles Unser, *Seed to Civilization: The Story of Food* (Cambridge: Harvard University Press, 1990); Anne Dorance, *Green Cargoes: The Story of the Transportation of Seeds and Plants from Their Original Homes to the Four Corners of the Earth* (Garden City, N.Y.: Doubleday, Doran and Co., 1945); Jack Harland, *Crops and Man,* 2d ed. (Madison, Wis.: American Society of Agronomy, 1992); Henry Hobhouse, *Seeds of Change: Five Plants that Transformed Mankind* (New York: Harper and Row, 1986); Alfred Crosby, *The Columbian Exchange: The Biological Consequences of 1492* (Westport, Conn.: Greenwood Press, 1972); idem, *Ecological Imperialism: The Biological Expansion of Europe, 900–1900* (Cambridge: Cambridge University Press, 1986); Sidney Mintz, *Crops and Human Culture,* Historical Essays on Rural Life (Marshall, Minn.: Society for the Study of Local and Regional History, 1994).

25. A lovely biographical introduction to economic botany is found in David Fairchild, *The World Was My Garden: Travels of a Plant Explorer* (New York: Charles Scribner's Sons, 1945).

26. In the 1980s, American Energy Farm Systems, headquartered in Marshall, promoted the notion that a common indigenous American weed, a potato-like tuber called the Jerusalem artichoke, would prove to be a miracle crop. They sold its seed as a new source of fuel, claiming that it would free both farmer and nation from their dependence on foreign oil and restore the true America and its Christian servant, the Midwestern farmer. A marvelous mixture of dreamers, unemployed fundamentalist ministers, scoundrels, true believers, and bogus scientists, the company, in pyramid fashion, sold approximately $30 million worth of artichoke seed to twenty-five hundred desperate farmers and small-time rural speculators in more than thirty states and three Canadian provinces in the space of eighteen months between 1981 and 1983. The company soon fell like a house of cards, leaving the average investor ten thousand dollars poorer and earning its three principals six months in jail. While in the end the affair affected the region's overall economy very little, it showed how myth, religion, salesmanship, nonsense, and pseudo-science can turn ordinary plants into miracle crops in desperate times. For more on the Jerusalem artichoke affair, see Joseph Amato, *The Great Jerusalem Artichoke Circus: The Buying and Selling of the American Dream* (Minneapolis: University of Minnesota Press, 1993).

27. Thomas Isern, *The Cultures of Agriculture on the North American Plains,* Rural and Regional Essay Series (Marshall, Minn.: Society for the Study of Local and Regional History, 1999).

28. For the range of plants and crops of early Blue Earth County farmers, see Kolnick, "Producer's Commonwealth," 66–90.

29. John Fraser Hart, *The Land That Feeds Us* (New York: W. W. Norton, 1991), 115. For a short history of corn, see Henry A. Wallace and William L. Brown, *Corn: Its Early Fathers,* rev. ed. (Ames: Iowa State University Press, 1988). For the sources, development, and changing place of corn in Midwestern agriculture, see Allan Bogue, *From Prairie to Corn Belt: Farming on the Illinois and Iowa Prairies in the Nineteenth Century* (Chicago: University of Chicago Press, 1963); Hart, *The Land,* 104–27; and Hudson, *Making the Corn Belt.*

30. Nass, "The Rural Experience," 131.

31. Hudson, *Making the Corn Belt,* 158–59.

32. See David Wright, *The Farm Chemurgic Movement and Agricultural Entrepreneurship between the Two World Wars,* Rural and Regional Essay Series (Marshall, Minn.: Society for the Study of Local and Regional History, 1998); U.S. Department of Agriculture, *Science and Farming: The Yearbook of Agriculture, 1943–47* (Washington, D.C.: Government Printing Office, 1947). On measuring the twentieth-century advance of science in shaping the land, see U.S. Department of Agriculture, *Science in Farming: The Yearbook of Agriculture* (Washington, D.C.: Government Printing Office, 1947).

33. For example, the gasoline tractor started displacing workhorses and the fields that fed them at rapid rates in the 1920s. By 1959 the agricultural census no longer recorded horses or mules. See Donald Durost and Warren Bailey, "What's Happened to Farming," in *Change in Rural America,* ed. Richard Rodefeld, Jan Flora, et al. (St. Louis: C. V. Mosby Co., 1978), 15.

34. For the recent search for new crops, see Gary Ritchie, ed., *New Agricultural Crops* (Boulder, Colo.: Westview Press, 1979); Jules Janick and James Simon, eds., *New Crops* (New York: John Wiley and Sons, 1993); U.S. Department of Agriculture, *New Crops, New Uses, New Markets: Industrial and Commercial Products from U.S. Agriculture, 1992 Yearbook of Agriculture* (Washington, D.C.: Government Printing Office, 1992); and Joseph Amato, *Jerusalem Artichoke Circus,* 1–14. On genetic diversity, see Kenny Ausubel, *Seeds of Change: The Living Treasure* (San Francisco: HarperCollins, 1994); Cary Fowler and Pat Mooney, *Shattering: Food, Politics, and the Loss of Genetic Diversity* (Tucson: University of Arizona Press, 1990).

35. For an introduction to garden plants and their diversity, see Kent Whealy and Arllys Adelmann, eds., *Seed Savers Exchange: The First Ten Years* (Decorah, Iowa: Seed Savers Publications, 1986).

36. The adaptation of the farm family to the changing farm economy, and the corresponding change in the nature of farm women's work, which involves leaving gardens, chickens, and eggs behind to go off to take up full-time work in banks, schools, industry, and elsewhere to supply needed cash and health insurance, constitutes a rich theme for local gender historians. See the *Pioneer Press,* St. Paul, Minn., June 27, 1999, special sections A and B.

37. On the potato in southwestern Minnesota, see Kolnick, "Producer's Commonwealth," 77. For an overview of the social and cultural history of the

potato, see Larry Zuckerman, *The Potato: How the Humble Spud Saved the World* (Boston: Faber and Faber, 1998).

38. For an introduction to the invasion of alien plants, see Crosby, *Columbian Exchange* and *Ecological Imperialism.* Two examples are tumbleweed, a Russian thistle accidentally brought to South Dakota, and crabgrass, originally a Polish millet that I assume also constituted an unwanted exotic "green cargo."

39. For an introduction to the land as an organism, see Aldo Leopold, *A Sand County Almanac* (1949; reprint, New York: Oxford University Press, 1968); Paul Gruchow, *Journal of a Prairie Year* (Minneapolis: University of Minnesota Press, 1985). For a brief survey of the land and contemporary agriculture, see Jan Wojick, *The Arguments of Agriculture* (West Lafayette, Ind.: Purdue University Press, 1989), and "Inside the Land Organism" (Stillwater, Minn.: Land Stewardship Project, n.d. [ca. 1980]).

CHAPTER 4. WRITING HISTORY THROUGH THE SENSES

1. For one example of this kind of history, a study of the acoustic past, see Bruce Smith, *The Acoustic World of Early Modern England* (Chicago: University of Chicago Press, 1999).

2. Joseph Amato, *Dust: A History of the Small and the Invisible* (Berkeley: University of California Press, 2000), esp. 67–91.

3. For this characterization of weather, see Edward Duensing and A. B. Millmoss, *Backyard and Beyond* (Golden, Colo.: Fulcrum Publishing, 1992), 124–25.

4. Vincent Dethier, *Crickets and Katydids, Concerts and Solos* (Cambridge: Harvard University Press, 1992), 2. Also see Gilbert Waldbauer, *Insects through the Seasons* (Cambridge: Harvard University Press, 1996), 35–38.

5. Dethier, *Crickets and Katydids,* 10.

6. Theodore Berland, *The Fight for Quiet* (Englewood Cliffs, N.J.: Prentice Hall, 1970), 29.

7. A report to this effect in the *Lyon County News* (March 3, 1881) is cited in MaryKay Broesder, *The Sounds of a Developing Prairie Town, Marshall, Minnesota: 1872–1918,* Historical Essays on Rural Life (Marshall, Minn.: Society for the Study of Local and Regional History, 1991).

8. For a recent auditory history of bells in traditional rural France, suggestive of what is possible for the Midwest, see Alain Corbin, *Village Bells: Sounds and Meaning in the Nineteenth-Century French Countryside* (New York: Columbia University Press, 1998).

9. Dethier, *Crickets and Katydids,* 14.

10. Henry David Thoreau, "Sounds," in *Walden* (New York: Penguin Books, 1983), 160. Aside from *Walden* itself, the breadth of Thoreau's writings as a regionalist and naturalist is on display in his *Natural History Essays* (Salt Lake City: Peregrine Smith Books, 1980).

11. Thoreau, *Walden,* 168.

12. Max Picard, *Le monde du silence* (Paris: Presses Universitaires de France, 1953), 155, 161–62.

13. For the rapid spread and importance of the radio in the countryside, see Hal Barron, *Mixed Harvest: The Second Great Transformation in the Rural*

North, 1870–1930 (Chapel Hill: University of North Carolina Press, 1997), 215–25 (the quotes are on pp. 217 and 221).

14. Edward Moe and Carl Taylor, *Culture of a Contemporary Rural Community, Irwin Iowa* (Washington, D.C.: U.S. Department of Agriculture, 1942).

15. For an example of the complexity of airport noise and abatement issues, see *Fact Book 1997* (Minneapolis: Metropolitan Airports Commission, Minneapolis–St. Paul, 1977), 4–2 to 4–10, and *Environmental Assessment for Extension of Runway 4–22 to 12,000 Feet* (Minneapolis: Metropolitan Airports Commission, n.d.), 4–1 to 4–30.

16. Antoine Compagnon, "Marcel Proust's *Remembrance of Things Past,*" in *Traditions,* vol. 2. of *Realms of Memory,* ed. Pierre Nora (New York: Columbia University Press, 1997), 211–46.

17. Gaetano Pennino, "I suoni e le voci," *Le forme del lavoro: Mestieri tradizionali in Sicilia* (Palermo: S. F. Flaccovio, 1988), 425.

18. No doubt, voices and sounds comfort humans. Parents speak an octave higher to their newborns, and whoever has not fallen asleep on the grassy banks of a babbling brook has not slept the sweetest sleep. At same time, the human ear can tolerate only certain sounds. More sensitive than the eye at picking up stimuli, "the range of sound energy that the human hear can hear is fantastic. Sharply painful sound is 10 million million [*sic*] times as powerful as the faintest audible sound. The ear can detect frequencies as high as 20,000 cycles per second, or Herz (Hz). . . . Under favorable conditions man may hear sounds so faint that [the sounds] might have been produced by the thermal motion of molecules. . . . Under optimum conditions frequency differences as small as two or three cycles per second and intensity differences of half a decibel can be detected. More than 300,000 tones of different frequency and/or intensity can be distinguished in the auditory area" (Berland, *The Fight for Quiet,* 7, 12).

19. A discussion of the etymological origin of *noise* is found in John Ayto, "Noise," in *Dictionary of Word Origins* (New York: Little, Brown and Company, 1990), 365.

20. Ibid., 45.

21. A useful guide, with bibliographic indications, is Samuel Rosen, "Noise Control," in *Encyclopedia Americana* vol. 20 (Danbury, Conn.: Grolier, 1999), 400–402.

22. See Eckart Klaus Roloff, "A Strange Silence about the Dangers of Noise," *German Tribune* (July 24, 1992): 12, 50, and Stephan Lebert, "Too Much Noise Not Only Causes Illness, It Can Also Impair Intellectual Powers" (November 27, 1992): 13–14.

23. Rural noises are partially governed by national and state standards and statutes. See the U.S. Code, especially Chapter 65—"Noise Control"—of Title 42, "The Public Health and Welfare," and parts of the regulations of the U.S. Department of Labor, Occupational Safety and Health Administration.

24. This ordinance was added to the Marshall City Code as Section 10.33, May 4, 1998.

25. Minnesota itself, which led the nation with its own Clean Air Act in the 1970s, also has a set of statutes regulating noise. Relying on national standards, they distinguish allowable noise levels for a range of areas, including diverse res-

idential, institutional, commercial, transportation, and manufacturing sites. They also put noise control under the supervision of the Minnesota Pollution Control Agency.

CHAPTER 5. ANGER

1. For a discussion of images and portrayals of Minnesota, see Joseph Amato and Anthony Amato, "Minnesota, Real and Imagined: A View from the Countryside," *Daedalus* (August 2000): 55–80.

2. Yi-Fu Tuan, *Landscapes of Fear* (Minneapolis: University of Minnesota Press, 1979), 144.

3. Starting in the 1860s and 1870s, the invention of barbed wire and fences allowed the division of livestock from grain, farm from farm, village from farm, and public from private land. See Wilbur Zelinsky, "Walls and Fences," in *Changing Rural Landscapes,* ed. Erwin Zube and Margaret Zube (Amherst: University of Massachusetts Press, 1955), 53–73.

4. See Janet Timmerman, *Draining the Great Oasis: Claiming Agricultural Land in Murray County, 1910–1915,* Historical Essays on Rural Life (Marshall, Minn.: Society for the Study of State and Local History, 1993).

5. Janet Liebl, "Whiskey's for Drinkin' and Water's for Fightin'," in *At the Headwaters: The 1993 Flood in Southwestern Minnesota* (Marshall, Minn.: Minnesota Conservation Corps / Southwest State University Flood Recovery Project, 1995), 21–22.

6. For more on the Farm Holiday Movement, especially in southwestern Minnesota, see David Nass, ed., *Holiday: Minnesotans Remember the Farmers' Holiday Association* (Marshall, Minn.: Plains Press, 1984).

7. Donata DeBruyckene, *You Can Never Say We Didn't Try: The National Farmers Organization in Lyon County, Minnesota,* Historical Essays on Rural Life (Marshall, Minn.: Society for the Study of Local and Regional History, 1990).

8. A useful unpublished student seminar paper on Groundswell is Rosemary Kodet, "Groundswell: The Populist Movement of the 1980s," Department of History, Southwest State University, 1994.

9. Joseph Amato, *When Father and Son Conspire: A Minnesota Farm Murder* (Ames: Iowa State University Press, 1988).

10. *Tracy Headlight Herald,* Tracy, Minn., March 24, 1999.

11. Prison Calendar, 1909–1931, vol. 22, Lyon County Records, archived at the History Center, Southwest State University.

12. Two models for exploring this cultural transformation in Europe are Eugen Weber, *Peasants into Frenchmen: The Modernization of Rural France, 1870–1914* (Stanford: Stanford University Press, 1976), and Jonas Frykman and Orvar Lögren, *Culture Builders: A Historical Anthropology of Middle-Class Life* (Baltimore: Johns Hopkins University Press, 1987).

13. The seminal work on the transformation of rural people in France is Weber's *Peasants into Frenchmen;* for a more general discussion, see Philippe Ariès and Georges Duby, eds., *History of Private Life,* vols. 4, 5, and 6 (Cambridge: Harvard University Press, 1989, 1990, 1991). Additionally, see my article "World

without Intimacy: A Portrait of a Time before We Were Intimate Individuals and Lovers," *International Social Science Review* 61, no. 4 (autumn 1986): 155–68. For a classic study of the articulation of manners and their spread, see Nobert Elias, *The Civilizing Process,* 3 vols. (New York: Pantheon Books, 1978). For a peculiar take on the process of cleanup, see my book *Dust: A History of the Small and the Invisible* (Berkeley: University of California Press, 1999), esp. 67–91.

14. For a range of articles tracing the penetration of rural peasant society by the civilizing forces of the nation, see *Conflicts and Divisions* and *Traditions,* vols. 1 and 2 of *Realms of Memory: The Construction of the French Past,* ed. Pierre Nora (New York: Columbia University Press, 1996, 1997).

15. Robert Muchembled, *L'Invention de l'homme moderne: Culture et sensibilité en France du XVe siècle au XVIIIe siècle* (Paris: Librairie Arthème Fayard, 1988). Also see his *Popular Culture and Elite Culture in France, 1400–1750* (Baton Rouge: Louisiana State University Press, 1985) and *La Violence au village: Sociabilité et comportements populaires en Artois du XVe au XVIIe siècle* (Brussels: Editions Brepols, 1989). Making a complex argument, Muchembled concludes that in the seventeenth and eighteenth centuries, as a result of changes in politics and society rather than of religion and morals, a new man emerged, master of himself and his own behavior, although traces of the older, more direct and violent, and less regulated man remained until 1914, which marked the beginning of a great act of state violence. See *L'Invention de l'homme moderne,* 203–89, 459.

16. For useful works on the transformation of nineteenth-century European society, see Frédéric Chauvaud, *Les passions villageoises au XIXe siècle: Les émotions rurales dans les pays de Beauce, du Hurepoix et du Montois* (Paris: Publisud, 1995), and Alain Corbin, *The Village of Cannibals: Rage and Murder in France, 1870* (Cambridge: Harvard University Press, 1992). Additionally, see Richard Cobb, *The Police and the People: French Popular Protest, 1789–1820* (Oxford: Oxford University Press, 1972); Pieter Spierenburg, *The Spectacle of Suffering: Executions and the Evolution of Repressions: From a Preindustrial Metropolis to the European Experience* (Cambridge: Cambridge University Press, 1984); idem, "The Body Injured: Violence and Physical Suffering in Daily Life," in *The Broken Spell: A Cultural and Anthropological History of Preindustrial Europe* (New Brunswick, N.J.: Rutgers University Press, 1991), 192–221; and Joseph Amato, *Victims and Values: A History and a Theory of Suffering* (New York: Praeger, 1990), 75–136.

17. Evelyn Ostlie, *Taming Death: An Early Norwegian Immigrant Church and Its Burial Customs in Western Minnesota,* Historical Essays on Rural Life (Marshall, Minn.: Society for the Study of Local and Regional History, 1992).

18. Carol Stearns and Peter Stearns, *Anger: The Struggle for Emotional Control in America's History* (Chicago: University of Chicago Press, 1986); see also Peter Stearns, "Suppressing Unpleasant Emotions: The Development of a Twentieth-Century American Style," in *Social History and Issues in Human Consciousness: Some Interdisciplinary Connections,* ed. Andrew Barnes and Peter Stearns (New York: New York University Press, 1989), 230–61.

19. For an introduction to the function of gossip, see Patricia Meyer Spacks, *Gossip* (Chicago: University of Chicago Press, 1986).

20. Interview by telephone with Dan Giles, April 3, 1998. For an early article on domestic violence and the legal system's response to it, see M. H. Field and H. F. Field, "Marital Violence and the Criminal Process," *Social Service Review* 47 (June 1973): 221–40.

21. For a discussion of the nuances inherent to the recent immigration to southwestern Minnesota and its accompanying societal changes, see Joseph Amato et al., *To Call It Home: The New Immigrants of Southwestern Minnesota* (Marshall, Minn.: Crossings Press, 1996).

22. For an example, see "K.K.K. a Reality in Pipestone," *Ivanhoe Times,* October 26, 1925.

23. For the work of the Minnesota Commission of Public Safety during World War I, see Carl Chrislock's *Watchdog of Loyalty: The Minnesota Commission of Public Safety during World War I* (St. Paul: Minnesota Historical Society Press, 1991). For specific regional instances of the targeting of immigrant communities, see also Robert Schoone-Jongen, *Patriotic Pressures: The Dutch Experience in Southwest Minnesota during World War I,* Historical Essays on Rural Life (Marshall, Minn.: Society for the Study of Local and Regional History, 1992), and Thomas McCausland, *Rally of Resolve: The Home Front in Lyon County,* Historical Essays on Rural Life (Marshall, Minn.: Society for the Study of Local and Regional History, 1990). For several incidents involving excessive expression of patriotism and anti-German sentiment in the region, see Radzilowksi, *Prairie Town,* 177–80.

24. For the ideological conflict involved between town and gown, professors and legionnaires, in Cottonwood, Minnesota, see the preface to Joseph Amato, *Guilt and Gratitude: A Study of the Origins of Contemporary Conscience* (Westport, Conn.: Greenwood Press, 1982), xiii–xxv; for student antiwar protest in Marshall, see Joseph Amato with John Radzilowski, *A New College on the Prairie: Southwest State University's First Twenty-Five Years, 1967–1992* (Marshall, Minn.: Crossings Press, 1992), 58.

25. Joseph Amato, *Servants of the Land: God, Family, and Farm, the Trinity of Belgian Economic Folkways in Southwestern Minnesota* (Marshall, Minn.: Crossings Press, 1990), 22.

26. Ibid., 25.

27. For an introduction to the history of gestures, see Jan Bremer and Herman Roodenburg, eds., *A Cultural History of Gesture* (Ithaca, N.Y.: Cornell University Press, 1991).

CHAPTER 6. THE CLANDESTINE

1. A useful introduction to aspects of the geography of the clandestine is Yi-Fu Tuan's *Landscapes of Fear* (Minneapolis: University of Minnesota Press, 1979).

2. Willa Cather, *The Professor's House* (New York: Alfred A. Knopf, 1953), 95.

3. *Independent,* Marshall, Minn., July 24, 1992.

4. Ibid., August 14, 1992, and February 24,1992.

5. *Minneapolis Star and Tribune,* December 5, 1999.

6. See Yi-Fu Tuan, *Landscapes of Fear;* Truman Capote, *In Cold Blood* (New York: NAL, 1965); Peter Davis, *Hometown: A Portrait of an American Community* (New York: Simon and Schuster, 1982); Calvin Trillin, "I Have Got Problems," *New Yorker* 61, no. 4 (March 18, 1985): 109–18; and Joseph Amato, *When Father and Son Conspire: A Minnesota Farm Murder* (Ames: Iowa State University Press, 1988).

7. For a recent example of the enduring power of incest over a rural family and a rural community, see Jane Smiley's novel *A Thousand Acres* (New York: Fawcett Columbia, 1992).

8. Starting in the 1970s, Southwest State University professors Barney Harney and Laren Barker, respectively of the psychology and biology departments, administered this survey annually in their conjoint Introduction to Human Sexuality class.

9. Hamlin Garland, *A Son of the Middle Border* (New York: The Macmillan Company, 1923), 251.

10. John Radzilowski, "Hidden Cosmos: The Life-Worlds of Polish Immigrants in Two Minnesota Communities, 1875–1925" (Ph.D. diss., Arizona State University, 1999), 180–86.

11. For the role of the press during World War I in Minnesota, see Carl Chrislock, *Watchdog of Loyalty: The Minnesota Commission of Public Safety during World War I* (St. Paul: Minnesota Historical Society Press, 1991); for the Dutch, see Robert Schoone-Jongen, *Patriotic Pressures: The Dutch Experience in Southwest Minnesota during World War I,* Historical Essays on Rural Life (Marshall, Minn.: Society for the Study of Local and Regional History, 1992).

12. *Ivanhoe Times,* Ivanhoe, Minn., October 26, 1923.

13. For a short history of the college, see Joseph Amato with John Radzilowski, *A New College on the Prairie: Southwest State University's First Twenty-Five Years, 1967–1992* (Marshall, Minn.: Crossings Press, 1992).

14. For a discussion of this incident, see Joseph Amato, *Guilt and Gratitude: A Study of the Origins of Contemporary Conscience* (Westport, Conn.: Greenwood Press, 1982), xiii–xxii.

15. For different accounts of the connection of this murder to the farm crisis, see Andrew Malcolm, *Final Harvest: An American Tragedy* (New York: Times Books, 1986), and Joseph Amato, *When Father and Son Conspire: A Minnesota Farm Murder* (Ames: Iowa State University Press, 1988).

16. For a full exposition of this episode, see Joseph Amato, *The Great Jerusalem Artichoke Circus: The Buying and Selling of the American Dream* (Minneapolis: University of Minnesota Press, 1993).

17. A single example of the potential for a history of scams is John Dillon's *Hind-Sights, or Looking Backwards at Swindlers* (New York: The Rural Publishing Company, 1911).

18. For an overview of recent regional immigration, see Joseph Amato, et al., *To Call It Home: The New Immigrants of Southwestern Minnesota* (Marshall, Minn.: Crossings Press, 1996).

19. *Independent,* Marshall, Minn., September 30, 1998.

20. For an interesting work on the wild, see Roger Bartra, *Wild Men in the Looking Glass: The Mythic Origins of European Otherness* (Ann Arbor: University of Michigan Press, 1994).

21. Michael Lesy, *The Wisconsin Death Trip* (New York: Pantheon Books, 1973).

22. For a developed discussion of these themes, see Joseph Amato, *Victim and Values: A History and a Theory of Suffering* (New York: Praeger, 1990), esp. 151–74.

CHAPTER 7. MADNESS

1. Even though the original trial records are no longer extant, presiding judge Noah Rosenbloom furnished me with his bench notes for the case of *State v. Elmer Le Roy Johnson,* and I had a copy of the competency hearing, *Lyon County v. Elmer Le Roy Johnson,* April 30, 1968.

2. The Minnesota Historical Society gave me access to these records on the condition that I not take down or refer to names. Rather than count all cases, I chose a dozen years at random, determined the average number of cases in those years, and multiplied the average by the sixty-seven-year period for which I had records.

3. I examined Lyon County insanity records from 1883 to 1950, with permission of the Minnesota Historical Society. I sought to quantify cases by diseases, residence, and ethnicity, but the small size of the sample, variations of form, and gaps in the records led me to simply choose three well-documented years.

4. For controversy surrounding the law of 1893 and court revisions to it in 1894, and an overview of the subsequent development of the law regarding commitment of the insane, see Don Martindale and Edith Martindale's *Social Psychiatry: Coping with Mental Illness, Alcoholism, and Drug Dependence* (St. Paul: Wind Flower, 1972), 36–51. The state legislature made revisions to the law in 1917, 1967, and 1982. Alterations in state petitions, certificates, and other pertinent forms were also made in 1893, 1907, 1911, 1917, and 1935.

5. Erickson's findings remain unpublished. Of more interest by its subject than its results is Frank Willis et al., "The First Mental Hospital for American Indians, 1900–1934," *Bulletin for the Menninger Clinic* 45 (1981): 149–54.

6. William Erickson, "Something Must Be Done for Them: Establishing Minnesota's First Hospital for the Insane," *Minnesota History* 53, no. 2 (summer 1992): 42–55.

7. William Erickson, former director of St. Peter's, was my primary source on the institution. I am indebted to him for a tour in the fall of 1995, several subsequent telephone conversations, and a lengthy letter, dated December 23, 1995. He lectured at Southwest State University on the origins of St. Peter's in the spring of 1996. For this text I have relied heavily on his article "Something Must Be Done for Them" and his book *This Great Charity: Minnesota's First Mental Hospital at St. Peter, Minnesota, 1866–1991* (St. Peter, Minn.: St. Peter Regional Treatment Center, 1991). Martindale and Martindale's *Social Psychiatry* gives a useful historical overview of the treatment of the insane in Minnesota. Ellen Dwire provides an overview of institutional life in *Home for the Mad: Life Inside Two Nineteenth-Century Asylums* (New Brunswick, N.J.: Rutgers University Press, 1987).

8. The heterogeneity of clientele proved the long-term test of asylums, according to Gerald Grob's introduction to Edward Jarvis, *Insanity and Idiocy in Massachusetts: Report of the Commission on Lunacy, 1855* (Cambridge: Harvard University Press, 1971), esp. 18–21. Also of use is Norman Dain, *Concepts of Insanity in the United States, 1789–1865* (New Brunswick, N.J.: Rutgers University Press, 1964).

9. Martindale and Martindale, *Social Psychiatry,* 10–11.

10. Dwire, *Homes for the Mad,* 216.

11. Martindale and Martindale, *Social Psychiatry,* 14.

12. In early-nineteenth-century London, the greatest ignominy of the poorhouse was to end up the dissected cadaver of emerging medical science's young anatomists.

13. Michel Foucault, in *Madness and Civilization* (New York: Random House, 1965), saw asylums as belonging to the Enlightenment project to control and rationalize humanity. David Rothman presents nuances of this view in *The Discovery of the Asylum: Social Order and Disorder in the New Republic* (New York: Little, Brown, 1971). Their interpretation is counterbalanced by Erickson's *This Great Charity* and Dwire's *Homes for the Mad.*

14. Starting in the early 1860s, Minnesota sent its insane at a per capita cost to Mount Pleasant in Iowa and St. Vincent's Institution for the Insane in St. Louis, until it opened St. Peter's. Erickson, "Something Must Be Done for Them," 45, and *This Great Charity,* 25.

15. By 1877, barely a decade after its founding, the problem of overcrowding at St. Peter's, which plagued the institution almost from its beginning, came to a head. In 1879, Rochester State Hospital, beginning as the Minnesota Inebriate Asylum in 1873, became the state's second hospital for the insane. In 1893 a third hospital was created at Fergus Falls; the care of inebriates was turned over to counties that same year.

16. Erickson, *This Great Charity,* 48.

17. Ibid., 52, 54, 48.

18. Useful for giving a sense of diagnosis in the interwar period is Morris Braude, *The Principles and Practice of Clinical Psychiatry* (Philadelphia: P. Blakiston's Sons, 1937), esp. 31–33.

19. Erickson, *This Great Charity,* 56.

20. Ibid., 57.

CHAPTER 8. MADAME BOVARY AND A LILAC SHIRT

1. Wallace Stegner, *Where the Bluebird Sings to the Lemonade Springs: Living and Writing in the West* (New York: Penguin, 1992), 202.

2. For a recent and useful anthology of Manfred's work, see *The Frederick Manfred Reader,* ed. John Rezmerski (Duluth, Minn.: Holy Cow! Press, 1996).

3. For a recent anthology of southwestern Minnesota writers and writing, see David Pichaske and Joseph Amato, eds., *Southwest Minnesota: The Land and the People* (Marshall, Minn.: Crossings Press, 1999). Also useful on rural writing is David Pichaske's *Late Harvest* (New York: Paragon House, 1992). For a useful guide to the farm novel, see Roy Meyer, *The Middle Western Farm Novel in the Twentieth Century* (Lincoln: University of Nebraska Press, 1965).

4. "Pro Patria," from *If I Die in a Combat Zone,* in Pichaske and Amato, *Southwest Minnesota;* the quote is on p. 112.

5. Leo Dangel, *Home from the Field: Collected Poems* (Granite Falls, Minn.: Spoon River Poetry Press, 1997). For a critical essay on Dangel's early poetry, see Philip Dacey, *Great River Review,* no. 22 (April 1993): 139–44.

6. Dangel, *Home from the Field,* 45.

7. Ibid., 85.

8. Ibid., 63.

9. Ibid., 208.

10. Ibid., 89.

11. Ibid., 162.

12. Ibid., 20.

13. Ibid., 43.

14. Ibid., 98–99.

15. Mark Schorer, *Sinclair Lewis: An American Life* (New York: McGraw-Hill, 1961), 296. Carol Kennicott can be considered more immediately to have been modeled on Lewis's own stepmother, as John T. Flanagan writes in *Minnesota's Literary Visitors* (n.p.: Pogo Press, 1993), 163–75.

16. Lewis Atherton, *Main Street on the Middle Border* (Bloomington: Indiana University Press, 1954), 109.

17. Radzilowski explored this elite group of founders in *Prairie Town: A History of Marshall, Minnesota, 1872–1997* (Marshall, Minn.: Lyon County Historical Society, 1997), 86–91.

18. Randy Abbott, Jr., "The Automobile Comes to Southwest Minnesota," Historical Essays on Rural Life (Marshall, Minn.: Society for the Study of Local and Regional History, 1993).

19. Sinclair Lewis, *Main Street, Lewis at Zenith: A Three-Novel Omnibus* (New York: Harcourt, Brace, and World, 1961), 31.

20. Ibid., 335.

21. Schorer, *Sinclair Lewis,* 295.

CHAPTER 9. THE RED ROCK

1. For a recent discussion of the place of rocks and mountains in naming locales, see Dan Flores, "The Rocky Mountain West: Fragile Space and Diverse Place," *Montana: The Magazine of Western History* (winter 1995): 46–56.

2. J. A. Grant, "Minnesota River Valley: Southwestern Minnesota," in *Geology of Minnesota: A Centennial Volume* (St. Paul: Minnesota Geological Survey, 1972), 177.

3. Ibid., 195.

4. For a technical geologic description of the rock, see George Austin, "The Sioux Quartzite, Southwestern Minnesota," *Geology of Minnesota,* 450–55.

5. For an overview of the history of this monument, see Hal Rothman, *Managing the Sacred and the Secular: An Administrative History of Pipestone National Monument* (Henderson, Nev.: National Park Service, 1992). For a discussion of the use of national monument designation in general, see Robert Righter, "National Monuments to National Parks: The Use of the Antiquities Act of 1906," *Western Historical Quarterly* 20 (August 1989): 281–301.

6. Robert Murray, *A History of the Pipestone National Monument* (Pipestone, Minn.: Pipestone Indian Shrine Association, in cooperation with the National Park Service, 1965), 11.

7. Ibid., 12.

8. Ibid., 13. The earliest indication of the quarry was offered in 1702 by Guillaume de l'Ilse and Paul Beaubien, "Notes on the Archaeology of Pipestone National Monument," in *The Red Pipestone Quarry of Minnesota,* compiled by Alan Woolworth for a special edition of the *Minnesota Archaeologist* 40, no. 1 (1981): 37.

9. Woolworth, *Red Pipestone Quarry,* 17. Also see Janet Timmerman, *Draining the Great Oasis: Claiming New Agricultural Land in Murray County, 1910–1915,* Historical Essays on Rural Life (Marshall, Minn.: Society for the Study of Local and Regional History, 1993).

10. Timmerman, *Great Oasis,* 19. For a relevant article, see William Corbett, "The Red Pipestone Quarry: The Yanktons Defend a Sacred Tradition, 1859–1929," *South Dakota History* 8 (1978): 99–116, and his master's thesis, "A History of the Red Pipestone Quarry and Pipestone National Monument" (University of South Dakota, Department of History, 1976).

11. Robert Murray, "Administrative History of Pipestone National Monument, Pipestone, Minnesota" (manuscript, Pipestone National Monument, 1965), 21.

12. Corbett, "History of the Red Pipestone Quarry," 39.

13. Corbett, "The Red Pipestone Quarry," 40.

14. Ibid., 44. Also see Dawn Hagen, "Protecting the Past, Saving the Stone: A Historical Study of the Exploitation of the Great Red Pipestone Quarry" (senior seminar paper, Southwest State University, Department of History, 1992), 13.

15. Noted in Alan Woolworth's unpublished reference guide to Minnesota History, "Minnesota's Legendary Pipestone Quarry" (St. Paul: Minnesota Historical Society, 1983), 6.

16. For an introduction to the highly complex subject of when and why native peoples used the pipe, see Robert Murray, "A Brief Survey of the Pipes and Smoking Customs of the Indians of the Northern Plains," in Woolworth, *Red Pipestone Quarry,* 81–95. Also of use is Robert Lowie, *Indians of the Plains* (Lincoln: University of Nebraska Press, 1954), 25–29; Frances Densmore, *Chippewa Customs* (St. Paul: Minnesota Historical Society Press, 1979), 143–44 and passim; Royal Hassrick, *The Sioux: Life and Customs of a Warrior Society* (Norman: University of Oklahoma Press, 1964); and Samuel Pond, *The Dakota or Sioux in Minnesota as They Were in 1834* (St. Paul: Minnesota Historical Society Press, 1986), 122–23.

17. Christopher Roelfsema-Hummel, "A Revisionist History of the Pipestone Quarries" (undergraduate paper, University of Wisconsin, Department of History, 1992), 3–4.

18. John Neihardt, *Black Elk Speaks, as told to John G. Neihardt* (New York: William Morrow and Company, 1932). Deloria's quotation is cited in Fergus Bordewich, *Killing the White Man's Indian: Inventing Native Americans at the End of the Twentieth Century* (New York: Anchor Books, 1996), 226.

19. Joseph Epes Brown, ed., *The Sacred Pipe: Black Elk's Account of the Seven Rites of the Oglala Sioux* (New York: Penguin Books, 1971), 25.

20. Alice Kehoe, "Primal Gaia: Primitivists and Plastic Medicine Men," in *The Invented Indian: Cultural Fictions and Government Policies,* ed. James A. Clifton (New Brunswick, N.J.: Transaction Publishers, 1990), 197.

21. Michael Steltenkamp, *Black Elk: Holy Man of the Oglala* (Norman: University of Oklahoma Press, 1993), xxi. For Black Elk's biography and his Catholic faith, see also Raymond DeMallie, ed., *The Sixth Grandfather: Black Elk's Teachings Given to John G. Neihardt* (Lincoln: University of Nebraska Press, 1984). For a recent attempt to discover similarities and parallels between the Dakota and Christian understandings of the world, see William Stolzman, S.J., *The Pipe and Christ* (Chamberlain, S.D.: Tipi Press, 1986).

22. For the process of reinvention in native culture, see Bordewich, *Killing the White Man's Indian;* Colin Calloways, ed., *New Directions in American Indian History* (Norman: University of Oklahoma Press, 1988), esp. 234–35; Clifton, *The Invented Indian;* and Hazel Hertzberg, *The Search for an American Indian Identity* (Syracuse, N.Y.: Syracuse University Press, 1971).

23. Rothman, *Managing the Sacred,* 202–18.

24. George Catlin, *Letters and Notes on the Manners, Customs, and Conditions of North American Indians,* 2 vols. (1844; reprint, New York: Dover, 1973).

25. Catlin, *North American Indians,* vol. 2, 256.

26. Ibid., 155.

27. Ibid., 156, 157.

28. Ibid., 164.

29. See Mentor Williams, ed., *Schoolcraft's Indian Legends* (East Lansing: Michigan State University Press, 1991), xxii–xxiv and 313–15. Also see Philip Mason, ed., *Schoolcraft's Ojibwa Lodge Stories: Life on the Lake Superior Frontier* (East Lansing, Mich.: Michigan State University Press, 1997).

30. Williams, *Schoolcraft's Indian Legends,* xxiii–xxiv.

31. See Philip Mason, ed., *Schoolcraft's Expedition to Lake Itasca* (East Lansing: Michigan State University Press, 1993).

32. For Longfellow's extensive European education and his dependence on Schoolcraft for the poem *Hiawatha,* see Chase Osborn and Stellanova Osborn, *Schoolcraft, Longfellow, "Hiawatha"* (Lancaster, Penn.: Jacques Cattell Press, 1942); for the quotation, see 26–27.

33. See Williams, *Schoolcraft's Indian Legends,* 313–15.

34. Henry Wadsworth Longfellow, *The Song of Hiawatha* (1855; reprint, London: Everyman, 1992), 5.

35. Ibid., 5.

36. Ibid., 152.

37. Ibid.

38. Ibid., 153.

39. Ibid., 160.

40. Quoted in Williams, *Schoolcraft's Indian Legends,* xix.

41. Only with the appearance of the *Myth of Hiawatha* did Schoolcraft make a connection between the Algonquin myth-hero Manabozho and the Iroquois political figure Hiawatha. See Williams, *Schoolcraft's Indian Legends,* xxiii.

42. "Longfellow, Henry Wadsworth," in *American Authors, 1600–1900,* ed. Stanley Kunitz and Howard Haycraft (New York: H. W. Wilson, 1938), 476–78.

43. Joseph Zaluky, " 'Fish' Jones and His Irresistible Longfellow Gardens," *Hennepin County History* (fall 1967): 7–17.

44. Cited in the pageant brochure, "Presenting the Annual Pageant, 'Song of Hiawatha,'" (Pipestone, Minn.: Pipestone Exchange Club, 1949).

45. For a booklet on Pipestone's Civil War veterans, see Pipestone County Genealogical Society, *Biographies of the Civil War Veterans Who Came to Pipestone County* (Pipestone, Minn.: Pipestone Publishing Company, 1991).

46. Roelfsema-Hummel, "A Revisionist History," 21; also see Karen Weets, "Vision Quest" (senior seminar paper, Southwest State University, Department of History, 1993), 1.

47. Christopher Roelfsema-Hummel, "Tycoons and Town Founders: Pipestone County Development" (unpublished paper, University of Minnesota, Morris, Department of History, 1993), 10, and Roelfsema-Hummel, "A Revisionist History," 15.

48. For a description of the town's Yankee fathers, see Roelfsema-Hummel, "Tycoons and Town Fathers," 15–22.

49. Cited in Roelfsema-Hummel, "A Revisionist History," 25.

50. Roelfsema-Hummel, "Tycoons and Town Founders," 12.

51. For the lives of the Close brothers and their ties to Iowa, the English colony Le Mars, and Pipestone, see Curtis Harnack, *Gentlemen on the Prairie* (Ames: Iowa State University Press, 1985); for their activities, see Roelfsema-Hummel, "Tycoons and Town Founders," 28–67.

52. Arthur P. Rose, *An Illustrated History of Rock and Pipestone Counties, Minnesota* (Luverne, Minn.: Northern History Publishing Company, 1911), 285.

53. Lee Olson, *Marmalade and Whiskey: British Remittance Men in the West* (Golden, Colo.: Fulcrum Publishing, 1993), 107–8.

54. Roelfsema-Hummel, "Tycoons and Town Founders," 53.

55. Ibid., 54.

56. Hagen, "Protecting the Past," 11.

57. Roelfsema-Hummel, "Tycoons and Town Founders," 56.

58. Ibid., 76–77.

59. Ibid., 65.

60. Ibid., 67.

61. Ibid., 57–58.

62. Roelfsema-Hummel, "Expanding Exploitation," in "A Revisionist History," 3–4.

63. Roelfsema-Hummel, "Tycoons and Town Founders," 71.

64. Ibid., 71–72, and Roelfsema-Hummel, "Expanding Exploitation," in "A Revisionist History," 6–7.

65. Rose, *Rock and Pipestone Counties,* 400–402.

66. Roelfsema-Hummel, "Tycoons and Town Founders," 8. See also Sandy Beckering, "Charles H. Bennett: A Man of Vision," *Coteau Heritage: Journal of the Pipestone County Heritage* 2, no. 1 (April 1989): 23.

67. Roelfsema-Hummel, "A Revisionist History," 16–18.

68. Ibid., 29.

69. Roelfsema-Hummel, "Expanding Exploitation," in "A Revisionist History," 8.

70. Ibid., 8–9.

71. Ibid., 10.

72. Pipestone School catalogue (Pipestone, Minn., 1914), 2–4.

73. Letter to editor of the *Pipestone County Star,* dated Chicago, September 20, 1893, *Pipestone Star,* September 22, 1893.

74. Valerie Cran, "The Selling of a New Prairie Town: Charles Bennett, Daniel Sweet, and the Booster Spirit of Pipestone Minnesota" (senior seminar paper, Southwest State University, Department of History, 1992), 18.

75. For an introduction to L. H. Moore, see *Pipestone County History* (Pipestone, Minn.: Pipestone Historical Society, 1984), 78. See also *Pipestone County Star,* May 8, 1980, 1–3.

76. Pipestone Genealogical Society, *Biographies of the Civil War Veterans,* 13.

77. For a treatment of Close residency and the immigrants they brought to town, see Harnack, *Gentlemen on the Prairie,* 188–89.

78. Olson, *Marmalade and Whiskey,* 108.

79. *Pipestone County Star,* April 10, 1917.

80. Ibid., May 22, 1917.

81. Robert Schoone-Jongen, *Patriotic Pressures: The Dutch Experience in Southwest Minnesota during World War I,* Historical Essays on Rural Life (Marshall, Minn.: Society for the Study of Local and Regional History, 1992), 4.

82. *History of Pipestone County in the World War* (Pipestone, Minn.: Leader Publishing Company, 1919).

83. For a general treatment of the Minnesota Commission of Public Safety, see Carl Chrislock, *Watchdog of Loyalty: The Minnesota Commission of Public Safety during World War I* (St. Paul: Minnesota Historical Society Press, 1991).

84. *Pipestone County Star,* May 21, 1918.

85. Chrislock, *Watchdog of Loyalty,* 5.

86. Ibid., 8.

87. "The Law Prevails, A Tussle with Saloons," *Pipestone County Star,* August 17, 1888.

88. Michael R. Worcester, "Order Number Ten: The Minnesota Commission of Public Safety vs. Pipestone County" (essay furnished to the author, Pipestone County Historical Museum), 5, 8.

89. Ibid., 9.

90. Roelfsema-Hummel, "Expanding Exploitation," in "A Revisionist History," 4, 13–27.

91. Scott Perrizo, personal e-mail correspondence, April 13, 2000.

CHAPTER 10. BUSINESS FIRST AND ALWAYS

1. Richard Davies, *Main Street Blues: The Decline of Small-Town America* (Columbus: Ohio State University Press, 1998).

2. Quoted in the *Oxford Book of Money* (Oxford: Oxford University Press, 1995), 359–60.

3. Quoted in ibid., 20.

4. Ibid., 37–38.

5. For Marshall, see John Radzilowski, *Prairie Town: A History of Marshall, Minnesota, 1872–1997* (Marshall, Minn.: Lyon County Historical Society, 1997). For the birth of railroad towns, see John C. Hudson, *Plains Country Towns* (Minneapolis: University of Minnesota Press, 1985).

6. Torgny Anderson, *The Centennial History of Lyon County* (Marshall, Minn.: Henle Publishing Company, 1970), 169.

7. See Hal Barron, *Mixed Harvest: The Second Great Transformation in the Rural North, 1870–1930* (Chapel Hill: University of North Carolina Press, 1997), 155–92.

8. Radzilowski, *Prairie Town,* 91–92.

9. Ibid., 87–94, 118–19.

10. Joseph Amato and John Radzilowski, *A Community of Strangers: Change, Turnover, Turbulence, and the Transformation of a Midwestern Country Town* (Marshall, Minn.: Crossings Press, 1999), 26.

11. Richard Lingeman, *Small Town America: A Narrative History, 1620 to the Present* (New York: G. P. Putnam's Sons, 1980), 429–30.

12. Joseph Amato, *A New College on the Prairie: Southwest State University's First Twenty-Five Years, 1967–1992* (Marshall, Minn.: Crossings Press, 1992), 16–18.

13. John Borchert, *Upper Midwest Urban Change in the 1960s* (Minneapolis: Upper Midwest Research and Development, 1968), 24.

14. Ibid., 25.

15. Amato, *A New College,* 13–21.

16. Ibid., 46.

17. Lingeman, *Small Town America,* 441.

18. Joseph Amato and John Meyer, *The Decline of Rural Minnesota* (Marshall, Minn.: Crossings Press, 1993).

19. U.S. Department of Agriculture, Economic Research Service Department, "Rural Change," in *Understanding Rural America* (Washington, D.C.: U.S. Department of Agriculture, 1991).

20. John Borchert, *Upper Midwest Urban Change,* 16.

21. U.S. Department of Agriculture, Economic Research Service, "Rural Diversity," in *Understanding Rural America* (Washington, D.C.: United States Department of Agriculture, 1991).

22. For a discussion of this natural decline, see Amato and Meyer, *Decline of Rural Minnesota,* 39–50.

23. Radzilowski, *Prairie Town,* 287.

24. Ibid., 285. For a parallel study, see Davies, *Main Street Blues,* 137–84.

25. Amy Glasmeier and Marie Howland, *From Combines to Computers: Rural Services and Development in the Age of Information Technology* (Albany: State University of New York Press, 1995), 93.

26. Ibid.

27. Amato and Meyer, *Decline of Rural Minnesota,* 14–15.

28. Jim Tate, "It's in the Crust," *Marshall Independent,* Marshall, Minn., December 5, 1998.

29. John Borchert, *America's Northern Heartland: An Economic and Historical Geography of the Upper Midwest* (Minneapolis: University of Minnesota Press, 1987), and William Cronon, *Nature's Metropolis: Chicago and the Great West* (New York: W. W. Norton, 1991).

CONCLUSION

1. William Cronon, *Nature's Metropolis: Chicago and the Great West* (New York: W. W. Norton, 1991); John C. Hudson, *Making the Corn Belt: A Geographical History of Middle Western Agriculture* (Bloomington: University of Indiana Press, 1994); John Borchert, *America's Northern Heartland: An Economic and Historical Geography of the Upper Midwest* (Minneapolis: University of Minnesota Press, 1987); and Andrew Cayton and Peter Onuf, *The Midwest and the Nation* (Bloomington: Indiana University Press, 1990).

2. Alexis de Tocqueville, *Democracy in America,* vol. 2 (New York: Vintage Books, 1957), 14.

3. See Joel Overholser, *Fort Benton: World's Innermost Port* (Fort Benton, Mont.: Rivers and Plains Society, 1987).

4. Jennifer Ackerman, *Notes from the Shore* (New York: Penguin Books, 1995), 72.

Acknowledgments and Sources

Long works create great indebtedness. Gratitude for this work was amassed over three decades of teaching at Southwest State University and the process of developing a rural studies curriculum and establishing a Center for Rural and Regional Studies.

My gratitude is owed to Southwest State University provost Randy Abbott, vice president Joann Fredrickson, former presidents Dennis Nielsen, Douglas Sweetland, and John Wefald, and deceased vice-president for university relations James Babcock, who generously allocated the university's own Gunlogson funds to the Center for Rural and Regional Studies. Additionally, state university librarians, especially Mary Jane Striegel and Nancy DeRoode, have found and procured for me the articles and books I needed, along with the helpful reference staff of the Wilson Library at the University of Minnesota. Shawn Hedman of computer services got me up and running after many an electronic breakdown.

My gratitude also joins a more intimate narrative of friendship and intellectual companionship. I still miss the original "history gang" of the 1970s and 1980s, composed of Maynard Brass, Thaddeus Radzilowski, David Nass, and Michael Kopp, and their minds and hearts.

As well, my gratitude follows a twenty-year path to the door of Jan Louwagie, coordinator of the university's history center and cofounder, treasurer, and do-it-all of our independent Society for the Study of Local and Regional History. A lasting debt also is owed other society members. Donata DeBruyckere has done yeoman service for the society and for me.

Kevin Stroup, southwest Minnesota native, friend, lawyer, and former student, has supplied me with countless insights into his home region. Janet Timmerman, who is always of good cheer and ready intelligence, has done the same.

Likewise, the center's new staff (who took up their posts when this book was well along the road to completion) also deserves acknowledgment. Geoff Cunfer helped me stay upright on "the slippery slopes of defining region," as did brand-new center fellow Molly Rozum, who was kind enough to share early chapters of her promising dissertation on the development of distinct grassland identities. My son Anthony Amato, who also works in the center, provided me with environmental and cultural insights. Center environmental educator Beth Spieles aided in the improvement of chapter 2 and Charles Kost, head of our geographic information systems program, enthusiastically created maps for this book. Julie Bach, Marianne Zarzana, and John Radzilowski helped me copy-edit part of an early draft of the book. Christina Kubat, student extraordinaire, proved immensely helpful in entering final revisions and corrections to the work.

Outside the university, I am indebted to editors Debra Miller and Ann Reagan of the Minnesota Historical Society, who supported this work in its early stages and were insightful critics as it took form. Alan Woolworth, independent fellow at the Minnesota Historical Society, and his colleague Scott Anfinson, state archaeologist, helped me form a sense of the presettlement ecology of southwestern Minnesota. Tom Isern of the University of North Dakota also provided beneficial criticism of an early draft of the book. Richard O. Davies of the University of Nevada, Reno, improved the work on several counts, in addition to supplying it with a foreword.

UCLA professor emeritus Eugen Weber has, over two decades, nudged me away from the general toward the particular and introduced me to master local historian Guy Thuillier. A two-hour meal with Thuillier has proved nearly a decade's intellectual feast. Professors and friends Leon Rappoport, Jeffrey Russell, and Steven Tonsor have intellectually nurtured me over half a lifetime.

Judge Bruce Christopherson helped me understand the changing faces of anger on the rural landscape. Judge Noah Rosenbloom of New Ulm, Minnesota, called my attention to a case of singular interest in the law's attempt to define insanity. Dr. William Erickson's writing counseled me on the regional history of madness, and I only regret we couldn't find a place for several photographs with which he furnished me. While Professor Tom Dilley helped me understand the geography of southwestern Minnesota, Mr. Christopher Roelfsema-Hummel, director of the Pipestone County Historical Museum, and his predecessor, Mr. Joseph Rambo, shaped my understanding of Pipestone's history.

Additionally, fifteen years of undergraduate teaching produced a river of history students who shared their thoughts on southwest Minnesota. Some of their papers were published in the Society for the Study of Local and Regional History's Essay Series, along with those of such visiting guest scholars as Robert Swierenga, Peter Mancall, David Wright, and Sidney Mintz. Together, our students and guest scholars have expanded my sense of place.

I express my fondest gratitude to Howard Boyer, former executive editor at the University of California Press, who accepted *Dust: A History of the Small and Invisible* and then to my delight welcomed to the press *Rethinking Home.* My indebtedness now includes new university press editor Blake Edgar, who significantly improved this book, as did keen and tenacious copy editors Erika Büky, who also cleaned up *Dust,* and Jacqueline Volin.

I conclude these acknowledgments with thanks to local readers who assured me in many kind ways that local history was worth doing, and to my wife, Catherine, who in so many ways made it possible.

SOURCES

My gratitude to my colleagues, students, and friends, and community members is inseparable from the written and oral sources that made *Rethinking Home* and my earlier books on rural and regional history possible. Local history and my autobiography are so closely linked that my work often seems more a fate than a choice. Accreted over decades fact by fact, anecdote by anecdote, insight by insight, my knowledge of southwest Minnesota became a passion and a destiny. Certain sources were an indispensable part of my transformation into a local historian.

My initiation to local history was the story of a father and son who murdered two bankers in 1983 in nearby Ruthton. In writing *When Father and Son Conspire: A Minnesota Farm Murder* (Ames: Iowa State University Press, 1988), local and statewide newspapers proved indispensable for assembling biographical material, explaining complex legal maneuvers, and recording reactions to the crime. Court records, which included Bureau of Criminal Apprehension investigative reports and laboratory work, material evidence to pleas and motions, and transcripts of hearings, provided evidence that I never could have assembled on my own.

At the same time, oral interviews proved wonderfully surprising, acquainting me with the inner dimension of a crime wrapped in illusion, deceit, and hate. Aside from helping me fulfill the journalist's burden of getting the facts straight, interviews helped me make sense of a profoundly irrational tale of a madness that brought a father and son to murder together, and to understand a national press that transformed the murder into an expression of the emerging national farm crisis.

The attention *When Father and Son Conspire* received christened me as a historian of southwestern Minnesota while teaching me to work imaginatively with myriad and diverse sources. Many conversations began, "Here's a story that you should write." The next story to which I yielded, after great reluctance, was a white-collar crime. *The Great Jerusalem Artichoke Circus: The Buying and Selling of the American Dream* (Minneapolis: University of Minnesota Press, 1993) tells the story of the largest horticultural hysteria in American history. This complex and multifaceted story, which cuts across the varied fields of agriculture, agronomy, alternative crops, individual biographies, business, energy, religion, sales, science, and technology, nearly drowned me in subjects and sources, although it also taught me how scarce and precious certain evidence is about particular human deeds and intentions. Newspapers again proved to be indispensable, furnishing brief summaries of complex business affairs, scientific matters, and legal actions, while legal documents provided immense gatherings of documentation and evidence at state, county, and federal expense. The company files and displays of American Energy Farm Systems, which perpetrated the swindle, presented me with shelves and shelves of "research," sales materials, minutes, and economic records, illustrating how much of contemporary history involves securing access to this kind of documentation. More than fifty oral interviews of principals, sellers, buyers, workers, creditors, prosecutors, and defenders, along with crop scientists, agronomists, and engineers, proved crucial for understanding this unique horticultural phenomenon, which revealed in the American mind of the early 1980s a mixture of fundamentalism, boosterism, Amway enthusiasm, xenophobia, and desperation for new crops. *The Great Jerusalem Artichoke Circus* confirmed my role as a local historian, bringing me new friends and awakening the now familiar bittersweet sense that my life is being measured out in books about transitory things and places.

In *Servants of the Land: God, Family, and Farm, the Trinity of Belgian Economic Folkways in Southwestern Minnesota* (Marshall, Minn.: Crossings Press, 1990), I pursued the culture of economics and the ethnicity of agriculture. I sought to grasp the underlying assumptions, principles, attitudes, and faith that accounted for the dominance of Lyon County's primary ethnic landholders, the Belgian and Dutch Catholics. In writing this history, I needed county histories, property records, deeds, and church histories. I also made use of oral histories; telephone books; visits to farms, villages, and cemeteries; and church, ethnic, and migration histories.

In the course of researching *Servants of the Land,* I began to realize the importance of genealogy to local history. Thanks to "the roots phenomenon," legions of amateurs across the world have invaded public libraries, cemeteries, rectories, courthouses, and other repositories in search of documents that might shed light on their family origins and histories and thus on the formation and development of localities. Collectively, genealogists detail the peculiar twists and turns of families, making lineage, once the reserved claim of royalty, the property of all and laying down a challenge to any historian who would separate history from the plight of individuals. *Servants of the Land* not only reconnected American families with their relatives overseas but also brought with it a sense that local historians do more than document places—they define them.

In *The Decline of Rural Minnesota* (Marshall, Minn.: Crossings Press, 1993) and *A Community of Strangers: Change, Turnover, Turbulence, and the Transformation of a Midwestern Country Town* (Marshall, Minn.: Crossings Press, 1999) I sought—with the help of my friends and colleagues David Pichaske, John Meyer, and John Radzilowski, respectively—to chart decline, change, and transformation. We made use of quantitative data found in national censuses, state economic reports, and local demographic, economic, and government records to enumerate total population numbers and calculate migration, turbulence rates, and institutional and community stability. Besides data on business history, we made use of county property records, lists of officeholders, and local tax records.

In a companion study of recent Asian, Latino, and African immigrants to eight southwestern Minnesota communities, Anthony Amato, John Radzilowski, Donata DeBruyckere, and I found that school records offered a decisive addition to the understanding of the composition of new regional migrant populations. In constructing our book *To Call It Home:*

The New Immigrants of Southwestern Minnesota (Marshall, Minn.: Crossings Press, 1996) we also drew on national and international studies of migration and ethnic patterns, consulted with a range of experts in these fields, and visited regional meatpacking companies that employ the new immigrants. Interviews with and reports from county officials, social workers, law enforcement officers, school administrators, and church officials provided insights into the presence, behavior, and culture of these nearly "invisible communities" in our midst.

A New College on the Prairie: Southwest State University's First Twenty-Five Years, 1967–1992 (Marshall, Minn.: Crossings Press, 1992) affirmed the importance of our history center and the university's archives. They furnished us with administrative documents, faculty and union documents, photographs, and editorial exchanges in the school newspaper and local newspaper. The files also contained anonymous letters, petitions, manifestos, posters, signs, and buttons that collectively expressed the tumultuous history of a young university, characterized by precipitous rises and declines in student enrollment, pervasive faculty-administration conflict, antiwar protests and racial clashes of exceptional dimension, and conflicts between college and town.

Working with Janet Timmerman and a handful of students, I produced a study of the 1993 flood that inundated the entire upper Mississippi basin and actually overwhelmed Marshall four times in the course of a single year. Our publication, *At the Headwaters: The 1993 Flood in Southwestern Minnesota* (Marshall, Minn.: Minnesota Conservation Corps / Southwest State University Flood Recovery Project, 1995), led us to make an extensive collection of local, regional, state, and national materials describing the flood's causes, origins, and consequences. Aside from gathering photographs, films, interviews, and documents on the flood's damage to life, property, land, and wildlife, we studied human reactions to the flood, the cleanup, and the proposed steps to mitigate damages from future floods. We considered what historians should preserve and make public from the flood, and we aimed our field trips at observing the lay of the land, noting wetlands and ditches, outlining watersheds, and identifying old and new flood-control structures. We supplemented our field research with interviews with farmers, city and county officials, and watershed association members. We followed this up with lengthy visits to the Department of Natural Resources and the St. Paul headquarters of the Army Corps of Engineers and correspondence with agencies whose sheer multitude resulted in one essay being titled "More Agencies Than You Can Shake a Stick At."

From our research on that project, one conclusion stands forth: local historians must follow many paths and trails. They must construct narratives with reference to national and even global factors, while reconstructing and telling stories of distinct places and individual incidents. They constantly will encounter the microcosm vanishing into the surrounding macrocosm, and vice-versa. They will discover that the best-laid plans for a year's discrete collecting always will tempt them with a decade of accumulating.

Yet there remains saving advice, if local historians discipline themselves: publication must serve as their North Star. Their dutiful preoccupation must be with the specific and pertinent evidence that allows them to imagine and reconstruct the local. They have to realize that a theoretical debate or even its resolution never satisfies their craft. For there is no history without an audience.

BOOKS AND PUBLICATIONS

Of course, I was indebted to many publications in developing my understanding of local and regional history and specifically in writing this book. I have listed here books and articles that I believe deserve special attention or might prove of particular interest to local historians. Many are found in the backnotes to individual chapters in this book.

For guides on writing local history, see *Local History, National Heritage* (Nashville, Tenn.: American Association for State and Local History, 1991); David Kyvig and Myron Marty, *Nearby History: Exploring the Past around You* (Nashville, Tenn.: American Association for State and Local History, 1982); Michael Kammen, *In the Past Lane: Historical Reflections on American Culture* (New York: Oxford University Press, 1997); and French regionalist Guy Thuillier and his colleague Jean Tulard's *Histoire locale et régionale* (Paris: Presses Universitaires de France, 1992).

For cultural histories and works that offer fresh approaches to rethinking local history, see Gaston Bachelard, *The Poetics of Space* (Boston: Beacon Press, 1969); Alain Corbin, *Village Bells: Sounds and Meaning in the Nineteenth-Century French Countryside* (New York: Columbia University Press, 1998); Alon Confino, *The Nation as a Local Metaphor: Württemberg, Imperial Germany, and National Memory, 1871–1918* (Chapel Hill: University of North Carolina Press, 1997); Paul Gruchow, *Grass Roots: The Universe of Home* (Minneapolis: Milkweed Editions, 1995); Eric Hobsbawm, *The Invention of Tradition* (Cambridge: Cambridge University Press, 1983); Michael Lesy, *The Wisconsin Death Trip* (New York: Pantheon Books, 1973); Tom Lutz, *Crying: The Natural and Cultural History of Crying* (New York: W. W. Norton, 1999); Geert Mak, *Jorwerd: The Death of the Village in Late Twentieth-Century Europe* (London: Harvill Press, 2000); William Miller, *The Anatomy of Disgust* (Cambridge: Harvard University Press, 1997); Steven Ozment, *Flesh and Spirit* (New York: Viking Press, 1999); Carol Stearns and Peter Stearns, *Anger: The Struggle for Emotional Control in America's History* (Chicago: University of Chicago Press, 1986); Peter Stearns, "Suppressing Unpleasant Emotions: The Development of a Twentieth-Century American Style," in *Social History and Issues in Human Consciousness: Some Interdisciplinary Connections,* ed. Andrew Barnes and Peter Stearns (New York: New York University Press, 1989); Yi-Fu Tuan, *Landscapes of Fear* (Minneapolis: University of Minnesota Press, 1979), and *Topophilia: A Study of Environmental Perception, Attitudes, and Values* (New York: Columbia University Press, 1974); and finally, André Vargnac, *Civilisation traditionnelle et genres de vie* (Paris: Editions Albin Michel, 1948), and Eugen Weber, *Peasants into Frenchmen: The Modernization of Rural France, 1870–1914* (Stanford: Stanford University Press, 1976).

For select books defining the transformation of the Midwest and its institutions and peoples, see Hal Barron, *Mixed Harvest: The Second Great Transformation in the Rural North, 1870–1930* (Chapel Hill: University of North Carolina Press, 1997); Theodore Blegen, *Minnesota: A History of the State* (Minneapolis: University of Minnesota Press, 1963); John Borchert, *America's Northern Heartland: An Economic and Historical Geography of the Upper Midwest* (Minneapolis: University of Minnesota Press, 1987); Andrew Cayton and Peter Onuf, *The Midwest and the Nation* (Bloomington: Indiana University Press, 1990); Clark Clifford, ed., *Minnesota in a Century of Change: The State and Its People since 1900* (St. Paul: Minnesota Historical Society Press, 1989); William Cronon, *Nature's Metropolis: Chicago and the Great West* (New York: W. W. Norton, 1991); James H. Madison, ed., *Heartland: Comparative Histories of the Midwestern States* (Bloomington: Indiana University Press, 1988); James Meinig, *Transcontinental America, 1850–1915* (New Haven: Yale University Press, 1998); James Shortridge, *The Middle West: Its Meaning in American Culture* (Lawrence: University Press of Kansas, 1989); John Fraser Hart, *The Land That Feeds Us* (New York: W. W. Norton, 1991); and John C. Hudson, *Plains Country Towns* (Minneapolis: University of Minnesota Press, 1985), and *Making the Corn Belt: A Geographical*

History of Middle Western Agriculture (Bloomington: Indiana University Press, 1994). Also of use are Thomas Isern, *The Cultures of Agriculture on the North American Plains,* Rural and Regional Essay Series (Marshall, Minn.: Society for the Study of Local and Regional History, 1999), and Erwin Zube and Margaret Zube, eds., *Changing Rural Landscapes* (Amherst: University of Massachusetts Press, 1955).

For introductory readings on ecological and environmental history, see Scott Anfinson, *Southwestern Minnesota Archaeology: Twelve Thousand Years in a Prairie Lake Region* (St. Paul: Minnesota Historical Society Press, 1997); William Cronon, *Changes in the Land: Indians, Colonists, and the Ecology of New England* (New York: Hill and Wang, 1985); Dan Flores, "Place: An Argument for Bioregional History," *Environmental History Review* 18 (winter 1994): 1–18; Kelly Kindscher, *Edible Wild Plants of the Prairie: An Ethnobotanical Guide* (Lawrence: University Press of Kansas, 1987); Richard Manning, *Grassland: The History, Biology, Politics, and Promise of the American Prairie* (New York: Penguin, 1997); Carolyn Merchant, *Ecological Revolutions: Nature, Gender, and Science* (Chapel Hill: University of North Carolina Press, 1989); James Parson, "On 'Bioregionalism' and 'Watershed Consciousness,'" *The Professional Geographer* (February 1985): 1–7; Hal Rothman, "Environmental History and Local History," *History News* (November–December 1993): 8–9; Timothy Silver, *A New Face of the Countryside: Indians, Colonists, and Slaves in South Atlantic Forests, 1500–1800* (Cambridge: Cambridge University Press, 1990); John R. Tester, *Minnesota's Natural Heritage: An Ecological Perspective* (Minneapolis: University of Minnesota Press, 1995); and the classic, William Thomas, ed., *Man's Role in Changing the Face of the Earth* (Chicago: University of Chicago Press, 1956).

For an overview of the prairie, see Gerald Friesen, *The Canadian Prairies: A History* (Toronto: University of Toronto Press, 1987); James Malin, *History and Ecology: Studies of the Grasslands* (Lincoln: University of Nebraska Press, 1984); Paul Gruchow, *Journal of a Prairie Year* (Minneapolis: University of Minnesota Press, 1985); Walter Prescott Webb, *The Great Plains* (New York: Grosset and Dunlap, 1931); William Least-Heat Moon, *PrairyErth* (Boston: Houghton Mifflin, 1991); Elliot West, *The Contested Plains: Indians, Gold Seekers, and the Rush to Colorado* (Lawrence: University Press of Kansas, 1998); Daniel Worster, *Under Western Skies: Nature and History in the American West* (Oxford: Oxford University Press, 1992); and Daniel Worster, ed., *The Ends of the Earth: Perspectives on Modern Environmental History* (Cambridge: Cambridge University Press, 1988).

For additional publications on Indian and white transformation of the American prairie landscape, see Dan Flores, "Bison Ecology and Bison Diplomacy: The Southern Plains from 1800 to 1850," *Journal of American History* 78 (September 1991): 465–85; James Sherow, "Working the Geodialectic: High Plains Indians and Their Horses in the Region of the Arkansas River Valley, 1800–1870," *Environmental History Review* 16 (summer 1992): 61–84; Stephen Pyne, *Fire in America: A Cultural History of Wildland and Rural Fire* (Seattle: University of Washington Press, 1997); and Richard White, *The Middle Ground: Indians, Empires, and Republics in the Great Lakes Region, 1650–1815* (Cambridge: Cambridge University Press, 1991).

Useful for writing the history of small rural towns are Lewis Atherton, *Main Street on the Middle Border* (Bloomington: Indiana University Press, 1954); Richard Davies, *Main Street Blues: The Decline of Small-Town America* (Columbus: Ohio State University Press, 1998); John Mack Faragher, *Sugar Creek: Life on the Illinois Prairie* (New Haven: Yale University Press, 1986); Peter Davis, *Hometown: A Portrait of an American Community* (New York: Simon and Schuster, 1982); Don Martindale and R. Galen Hanson, *Small Town and the Nation: The Conflict of Local and Translocal Forces* (Westport, Conn.: Greenwood Press, 1969); C. Tolbert, *Constructing Townscapes: Space and Society in Antebellum Tennessee* (Chapel Hill: University of North Carolina Press, 1999); and Arthur Vidich and Joseph Bensman, *Small Town in Mass Society: Class, Power, and Religion in a Rural Community* (Garden City, N.Y.: Anchor / Doubleday, 1958).

For guides to the history of agriculture, see Allan Bogue, *From Prairie to Corn Belt: Farming on the Illinois and Iowa Prairies in the Nineteenth Century* (Chicago: University of Chicago Press, 1963); David Danbom, *Born in the Country: A History of Rural America* (Baltimore: Johns Hopkins University Press, 1995); R. Douglas Hurt, *American Agriculture: A Brief History* (Ames: Iowa State University Press, 1994); Morton Rothstein, "Writing American Agricultural History," Historical Essays on Rural Life (Marshall, Minn.: Society for the Study of Local and Regional History, 1996).

For select books on Midwestern literature, see John T. Flanagan, *Minnesota's Literary Visitors* (n.p.: Pogo Press, 1993); David Pichaske, *Late Harvest* (New York: Paragon House, 1992); David Pichaske and Joseph Amato, eds. *Southwest Minnesota: The Land and the People* (Marshall, Minn.: Crossings Press, 1999); Roy Meyer, *The Middle Western Farm*

Novel in the Twentieth Century (Lincoln: University of Nebraska Press, 1965).

For an introduction to peoples of the northern prairie, see Allen Noble, ed., *To Build in a New Land: Ethnic Landscapes in North America* (Baltimore: Johns Hopkins University Press, 1992); Frederick C. Luebke, ed., *Ethnicity on the Great Plains* (Lincoln: University of Nebraska Press, 1980); June Drenning Holmquist, ed., *They Chose Minnesota: A Survey of the State's Ethnic Groups* (St. Paul: Minnesota Historical Society Press, 1981); Robert Ostergren, *A Community Transplanted: The Trans-Atlantic Experience of a Swedish Immigrant Settlement in the Upper Middle West, 1835–1915* (Madison: University of Wisconsin Press, 1988).

For critical studies of Native American identity, see Fergus Bordewich, *Killing the White Man's Indian: Inventing Native Americans at the End of the Twentieth Century* (New York: Anchor Books, 1996); Collin Calloways, ed., *New Directions in American Indian History* (Norman: University of Oklahoma Press, 1988); James A. Clifton, ed., *The Invented Indian: Cultural Fictions and Government Policies* (New Brunswick, N.J.: Transaction Publishers, 1990); Hazel Hertzberg, *The Search for an American Indian Identity* (Syracuse, N.Y.: Syracuse University Press, 1971); and Shepard Krech III, *The Ecological Indian: Myth and History* (New York: W. W. Norton, 1999).

Useful for women's history are Deborah Fink, *Agrarian Women: Wives and Mothers in Rural Nebraska, 1880–1940* (Chapel Hill: University of North Carolina Press, 1992); Glenda Riley, *Frontierswomen: The Iowa Experience* (Ames: Iowa State University Press, 1981); and Rachel Ann Rosenfeld, *Farm Women: Work, Farm, and Family in the United States* (Chapel Hill: University of North Carolina Press, 1985).

Finally, local historians must use classic historical and literary studies of place to expand their imagination of themes and sources. To mind come Natalie Davis, *The Return of Martin Guerre* (Cambridge: Harvard University Press, 1983); Emile Guillaumin, *Life of the Simple Man* (Hanover, N.H.: University Press of New England, 1983); and Carlo Ginzburg, *The Cheese and the Worms: The Cosmos of a Sixteenth-Century Miller,* trans. John and Anne Tedeschi (Baltimore: Johns Hopkins University Press, 1980).

I conclude by throwing local historians into their favorite briar patch. They should, I suggest, dedicate a part of their travels to finding pearls of local archives and publications. My recent travels assure me that these pearls do exist. On a canoeing trip in Montana, I discovered in Fort Benton a lovely local historical archive that threw light on the town known as "the world's innermost port"—a geographic crossroads of western exploration and domination. The archives grew out of the accumulated work and records of the town's lifelong journalist, Joel Overholser.

On the very eve of writing this bibliography, in the autumn of 2000, a speaking engagement took me to the University of Louisiana at Lafayette. There I discovered the Center for Louisiana Studies. A group of dedicated state and local historians, among them Glenn Conrad, Carl Brasseau, Vaughan Baker, and Amos Simpson, staff and support it. Their three decades of dedication have yielded a plethora of published documents and critical secondary work. Responsive to recent trends in national, social, gender, and race historiography, their works span the breadth of material and cultural history of Louisiana. Well aware of the overarching influences of international politics and commodity prices, they have not renounced singular histories of Louisiana's diverse ecological and cultural regions.

Index

Compositor:	Impressions Book & Journal Services, Inc.
Text:	10/13 Sabon
Display:	Sabon
Printer and Binder:	Edwards Brothers, Inc.